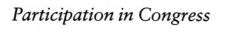

Participation in Congress

RICHARD L. HALL

Participation in Congress

Yale University Press
New Haven and London

Published with assistance from
the Mary Cady Tew Memorial Fund.

Printed in the United States of America.

Library of Congress Cataloging-in-Publication Data

Hall, Richard L.
    Participation in Congress / Richard L. Hall.
      p. cm.
    Includes bibliographical references and index.
    ISBN 0-300-06811-5 (cloth : alk. paper)
        0-300-07651-7 (pbk. : alk. paper)

    1. United States.   Congress — Committees.   2. Legislators — United
States.   3. Political participation — United States.   I. Title.
JK1029.H25   1996
328.73'0765 — dc20   96–15778

A catalogue record for this book is available from the British Library.
The paper in this book meets the guidelines for permanence and durability of the
Committee on Production Guidelines for Book Longevity of the Council on Li-
brary Resources.

10 9 8 7 6 5 4 3 2

To Vickie, Kelly, and Steven

Contents

Tables

Acknowledgments

The unindicted co-conspirators on this book are many. The identities of some are easier to detect than others, however, such that I feel the need to implicate publicly the most notorious of those who contributed to the intellectual crimes and misdemeanors that appear in these pages.

I will finger first the principal accessory before the fact, John Kingdon. John has been mentor, critic, and friend from the earliest stages of this study. He more than anyone is responsible for encouraging me to transform it into a book-length treatise, and he has offered good counsel, penetrating chapter-by-chapter criticism, and moral support over a long period. Similarly culpable are Richard Fenno and William Keech. Both gave essential guidance as I plotted the pilot project from which this book ultimately emerged, and both have encouraged and otherwise boosted its development at subsequent turns. Don Herzog and Don Kinder provided excellent criticism and at various times took my confession without turning me over to the proper authorities. Without these good friends and colleagues, no doubt I would have given up on the project and turned my energies toward becoming a useful member of society. I thank them for saving me from that fate.

Numerous others provided comments or criticism at various stages of the project that helped me to perpetrate this book. I would especially like to thank John Chamberlin, Paul Courant, Doug Dion, John E. Jackson, David C. King,

Keith Krehbiel, Michael Lienesch, Gary McKissick, Donald Searing, and Rob Worden. Whatever intellectual merit one may find in the ideas and arguments contained here is also traceable to the teachings and writings of Barbara Avery, Ted Christiansen, Lane Davis, Paul Kress, John S. Nelson, and Kenneth Shepsle. This was unbeknownst to them, however, such that they should be held harmless in any proceedings that may be brought against me.

Several persons provided valuable research or other assistance and thus aided and abetted what I have done. I would like to thank Larry Evans, Rich Forshee, Janet Newcity, and Molly Shaffer. Mary Breijak, Wendy Niemi, Tonia Short, and especially Susan Abel and Susan Laity provided timely and valuable editorial assistance. Among those I will not name are the staffers, members of Congress, and other participant-observers who generously provided the time and patience required for the extensive interviews upon which *Participation in Congress* heavily depends.

For financial support, I am indebted to the Everett McKinley Dirksen Research Center, the National Science Foundation, the University of Michigan Office of Vice President for Research, and the University of Michigan School of Public Policy. No less important supporters and patrons include Marc and Paula Davis, John and Clyrene Hall, Elizabeth Johnson, Steve Rossi, and especially Betsy and Chuck Sigman. Thanks to them all.

This book is dedicated to my wife, Vickie, my daughter, Kelly, and my son, Steven. Vickie's love and support brought the book to fruition, despite numerous delays. Kelly and Steve showed patience beyond their years and the good sense to ignore what I was doing.

Participation in Congress

Introduction

For every issue that comes before them, there are essentially two decisions that each member of Congress must make: what position to take and how active to be. A rich literature within political science and economics is devoted to the first, exploring the causes and consequences of members' voting decisions in committee and on the floor. By comparison, almost nothing is known about the decisions that members make every day, issue by issue, regarding how much they will participate in the legislative deliberations of their chamber. Such decisions are the focus of this book.

Legislative Participation and the Practice of Representation

There are several reasons to suggest that this focus is important if we are to understand and evaluate how Congress deliberates on and ultimately decides matters of public policy. The first and what I take to be the most important has to do with the capacities of Congress as a representative body. One of the hallmarks of representative assemblies, John Stuart Mill tells us, is that they bring together diverse parties with different views, values, and political interests.[1] The assembly makes possible a deliberation in which conflicting

1. See Mill 1975 [1861], chap. 5, especially pp. 215, 226–28.

judgments about the public good, or even the efficient promotion of narrow interests, can be examined, debated, and resolved. And through such a process the actions of government achieve legitimacy. Citizens from far quarters harboring very different interests and opinions participate through their agents. By exercising their franchise in fair and competitive legislative elections, citizens give their consent to those who would act on their behalf.

Such an idyllic view of the representative process, however, turns partly on the assumption that once elected, the citizens' agents themselves participate in legislative decisions. As I discuss in the following pages, this is an assumption that is not easily sustained. Participation in Congress is seldom universal. It is never equal. Although most (sometimes all) members vote when specific decisions come to a formal roll call on the chamber floor, floor voting is only one and probably not the most important form of participation in the legislative process. Building a coalition for a legislative package, drafting particular amendments, planning and executing parliamentary strategy, bargaining with or persuading colleagues to adopt one's point of view—all these activities weigh more heavily than voting in the decision-making calculus of most bills, especially in a legislature where committees, anterooms, and staff meetings are the principal forums for deliberation and decision. In such activities, participation is highly selective. Indeed, few but the most salient or controversial policy choices elicit significant involvement by more than a small group of members, despite the fact that all enjoy the same constitutional sanction to act.

Such patterns of behavior, I believe, render the practice of representation more than a little problematic, perhaps paradoxical. More specifically, the selective nature of legislative participation leads one to somewhat different assessments of representation in Congress, depending on the level at which one's standard of representation is pitched. In representation, as in other things, what is right for individual members is not necessarily right for the institution.

By far the most common approach has been to view representation at the individual level or, more accurately, at the level of the district-member (or principal-agent) dyad. Representation, in turn, is thought to be strong when the dyadic relationships are strong—that is, when members act like good "delegates," adopting positions in the legislature that are consistent with the policy positions or ideologies of their constituents. Thus have scholars for four decades evaluated the health of representation by examining the congruence between constituents' opinions and the voting behavior of their elected representatives.[2]

---

2. The seminal statement of the congruence model is Miller and Stokes 1963, though related and important work on constituency influence and roll call voting predates it. See,

The study of legislative participation takes this line of research in what I believe to be a new and fruitful direction. Whatever connection there might be between district opinions and member positions, members can be responsive to their constituents in an altogether different, perhaps more important sense during legislative action on the various matters that come before Congress. The distinction that we require — one that I will make much of in the pages to come — is between what formal theorists refer to as *revealed preferences* and what I will refer to here as *revealed intensities*. If the preferences of members are revealed (more or less) in their votes on a particular issue, their intensities are revealed by the time and legislative effort they devote to it.[3] The relevance of the distinction to representation is that members may respond to constituent opinion through their voting behavior, but they may also reflect the intensity of constituent interests through the time and energy they expend. The good delegate, that is, should not only adopt the electorally correct position; she should invest herself and her office heavily in legislative contests where her constituents have a clear and abiding interest, issues where they stand much to gain or lose, with the consequence that she will give shorter shrift to issues unlikely to evoke strong feelings back home. The representative from South Dakota who concentrates legislative time on South Africa, and the senator from South Carolina who takes little interest in textile tariffs, whatever their positions and whatever *we* may think of their actions, are not being ideal district delegates.

Do members of Congress act like good delegates of their districts? While the evidence from the analysis of members' voting behavior is mixed, the conclusion I will draw from the analysis of legislative participation is quite clear. Members of Congress are quite sensitive to the intensity of district interests, as those interests are variously evoked by legislative matters that come before their chamber. When members perceive that a bill is directly relevant to the district they represent, they are more likely to become actively involved, and once involved, more likely to invest significant amounts of their time, energy,

---

for example, MacRae 1958. For critical reviews of the subsequent literature on representation, see Fiorina 1974, chap. 1; Eulau and Karps 1977; Jewell 1983; Kingdon 1977.

3. Strictly speaking, utility theory in formal economics does not admit of a distinction between preference and intensity (see, for instance, Abrams 1980, 78–84). Fundamental problems arise, however, when one moves from the abstract concept of preference to its supposed substantive referent in an unreified legislative context. Specifically, the economist's concept of preference is not isomorphic to the position a member reveals through votes, even sincere votes. Only by making extraordinarily dubious assumptions, for instance, can one claim to recover the willingness-to-pay-function from information that is contained in roll calls. I discuss in Chapter 9 the implications of the concept of revealed intensity for positive theories of legislative choice. See also Hall 1995.

and staff effort in the legislative action. Although there are variations that will warrant our attention and although constituents' interests are not the only (nor always the most important) determinant of legislative participation, the general finding that they matter holds true across policy domains (agriculture, human resources, energy, and commerce), decision-making forums (behind-the-scenes negotiations, public debate), and the several stages in a sequential legislative process (subcommittee, committee, floor). According to the delegate standard of legislative behavior, then, the evidence presented in these pages should prove reassuring to people who worry about the responsiveness of representatives to constituents at a time when cynicism about incumbent politicians still runs high and the incidence of high-priced, media-centered campaigns is on the rise.

The delegate standard applied to district-member relationships, however, does not tell us everything that we need to know about the practice of representation in Congress. To assume that the examination of 535 dyadic relationships can, in uncomplicated fashion, permit us to assess the performance of a representative institution is to commit, if not a fallacy of composition, a basic mistake in reasoning about the nature of collective action in complex organizations. The standard more appropriately and more commonly (if implicitly) applied to the evaluation of legislative institutions is something like what Chamberlin and Courant (1983) refer to as the "representativeness of deliberations." According to this standard, the electoral accountability of members to distant and different constituencies is not so much an end in itself as it is an imperfect means to a larger end — the creation of an assembly that roughly resembles the larger population in the views, values, and interests to which it might give expression in a process of informed deliberation and debate.[4] Representation is a process of citizen participation once removed.

According to this standard, however, the selective participation of members

4. This view is central to discussions of representation and republican government in both Mill and Madison. That it is an important standard by which members themselves judge the legitimacy of legislative institutions is evident in a number of formal practices in the contemporary Congress and most Western assemblies. For instance, most parliamentary systems take seriously the rights of the loyal opposition to challenge and criticize the majority's position, even though the ultimate policy choice is, more often than not, a fait accompli. Likewise, although the standing rules of both chambers of Congress are drafted entirely by the majority, it typically fashions those rules in a way that gives considerable representation to the minority (for example, on standing committees and at House-Senate conferences) and numerous other opportunities for the minority to participate, despite the fact that the opportunities are frequently exploited to delay or prevent the majority from enacting its program.

in legislative decision making must be viewed with considerable suspicion. The point here is not that all duly elected representatives must be involved equally in every decision. Indeed, large organizations achieve important gains in both information and efficiency by encouraging their members to specialize, to concentrate on some matters more than others and thus acquire the expertise necessary to successfully address complex questions in a timely manner.[5] In leaving most of the legislative labor to a particular few, in turn, the chamber may be simply *delegating* authority to a subset of individuals whose role it is to serve as agents of the house. That is, the representativeness of the institution can, in theory, be preserved if specialists act as delegates of a chamber of delegates. Representation becomes something like citizen participation *twice* removed.

But the practice of specialization and the representativeness of deliberations reside together in an uneasy tension. If a small number of legislators assume responsibility for some particular issue, then we must worry a good deal about whether those participants are themselves representative of the larger chamber, at least with respect to the views and values relevant to the matter at hand. Participation in Congress, for the most part, is not a matter of institutional design or authoritative delegation; for the most part, it is a matter of individual choice. And as the following chapters will show, there are good theoretical reasons and considerable evidence to suggest that the members active on any given matter often will *not* reflect the values and interests apparent in the chamber, and members more representative of the chamber, in turn, often lack incentives to monitor what the interested and active do.

More specifically, this worry becomes particularly strong precisely in cases where the connection between legislative participation and the interests of the constituency is strongest. The relationship is conditional in important ways, on which I will elaborate; the basic paradox, though, is this: the more responsive members are to intense constituency interests when making decisions about participation, the less representative the deliberations of the chamber are likely to be. The nature and conditions of this relationship are central issues in the evaluation of Congress as a representative institution, issues to which I return in the concluding chapter.

Legislative Participation and the Nature of Collective Choice

If the study of legislative participation is important for understanding the practice of representation in Congress, it is intimately tied to several other,

---

5. See Krehbiel 1991 for a thorough elaboration of such advantages.

closely related issues in the study of democratic institutions. Prominent among these is the practice of collective choice in what is, ostensibly, a majority-rule assembly. By what manner of mathematics are the preferences of individual members summarized into a collective action sanctioned by the group? Much of the theoretical work in which this question is taken up begins with the (often unexamined) assumption that the principal means by which collective choices are made in Congress is simple majority vote — that is, a decision process in which each individual member enjoys an equal share. Thus does Duncan Black (1958) argue that if member preferences are ordered along a single dimension and the distribution of preferences is single-peaked, the proper prediction is that the collective outcome will be the position of the median voter. The median-voter theorem, in turn, serves as an important point of departure for a substantial body of work in the field of legislative choice.

The premise of this book, however, is that the (sometimes qualified)[6] egalitarianism implied by majority-rule voting models is highly problematic, at least insofar as one's ultimate concern is with explaining real-world processes. Dahl captured this point over three decades ago: "In the actual world of governmental politics in the United States, the only stage at which [majority rule] is at all closely approximated seems to be during vote counting in elections and legislative bodies. In the pre-voting stage many influences, including those of superior wealth and control over organizational resources, so greatly exaggerate the power of the few as compared with the many that the social processes leading up to the process of voting may properly be spoken of as highly inegalitarian and undemocratic" (1956, 66).

To put it somewhat differently, majoritarian voting tells us only part of what we need to know. Again, the distinction that bears emphasizing is between revealed preferences and revealed intensities. Votes capture the former, not the latter. But members who wish to affect specific outcomes have much more to invest than their votes. Their legislative time and energy, staff effort, and political capital, borrowed or accrued, can be variously invested or conserved in the legislative competition over the issues that come before the chamber. Members with relatively strong interests in a given issue expect greater benefits from such investments; they are thus more inclined to participate and,

6. Qualified in the sense that a fair amount of theoretical work on legislative choice has emphasized the differentially sought and unevenly distributed procedural advantages that structure the institutional context in which majoritarian voting takes place, a matter I discuss later. See, for instance, Shepsle 1978; 1979; Shepsle and Weingast 1987a; Weingast and Marshall 1988. For a review of the relevant institutionalist literature, see Shepsle and Weingast 1995.

when participating, to pursue their positions more vigorously. Members with little interest in the issue, by contrast, are more likely to emphasize the opportunity costs of involvement, conserving their resources for what for them are politically more profitable issues. Moreover, members are unevenly endowed with the legislative resources to invest. For this reason as well, the intensity that they *reveal* in their participation (which is the intensity that gets registered in the collective-choice process) is highly variable. It reflects (among other things) the intensity of their personal or political interest in the matter; the amount of resources that they have to commit; and, under certain specifiable conditions, the strategic calculations they will make regarding the expected return on their resource investments. In sum, one needs to think not only about what members want legislatively but also about their willingness and ability to pay what it takes to get it.

If differences in members' revealed preferences may make a difference in collective outcomes, however, what is the effect of differences in revealed intensities? According to Dahl, the effect is seldom trivial; in the United States, he concludes, majorities seldom rule; intense minorities do (1956, chapter 5). In other work on collective choice, the point has been more formally elaborated. Taking issue with Black and his theoretical successors, John Jackson (1973) demonstrated that the practical equivalent of the median-voter result occurs in cases where preferences are independent of intensities. "If people's preferences and the weight they give to each issue are correlated . . . then a nonmean position which accommodates each of the more intense preferences can defeat the mean strategy." Or, stated somewhat differently, "In general, the points which can defeat the mean will be in the direction of the correlation between preferences and intensities." Moreover, Jackson speculated that such relationships are common in several important areas of public policy.

The importance of differentiable intensities has been a central if too-implicit theme in distributive theories of legislative organization and collective choice as well. On the multiple matters that come before them, members have heterogeneous preferences and thus stand to capture gains from ongoing legislative exchange. According to this view, a relatively uninterested chamber majority trades away to particular committees its constitutional right to decide on particular issues, while its numerous members, in return, anticipate procedural advantages in domains of their own choosing. The allocation of power over the agenda and other parliamentary rights, the assignment of restrictive rules to bills in the House, and the procedural advantages awarded committees at the postfloor stage restrain agents of nominal majorities from undoing, bill by bill, the cross-policy logrolling arrangements that redound to the electoral benefit of legislative incumbents. Policy benefits, then, are distributed to members whose districts value them most. Thus structured, the legislative world works out a good deal better for every member than the War of All Against All.

From the perspective I take in this book, however, two missing links become apparent in this line of theorizing. First, distributive theory provides no conceptual distinction between the direction of preferences and the intensity of interests. To make such a distinction strikes me as crucial if distributive theory is to progress. Members trade on interests, which are heterogeneous in intensity across issues, not on preferences, at least insofar as preferences are revealed by the positions that members express in their votes in majority-rule voting games. Second, distributive theories of legislative choice rest on the view that members' interests are unconditionally linked with electoral self-interest and hence with the interests of their constituency. This is a substantively important but contestable empirical question, one that I will investigate in systematic fashion. A consequence, I hope, will be to establish better behavioral foundations for the distributive impulses of Congress while clarifying the conditions under which those impulses are likely to give way to more informed, relatively majoritarian forces — a tendency that appears prominent in institutionalist theory with very different and relatively recent origins (see especially Krehbiel 1991).

In the following pages, I take up a form of behavior that has been largely ignored by legislative scholars but that should have important consequences for the empirical study of collective choice. Indeed, for most members on most issues, the scarcity of time and legislative resources combined with a relatively low level of interest leads them to abdicate what formal legislative authority they enjoy. They simply do not participate, and they pay little attention to those who do. In some cases that I will recount, a standing committee of reputed legislative specialists reduces to only two or three players, who bargain among themselves with relative impunity on significant (though not necessarily salient) matters of public policy. If legislating is a game, in other words, it is a game in which the number and identities of the players are not predetermined. These features arise endogenously as the game gets played. Stated somewhat differently, a model of legislative choice must tell us not only how the preferences of the players become aggregated but also how nominal members come to be players in the first place. More generally, the patterns of activity and abdication in Congress are central to understanding the fluid distribution of influence in a decision-making process that is too often assumed to be genuinely majoritarian.

Legislative Participants and Other Institutional Actors

Finally, members' choices about whether and to what extent they will participate are taken to be important by a good number of actors in the policy process and should thus help us to understand the priorities of those in and around Congress. From the point of view of members themselves, in fact, such choices are more frequent, more complicated, and typically more consequential than the much more visible and more frequently investigated voting decision. Members make decisions about their legislative priorities on an ongoing basis, as new issues, new opportunities, and new demands arise. These choices, in turn, affect the achievement of their objectives both within the institution — establishing a favorable reputation, staking out legislative territory, promoting particular visions of good policy, or enacting specific legislative provisions — and outside it: responding to and thus gaining favor with important groups and constituencies, increasing one's visibility in either the local or national media, and raising campaign funds. As Bauer, Pool, and Dexter observe, the member's principal dilemma is "not how to vote but what to do with his time, how to allocate his resources, and where to put his energy" (1963, 405). If anything, that observation is truer now than it was during the prereform period in which it was written.

Other actors as well have a keen interest in who participates on given issues. Expectations about the identity of the participants and the intensity of their participation inform the strategies that key outsiders employ to achieve specific policy objectives. Interest groups deploy their lobbyists, donate money, gather political intelligence, and provide technical expertise in an effort not so much to buy support as to mobilize their supporters (Hall and Wayman 1990). Agency bureaucrats cultivate relationships with individuals willing to serve as active champions of the agency point of view — individuals who will intervene when a proposed action threatens agency programs or who will serve as coalition leaders for proposals that would enhance the budget or autonomy of the agency (Arnold 1979, especially 40–42, 98–100). And presidents and other party leaders pursuing legislative programs depend heavily not simply on the voting loyalty of the party rank and file but on the willingness of particular members to, in Capitol Hill parlance, "carry their water."

If we are to understand fully the nature of the relationships between legislators and interest groups, between legislators and bureaucrats, between legislators and party leaders, and between legislators and the president, legislative participation must come squarely into focus. In this book I will point to several new and potentially fruitful directions for the study of political institutions and representative government. I will briefly explore several of those directions at the end of the book.

Who Participates and Why?

This work thus rests on a simple but important observation about the nature of decision making in legislative assemblies: not all members are equally involved in each legislative decision. I start with the assumption that the patterns of involvement will prove important for understanding the nature and quality of representation, the variable exercise of influence in the calculus of legislative consent, and the nature of the relationships between actors in Congress and other major actors in the national policy-making process. Hence, I set out to explore when and why members participate.

The book's principal purpose, then, is to develop and test a theory of legislative participation. Developing such a theory requires that one take note of several preliminaries. The most important is this: unlike more bureaucratic organizations, the "division of labor" visible in Congress is not authoritatively imposed. It bubbles up, as it were, from individual members' day-to-day choices about which matters warrant their time, energy, and staff attention.

This is a simple point, one that I will establish more clearly in the following pages. But it reflects a view of legislative organization qualitatively different from both old and new institutionalist accounts of Congress. The conventional view is simply that Congress has something approximating an identifiable division of labor, institutionalized in the structure of its committee and subcommittee system — the jurisdictional boundaries and membership rolls that are formally adopted at the beginning of a congress and, barring extraordinary circumstances, are exogenous to the host of specific issues the chamber takes up over the ensuing two-year period. A substantial body of scholarship has been devoted to the committee assignment process and the patterns of committee membership,[7] on the eminently reasonable assumption that the identity, attributes, and interests of the legislative laborers in a particular policy domain make a difference in the sorts of policies that are developed.

---

7. Regarding committee assignments, see especially Eulau 1984; Fenno 1973a, chap. 1; Shepsle 1978. For a recent book that disputes the conventional view about committee self-selection and its consequences, see Krehbiel 1991. A growing number of works have explored the hypothesis that committee composition is biased in systematic ways. See, for example, Cox and McCubbins 1993; Hall and Grofman 1990; Krehbiel 1990; Londregan and Snyder 1994.

Committees and subcommittees have thus become the stylized answers to the unhappily implicit question, Who participates in Congress? But they are not very good answers, for two reasons. They are empirically imprecise. And they are theoretically misleading.

Most of the legislative work in Congress does in fact occur in committees and subcommittees. That is, it is true that the serious actors in the legislative process tend to be members of the committee with jurisdiction. But the converse is not true. Committee members need not be — on most bills, tend not to be — serious actors. Even on relatively narrow or specialized committees or subcommittees, the subset of members who are much more than passive observers on any given matter is small, seldom over half, with the membership of that subset changing, sometimes dramatically, from bill to bill. And the tendency for serious legislative actors to come from the relevant committee or subcommittee is only a central tendency, around which there is considerable variation. In the Senate, the chamber floor has long been an important forum for serious, albeit selective, participation by committee nonmembers. And over the past decade, participation on the House floor has become increasingly common.[8]

In sum, committees and subcommittees are central to answering the question of who participates in Congress. Indeed, they are prominent in both the theoretical account and the empirical design of this study. But they constitute only a point of departure, not a satisfactory answer. Taking them for a satisfactory answer, in fact, can be theoretically misleading. By focusing on the formal institutional units, we too-conveniently label as institutional or structural something that is better understood as a behavioral phenomenon (albeit subject to institutional constraints). Taken literally, at least, the view that committees constitute a system by which the organization divides labor — thereby achieving specialization, expertise, and greater organizational efficiency — founders on an important behavioral puzzle. Legislative labor in Congress is required of no one. Few specific tasks are assigned; no production quotas are set. No sanctions await senators and representatives who show up late, disappear when a constituent calls or the golfing weather is good, or otherwise labor little in legislative decision making. (On the contrary, Fenno suggests that such behavior might lead one to be reelected [1978, chapter 6]; the wag might say that it leads one to become vice president.) Why, then, does anyone do the organization's work? Unlike a private firm, Congress has little

8. This is evident in the growth in amending activity on the House and Senate floors. See especially Smith 1989; Sinclair 1989.

capacity to address the classic Olsonian free-rider problem. The legislative labor it might divide and assign to promote its collective objectives the individual members are under no obligation to do.

Why do members participate in the decision making on particular issues? In its most abstract form, the theory I develop here is one of purposive behavior in an institutional context. The principal objects of study, that is, are individual choices, not institutional designs or organizational functions. At the same time, however, individuals make choices subject to institutional constraints — preexisting institutional arrangements or procedural prerogatives that benefit some more than others. To paraphrase Shepsle's view of members' assignment behavior (1978, 6–7), each legislator contemplating involvement in a particular matter entertains certain interests, possesses behavioral alternatives, chooses from among the latter with an eye to the former, and is constrained in her choices by the information and other resources available to her (and to her potential legislative competitors) and by the institutionally provided opportunities to act.

Even after one has adopted this general formula, however, much remains to be done by way of developing a satisfactory theory of participation. One must turn the economist's language of constrained optimization into a more precisely elaborated statement about the interests and constraints that matter and the conditions under which they matter. What are the specific behavioral alternatives from which members choose? What interests and incentives incline members to participate (or abdicate), and under what conditions? What resources most significantly affect members' ability to get involved in specific issues? And which institutional arrangements give which members special access to, or bar entry to, the deliberative process on the various bills before their chamber? Such are the specific questions taken up in the following chapters.

An Overview of the Study

The first problems to confront in the investigation of legislative participation are conceptual. How do we characterize the behavioral alternatives we might loosely refer to as participation? As others have observed in the study of the subject at the mass level, political participation refers to no single, identifiable act. Rather, it subsumes a number of different and specific political activities. In Chapter 2 I take up the concept, define two analytically distinct modes of legislative participation, develop valid and reliable indicators of each, and use them to map the patterns of activity and abdication in the decision making of three House committees.

Chapters 3 and 4 lay out a theory of participation, tailored to the context of decision making in committee, where the preponderance of deliberative business takes place. As suggested earlier, the theory starts from the premise that legislators are purposive actors, but it proceeds in two ways that distinguish it from standard economic theory. First, it reflects a broad approach to the sorts of motives and calculations that one must include under the rubric of interest. While constituency considerations are certainly important, neither reelection per se nor "self-interest" as it is conventionally construed can carry the explanatory weight that scholars so often assert. Second, it relaxes the standard assumption that goals or interests are stable, ordered elements of the elite psyche. If, as Fenno (1973) says, not all representatives are alike in the interests they adopt, not all issues are alike in the way they impinge on particular interests. The intensity of any given interest, I argue, is contingent on the object of legislative action, subjectively perceived by the actor, and its effect on member behavior is itself contingent on strategic considerations stemming from the political context. At the same time, however, this account does not presume to capture all of the various layers of the different interests that sometimes enter members' decisions. In particular, I have argued elsewhere that moneyed interest groups, through their investment of campaign contributions and lobbying efforts, mobilize otherwise sympathetic members to participate on legislative matters that the groups care about (Hall and Wayman 1990; Hall 1994b). The extent to which intra- and extra-district group interests influence members' perceptions of interest, unfortunately, is a matter that I cannot unravel, given the data available. The basic model I develop and test in this book, then, should be taken as a point of departure for future work on such questions.

If members are led to participate because of the interests that particular bills evoke, they also face a variable set of opportunity costs and resource constraints that structure their ability to act. Some start with greater advantages — in political experience, substantive expertise, and lines of political communication. Some enjoy certain institutional endowments — formal positions, additional staff, procedural prerogatives — that enhance their ability to pay the information and transaction costs that significant participation entails. In Chapter 4 I specify a set of factors that structure those costs as they vary member to member and bill to bill, and I contrast the resulting hypotheses with those of sociological theory — the prescriptive and proscriptive norms thought to have structured legislative participation in an earlier era but whose vitality, numerous scholars have maintained, has waned in the postreform period. I argue that those norms have not, in fact, waned. Rather, the theory of legislative information and transaction costs that I elaborate in Chapter 4 implies that those norms never were very important in the prereform period.

In their place I provide an account of rational apprenticeship and rational specialization that comprehends both pre- and postreform behavioral patterns.

The ensuing chapters offer a systematic effort to test the theory empirically. I attempt to explain who participates and why, giving appropriate attention to the institutional contexts and circumstances affecting members of Congress at different stages of the legislative process. In Chapter 5 I translate the theory into a model of participation at the subcommittee stage, applicable to both the formal markup of legislation and the informal processes of setting the agenda and negotiating behind the scenes, and I estimate it with subcommittee data from three House committees. In Chapter 6 I extend the model to full-committee deliberations, adding behavioral data from a prereform congress in order to test the sociological theory of participation on its strongest ground and the optimization theory on its weakest.

In Chapter 7 I investigate participation on the House floor, adapting the theory to comprehend the somewhat different opportunities and constraints that operate when deliberations move into full view of the larger legislative assembly. In Chapter 8 I explore the robustness of my principal findings by replicating much of the original analysis with data from the same three committees in a recent congress—the 103rd (1993–94). The reader concerned about the potentially time-bound nature of the foregoing results will be reassured by the evidence in Chapter 8 that the model generalizes to a different postreform congress, dealing with a different administration (of a different party) and confronting a different agenda. I also extend my discussion to participation in the U.S. Senate, providing a brief comparative analysis of participation on ten bills marked up in the corresponding committees of both House and Senate. I conclude by exploring the implications that the procedural reforms of the 104th Republican Congress have for participation and discuss what I take to be several promising lines for further research on legislative participation.

In the final chapter, I return to the larger consequences of selective participation for our understanding and evaluation of congressional decision making. By more carefully examining the interests and attributes of legislative participants, I explore the conditions under which the representativeness of legislative deliberations breaks down under legislative procedures designed to empower majoritarian forces. I discuss the implications of these findings for issues of legislative organization. And I explore their implications for future work on individual behavior, collective choice, and democratic consent in Congress.

Preliminaries of Data and Design

Most of the data for this study are drawn from samples of bills and members from three House committees: Agriculture, Energy and Commerce, and Education and Labor. But the theory of participation developed and tested here should prove applicable to other policy domains and other sets of legislators as well.

This expectation follows directly from a premise central to this study: that different issues are differently perceived by different actors and evoke different behavioral responses. Taken together, the policy jurisdictions examined here probably capture variation along most of the relevant issue dimensions and most of the actor attributes that one might seek in a study more comprehensive in scope.

In terms of issue salience, the jurisdiction of the House Energy and Commerce Committee encompassed many of the major issues of the day (see King 1994). A number of them were subjects of bills sampled here: clean water, clean air, health care, Superfund, and a major regulation of the telephone industry in the aftermath of the AT&T divestiture. Although the Education and Labor Committee was not the hotbed of salient, highly charged issues that it had been, say, in the late 1960s, it too addressed issues of considerable national importance, which are analyzed in this study. The growing concern with educational achievement and teacher quality; the public discomfiture over cutbacks in school nutrition and programs for the elderly; job training and high levels of structural unemployment; workplace safety and health — each of these issues fell within the committee's theater of operations. Finally, Agriculture stands closer to the other end of the continuum in terms of the general versus parochial nature of its jurisdiction. But even in the agriculture area, there was considerable variation apparent in the data. For instance, during the 97th Congress a four-year omnibus farm bill was developed and enacted. Billions of dollars in federal expenditures on substantive policies were at stake at a time when budget cutting was the watchword and David Stockman, director of the Office of Management and Budget (OMB) under Reagan, was the man of the day. Agriculture programs — notably the federal food stamp program and dairy price supports — thus received considerable national attention and have continued to do so.

The jurisdictions of all three committees thus include, in varying degrees, issues of national salience; however, all three deal with a large number of minor, routine, or noncontroversial bills as well — the sorts of bills that count for much of what Congress and its committees do. By taking saturation samples of bills from these three jurisdictions (see Appendix A), I thus capture a great deal of variation in the prominence of the issues that members confronted, variation that should roughly approximate the legislative work of the larger House.

These areas provide a good mix of issues with regard to policy scope, as well. House Commerce is renowned for the broad sweep of its jurisdiction. Given the committee's responsibility for such issues as air and water quality, hazardous waste, telecommunications, transportation, health, energy, and consumer issues, the reputed map of the world on a committee room's wall entitled "the jurisdiction of Energy and Commerce" is not far from the truth. At the other end of the scale, Agriculture has the narrowest and most homogeneous jurisdiction among the major House committees: it deals almost exclusively with issues of concern in rural areas. Education and Labor falls somewhere between the other two in the diversity of issues and interests it handles. One subcommittee, for instance, held jurisdiction over migrant labor law, the minimum wage, wage discrimination, the Davis-Bacon Act, and other federal laws regulating both private and public employers. Another subcommittee dealt with several significant social welfare programs, including programs and services for the elderly and the poor and laws governing the care and treatment of children. The jurisdiction of the Elementary and Secondary Education Subcommittee extended to issues of federal aid to education, teacher training, and equal educational opportunity. And other subcommittees held jurisdiction over such matters as national service programs, college loans and Pell Grants, health care, and vocational rehabilitation. In sum, Education and Labor has long been something of a holding company for distinct and qualitatively different subjurisdictions. The same can be said more or less (Commerce more, Agriculture less) for the other two committees as well.

Finally, the committee samples include more than one-fifth of the total House membership and reveal substantial variation in members' occupational backgrounds, geographical roots, and ideologies, and in the economies and demographics of the districts they represent. In party, gender, and seniority, the members included in the several committee samples closely mirror the committee members as a whole. And in Chapter 7 I examine the floor participation of the full House population.

A few words are in order, however, about the distortions imposed by the choice of these jurisdictions and the committees of members that own them. As Fenno (1973a) has noted, "committees differ," and only three committees are directly studied here. The three were chosen, however, to capture variation across the general categories in Fenno's classic comparative committee study. Education and Labor is one of the "policy" committees on which Fenno focused. Agriculture is reputed to be the classic constituency-oriented committee in the House. And Commerce ranks just behind Appropriations and Ways and Means in its attractiveness and the status within the institution that membership on it confers. More important, my findings remain quite stable from one committee to the next. That is, the model proves general, even if differences in the nature of committee jurisdictions and memberships produce distributions on the key explanatory variables that are actually quite different. Individual-level, issue-specific data on post-assignment behavior, moreover, provide a firmer basis for exploring the substantive committee differences that do exist.

Whatever the limits of the empirical focus of this study, I believe that they are offset by several important advantages. Given the undeveloped state of research on this form of legislative behavior, my focus on a manageable number of members, issues, committees, and congresses permitted badly needed analytical depth. I rely in this study on two sorts of data, both time consuming to gather but rich in what they can tell us about legislative decision making. The first is archival. Data on floor participation are easily obtained from the Congressional Record, but similar data on individuals' participation in committee markups are mostly culled from unpublished records on file in committee offices. As a general rule, those records can be neither borrowed nor photocopied, so that the data collection and coding can be done only through tedious note taking in Washington, at the convenience of committee office employees. The records I reviewed comprise hundreds of pages of detailed minutes and thousands of pages of unedited verbatim transcripts.

The second sort of data comes from interviews with congressional staffers. The committee records seemed remarkably detailed and complete, yet my preliminary research indicated that much about committee decision making was not revealed there. Hence, I conducted interviews with the professional committee and subcommittee staff members who had responsibility for staffing each bill in my sample on both sides of the aisle, as well as interviews with one or more staffers in each of the members' personal offices. In all, I conducted more than two hundred interviews, many of them requiring more than one sitting.

Finally, I supplemented both the archival and interview data with occasional open-ended interviews with members, staffers, agency personnel, and lobbyists, and with what Fenno would call "soaking and poking, or just hanging around" (1978, 249) a number of different committees in both the House and the Senate. If such an experience does not provide what normally gets labeled as data, it certainly improves the ability of the researcher to do better in the (unscientific) social-scientific enterprise of moving from results to interpretations. And in the end, of course, the interpretations are what count.

PART I

A Theory of Legislative Participation

The Nature of Legislative Participation

The congressman is typically thrust unprepared into a specialized milieu and confronted with a massive volume of highly technical legislation, with most of which he can deal only superficially. Counting on the assistance of a modest staff, he must work within the framework of a committee structure and is burdened with the additional task of servicing myriad personal requests from his constituents. These pressures combine to make time one of the congressman's most critical resources and the study of its allocation and husbanding a key to the legislative process. — Raymond Bauer, Ithiel de Sola Pool, and Lewis A. Dexter, *American Business and Public Policy*

Congressional committees and subcommittees have long been touted as the institutions of legislative learning, the places where members can concentrate on and thereby master a manageable number of issues. By providing a system through which members might specialize, the organization is thought to acquire, in turn, the expertise it needs to generate informed majoritarian choices (Krehbiel 1991), better policies in response to complex problems, and a greater capacity to match wits with the executive branch. No doubt there is a good measure of truth in this view. In the contemporary Congress, it remains the case that most of the specialized legislative work occurs "within the framework of a committee structure." But as Bauer and his colleagues also suggest in the quotation that opens this chapter, it has not been true for more than three decades that the ostensible division of labor within Congress renders the member's legislative work manageable, much less masterful. Legislative time is invariably short, and the increasing demands placed upon it have only made its allocation and husbanding both more important and more problematic.

The Shortness of Legislative Time

Various statistics reveal the historical trends in several legislative activities that compete for the typical House member's time. Since Bauer and his associates completed their research in the early 1960s, for instance, the average number of panel assignments in the House member's portfolio, and the number of committee meetings, has gone up by more than half. The number of hours in session has increased by a third. And while their number has dropped considerably in the past ten years, the trips that the typical member takes to vote on the House floor has more than quadrupled, going from 240 in the 87th Congress (1961–62) to 1,122 in the 103rd (1993–94)—about three votes a day while the House is in session. Likewise, there has been an increase in the activities of various quasi-legislative organizations to which most members belong, as reflected in the growth of congressional caucuses. An investigation by Susan Hammond reveals that by the late 1960s there were only two caucuses in the House; by 1986 there were ninety. Over the same period, the number of bicameral caucuses jumped from one to twenty-five (Hammond 1989, 355).

As if such responsibilities were not taxing enough, the extra legislative demands on members and on their office staff have also increased over the same period. The average number of days the House member spent in the district jumped from about 25 per congress in the early 1960s to more than 250 per congress in the early 1980s (Parker 1989, 30). Congressional offices now generate from five to ten times as much mail as they did three decades ago (Ornstein et al., 1990, 164). And over the same period, constituency casework has skyrocketed (Fiorina 1989; Parker 1986). Yet even these trends do not compare to the trajectory in the attention legislators pay to the business of campaign fundraising. Although the available time-series data do not stretch back as far as 1974, the average amount of money that the typical House member feels compelled to raise has jumped by a factor of six since then. One member estimated that he now spends 20 percent of his time calling or meeting with prospective donors, an estimate that squares with the reports of other members frustrated by the time required to finance a high-cost campaign. Members of Congress, one recent study concludes, "have been forced to follow a never-ending money chase. They spend countless hours and tremendous energy in fundraising, often to the detriment of their legislative duties" (Magleby and Nelson 1990, 1–2).

Not surprisingly, the effects of these various demands find their way into the perceptions that members have of their jobs. Elizabeth Drew quotes one representative: " 'There are just too many votes, too many issues, too many meetings, too many attention-demanding situations. We're going to committee meetings, subcommittee meetings, caucuses—a caucus of the class with which you were elected here, the rural caucus, the steel caucus, you name it—and we're seeing constituents and returning phone calls and trying to rush back and forth to the district, and then we're supposed to understand what we're voting on when we get to the House floor' " (quoted in O'Donnell 1981, 128). Similar themes run through the interviews I conducted with current and former members of Congress:

> I feel like I'm spread thin all the time. There's never any time to read or think an issue through or anything like that.
>
> In my opinion, the workload is inestimable. I feel like I'm just treading water most of the time.
>
> I read somewhere that the workload of each member's office had doubled every five years since 1935. . . . [Our] days are so fractured with competing claims that [we] cannot concentrate on careful legislative work.
>
> The main thing I'd point to is the confusion, the lack of preparation. If I'm going to do the job I came here to do, I need to do more than just read a text. I've done it, literally, but it's a lousy way to operate. I don't know what I'd do if a page was missing or out of order or something. . . . There are times when I say to myself, I don't need this, I don't need to subject myself to this bullshit.

In sum, the limits of time and the press of legislative and nonlegislative demands are substantial and have become increasingly so in recent years. The consequences of these demands are everywhere apparent, especially in the place where most of the legislative work takes place and where specialization and informed deliberation are supposed to occur. Quite simply, participation in one's own committees is a sometimes thing. Drawing on interviews that were conducted about the time that Bauer and his colleagues were writing, Charles Clapp concluded that less than half of a committee's members regularly participated in its deliberations (1963, 266). Scattered committee studies over the past two decades support less generous descriptions. In his study of the House Ways and Means Committee, John Manley found that on many important issues, a "subgroup" within the committee, sometimes as small as three individuals, "dominated the executive session deliberations" (1970, 74). More recently, Lynette Perkins found that two-thirds of the House Judiciary Committee's membership were described by committee staff as "minimally present," "not interested," or "not around much" (1980, 378–79). And James Payne's study of the House banking and public works hearings revealed that the preponderance of members fall into a category of low participation (1980; see also Burgin 1991).

My survey of legislative staffers in member's personal offices provided similar accounts:

> There are weeks where if he makes it to half of his committee meetings, he's doing well.

He had a conflict, but the point is that members always have conflicts. They have to be in two places at once, so they have to choose: Which issue is more important to me?

Legislatively, there are maybe six or so areas we really end up getting involved in, and all these other things are just blips that show up on the screen and disappear. There just isn't time.

Half of his time is spent committee-hopping. We had put together this amendment that he wanted to offer to the higher ed. bill. . . . The markup's half over before he shows up. He gets in there, asks a couple of questions, offers the amendment. Not two minutes later, our A.A. [administrative assistant] comes and pulls him out in the hall to meet with some guy from the district. By then he's late for another meeting; then there's another floor vote; then he heads off for a fundraiser or something. Then he gets on a plane and flies back to the district, and he doesn't even find out what happened until the following Tuesday. . . . Oh, and he forgot to leave his proxy, so he didn't even end up voting for his own amendment!

Similar observations could be quoted by the dozens, but the basic point should be clear enough. Congressmen in committees simply have too much to do legislatively and too little time, energy, and other legislative resources to do it. They cannot take on every issue; they must choose. The resulting pattern of frustration has been generally confirmed in a survey administered by the House Commission on Administrative Review. Summarizing the responses from that survey, Thomas O'Donnell concludes that House members' "ability to concentrate time on any single activity is severely constrained by the abundance and complexity of the demands that confront them" (1981, 138).

The Concept of Legislative Participation

The selective nature of legislative participation is thus revealed in a wide range of sources, yet no systematic study has been made of such behavior. Where the subject is treated at all, it is rarely more than a passing concern in a larger examination of legislative life. Because of the relative inaccessibility of committee data, furthermore, the scattered studies that have touched on the subject have been almost exclusively based on interviews, so that most contain only general descriptions of committee participation patterns. No sustained theoretical treatments exist.

In the study of legislative participation, then, the first problems one must confront are conceptual and methodological. Unlike other, more widely studied forms of legislative behavior (the roll call vote, the committee assignment request), participation refers to no single, identifiable act. Rather, it is a general category that subsumes a range of different, more or less significant, more or less visible activities. Our first task, then, is to consider how the concept is to be drawn.

THE CONCEPT OF PARTICIPATION AND THE
PRACTICE OF DEMOCRATIC CONSENT

In a passage that has been quoted by congressional scholars ad nauseam ever since (I shan't break the tradition here), a young political scientist by the name of Woodrow Wilson described the United States Congress as a creature of its own committees, holding session merely "to sanction [their] conclusions as rapidly as possible." As a matter of empirical political science, it turns out, Wilson's claim was simply wrong, so it may be for the best that he later pursued another line of work. But the distinction he made between the "public exhibition" of the House floor and the serious legislative work that presumably took place elsewhere raises a more general issue for the study of legislative participation.

Quite simply, the issue is this: What counts as participation? Some of the observable legislative activities that members perform day to day, whether in committee or on the floor, have little effect on the shape of the legislation that ultimately gets approved (or defeated). Indeed, in some circumstances, members take action that they do not expect, perhaps do not even intend, to have any immediate legislative consequences. For instance, the political maverick may offer an amendment intended to illustrate some flaw in the majority's position, knowing that the amendment will not be seriously considered; or the minority party may stake out its own legislative agenda in the form of a substitute bill, realizing that it will not pass; or, more frequently, members of both parties may vote (or change a vote) on the House floor with the intent of publicly recording a position, knowing full well that their vote will have no effect on the outcome.

In thinking about legislative participation, in short, the temptation is to distinguish between two different sorts of activities — those which are substantive and serious and those which are legislatively superfluous or symbolic. By implication, it is the former, not the latter, with which students of congressional behavior ought to be concerned.

As a point of conceptual departure, this strikes me as a temptation that ought to be strongly resisted. The reason is not that there are serious practical problems with implementing such a distinction, though that is certainly true.[1]

---

1. Absent information regarding members' private intentions and expectations, conjecture is the only method available to classify different kinds of legislative acts by differ-

Rather, the main reason goes to an important justification for studying legislative participation in the first place, that participation by the citizens' several agents and hence the expression of a wide range of alternative points of view is central to the practice of democratic consent. It will invariably happen during legislative deliberations that certain views and interests get expressed that will almost certainly fail. But that does not render them meaningless or merely symbolic. Quite the contrary. The idea of consent becomes important in democratic theory precisely in the case where the views of some minority do not prevail, where a minority thus disagrees with the collective choice made by the polity. Participation is what obligates the minority to an outcome it does not like. Put somewhat differently, participation (perhaps once or twice removed) is the solution liberal democracy offers to the puzzle, How is it that free agents can agree *to* something they do not agree *with?* Thus do most Western assemblies take seriously the rights of the opposition to challenge and criticize the majority's proposals. Without the ability to exercise such rights, the legitimacy of representative government quickly dissolves.[2]

Moreover, proposals that appear to be no more than symbolic gestures can serve all manner of other legislative purposes. Destined to fail in the short run, such proposals might stake out a bargaining position for subsequent stages of the legislative process, say, a House-Senate conference or negotiations with the White House. Or they might accentuate partisan differences that form the backdrop for some future electoral contest, thereby improving the accountability of agents to their districts. Still other proposals might be offered with an eye to affecting some future agenda, a process that Kingdon refers to as "softening up" the relevant policy community or attentive public (1984, 134–37).

In sum, it would not only be operationally difficult (perhaps impossible) for the researcher to categorize the seriousness or superfluity of particular actions, it is misguided on other grounds as well. Actions that appear to have no discernible effect on the legislation in question cannot be assumed unimportant in the larger processes of representation, partisan competition, and agenda formation. Moreover, to do so implies the ancillary assumption that reasonably rational legislators, who already suffer from serious time constraints, will spend nontrivial amounts of their time on trivial pursuits. In the

---

ent members at different moments as "serious" or "superfluous." It is certainly difficult to imagine what coding criteria one would produce to substantiate such distinctions, and even harder to imagine how the criteria could be applied to the reading of a paper record of legislative action.

2. On the importance of representation to theories of democratic consent and political obligation, see Herzog 1989, chap. 6.

analysis that follows, I will thus assume that the various legislative activities which members pursue for any given bill warrant our attention. What consequences particular activities might have for the practice of representation and the exercise of influence (among other things) are separate but important questions, the exploration of which I return to in the final chapter.[3]

TWO MODES OF LEGISLATIVE PARTICIPATION

To say that we should not dismiss particular actions a priori, however, is not to say that they are interchangeable, that distinctions appropriate to the purpose cannot be made between them. On this point, I borrow a lesson from Verba and Nie's well-known study of political participation in the mass public (1972). Verba and Nie argue that the participation of individual citizens can vary not only in degree but in kind. Differences in the kind of participation, in turn, can be of substantial theoretical importance: "Both the process of coming to participate and the consequences differ depending on the kind of act involved" (Verba and Nie, 1972, 45). They identify several kinds of participation at the mass level and label them *modes of participation,* a term that I will borrow here. What (if any) are the different modes of participation in legislative decision making?

Based on several in-depth case studies of legislative politics and a series of exploratory interviews, I identified two modes, which I will refer to as *formal* and *informal* participation. Much of a committee's decision-making activity takes place in formal committee and subcommittee markup sessions. Here the central and often the most controversial issues of a bill are taken up for collective consideration; specific provisions and counterproposals are debated; and the legislation is summarized, sometimes section by section, then amended and voted on. Rules of parliamentary procedure are in force, but nothing like the restrictive rules often imposed on the House floor operate in committee; hence all committee members enjoy the formal right to participate. Since the reforms of the early 1970s, moreover, the vast majority of markups have been held in open session, so that formal participation has also been public participation. Such meetings, in fact, tend to be very well attended by committee outsiders: if not by the national press, certainly by representatives of the various organized interests likely to be affected by the matter at hand.

3. This point bears emphasizing. Participation does not imply influence over alternative policy choices. While the study of legislative participation should enhance our understanding of influence in that the two phenomena, I believe, are causally (but conditionally) related, the two concepts must be kept distinct. It is the former, behavioral phenomenon that is the focus of this book. See Hall (1992) where I draw the distinction sharply and attempt to measure each phenomenon separately.

At the same time, much of a committee's decision-making activity occurs *informally* — outside the context of an official markup. Two characteristics distinguish such activity. The first is that once one leaves the glare of the committee meeting room, most of the legislative action becomes nonpublic. Journalists and lobbyists are often excluded; meeting times and places are not announced; official records are rarely kept; majority-rule mechanisms are seldom applied. Indeed, much of the serious deliberating takes place over the phone, on the floor, in the anterooms, and through various memos and letters that circulate among the principal players. In short, while committees in the postreform Congress are no longer the "dim dungeons of silence" (Wilson 1956 [1885], 63) they once were, much of their work is still done in the dark, at least insofar as the public and the press are concerned.

The second distinguishing feature of this behind-the-scenes work is that most of it is conducted by staff. One of the first lessons that a neophyte legislator learns is that while the demands placed upon him seem to expand geometrically, the supply of time available to meet those demands is, by virtue of universal law, inelastic. Faced with the press of excessive obligations and the frequent prospect of needing to be two places at once, members have responded by relying increasingly on staff. Salisbury and Shepsle (1981a, 1981b) thus observe that the actor in congressional decision making is no longer the member but his *enterprise,* an organization of 20 to 120 agents for which the member serves as principal. Staff negotiations and interactions have become a "substitute for direct conversations and deliberations among members," and much of what members do in person is prefigured by the options and information that staffers supply (Malbin 1979, chapter 1 and p. 245). The study of legislative participation, then, must extend not only to the member but to the enterprise. Invisible in the official action of the committee markup, the role of that enterprise is everywhere evident in the legislative deliberations that occur behind the scenes.

Participants from both parties repeatedly stressed the significance of these informal deliberations. One of the most important stages in the decision-making process, for instance, comes when the principal players formulate the provisions of the original markup vehicle. But members and their staffs participate in other informal ways as well. Working out subsequent compromises, planning party strategy, building support for particular initiatives — all these activities can have an important effect on the legislation that makes its way through the process. Views or interests that are not represented in the premarkup discussions are less likely to receive a full and fair hearing at subsequent stages.

Although the formal and informal may be analytically distinguishable modes of behavior, however, they should not be unrelated. Even if key provisions are proposed and discussed prior to markup, they are typically summarized and justified, and where controversial, they are either ratified or rejected in open session. Thus even though much may go on outside the markup, the markup both serves as an indicator of who has participated behind the scenes and is itself an important forum for policy making. Just how good an indicator it is, however, varies from bill to bill. Formal markups are sometimes fast, pro forma affairs, revealing the roles played by only the two or three major players. This point was repeated several times by committee staffers as I conducted my first few interviews. After mentioning that I had already spent considerable time reading several hundred pages of markup transcripts for the 1982 Job Training Partnership Act, I asked one veteran staffer if she would agree to an interview. She responded, only partly in jest, "I guess I'll have to. You sure can't tell from our markup what went on." Other staffers gave blow-by-blow accounts of particular bills for which the markup was preceded by several days of staff meetings and lengthy exchanges between staffers and their bosses. In short, the records of committee and subcommittee markups undoubtedly tell us much of the committee decision-making story, yet the researcher who relies exclusively on such records acquires a picture of members' behavior but misses the actions of their support staff. Such an oversight introduces potentially significant measurement error.

The primary justification for treating formal and informal participation as analytically distinct modes, however, is theoretical, not methodological. To paraphrase the language of Verba and Nie, public and nonpublic participation may differ in both their causes and their effects. This possibility is suggested by the oft-cited distinction between legislative "show horses" and "workhorses" (Clapp 1963; Matthews 1959; Payne 1980). Workhorses are members who shun publicity and tend to their legislative duties; their goal is to gain "the respect of their colleagues" (Matthews 1959, 1067) and thereby affect the shape of the legislation their chamber produces. They are "quiet, influential types" (Payne 1980, 429). Show horses, on the other hand, seek publicity and presumably neglect detailed legislative work. Their audience is not so much their colleagues as it is some current or future constituency whose interests they have an incentive to represent. As a result, their actions are less likely to have a significant legislative effect within their chamber.

Of course, such characterizations refer to ideal types, not real individuals. And as I have already suggested, the view that position taking and other forms of symbolic action are irrelevant politically simply because they are inconsequential legislatively is difficult to justify, unless one's sole concern is the prediction of outcomes, not the practice of representation. But the workhorse–

show horse distinction does suggest that legislative participation may have two theoretically distinct dimensions, which are reflected more or less in the behavior of different legislators as they speak (sometimes simultaneously) to different audiences. Specifically, although formal and informal participation may be related and though both are substantively important in the decision-making process, the public nature of formal sessions makes them a more likely arena for "show horse" legislative behavior motivated more by constituency concerns; informal participation is more likely to elicit the workhorse contributions motivated more by policy concerns. Such hypotheses will be elaborated in greater depth in the next chapter. For now, the simple assumption is that full understanding of the nature of legislative participation depends on information regarding both modes.

PARTICIPATION AND SPECIALIZATION: A CONCEPTUAL DIGRESSION

When the subject has arisen in past research on legislative behavior, the discussion of participation has invariably been tied to the concept of specialization, or *participation* and *specialization* have even been used synonymously. In his classic work on committee decision making, for instance, Fenno (1973a) collapses any conceptual distinctions one might imagine between the two, examining committee differences in light of their varying "participation-specialization norms." Recent important work on the theory of legislative organization, in contrast, has refocused attention on specialization as a public good-producing activity, in that it increases the information available to chamber majorities seeking policies most likely to produce the real-world changes they desire (Gilligan and Krehbiel 1990; Krehbiel 1991). The conceptual boundaries of the term, however, are no clearer in the recent work.

The distinction between participation and specialization thus warrants a brief digression. Participation refers simply to observable behavior in a particular decision-making forum; it can range from absence or abstention to active involvement, such as "taking the lead" in pushing (or opposing) a particular proposal.[4] It is also possible to describe legislative participation at different levels of analysis, depending on the scholar's purpose — a member's participation on a specific issue or his participation across a range of issues that come before his subcommittees, committees, or chamber. What we typically label specialization, on the other hand, is defined by the intersection of two separate conceptual dimensions. One of these is the breadth of participa-

4. In this respect, legislative entrepreneurship — a central but little understood phenomenon in legislative agenda setting (Kingdon 1984) and coalition building (Arnold 1990) — is but a special case of participation.

Table 2.1   Participation, Expertise, and
Specialization: A Conceptual Clarification

	Participation	
Expertise	Narrow	Broad
Low	Apprentice	Generalist
High	Specialist	—

tion: a specialist is one who participates in a particular, often narrowly circum-scribed jurisdiction. Thus when I say to some audience that I am a specialist in legislative politics, I intend to convey that I focus most of my research and teaching efforts in that particular area, rather than, say, presidential character, East European ethnic conflict, or seventeenth-century Puritan election ser-mons. But the notion of specialization implies something more than selective attention to some particular field of endeavor. Specialization is an activity whose intended if not realized consequence is the acquisition of *expertise*. Thus the term *specialist* is often used synonymously with the term *expert*.

It nevertheless bears emphasizing that these two conceptual dimensions — narrow focus and the acquisition of expertise — are related. It is generally necessary to focus one's attention narrowly in order to obtain exceptional expertise in the chosen field. Of course, an almost exclusive research focus on legislative politics does not guarantee expert knowledge in that area. But gen-erally speaking, the concentrated investment of time and energy in a particular area does tend to produce greater policy-related knowledge — what we would normally refer to as expertise.

The two-dimensional nature of specialization and its relation to legislative participation is illustrated in table 2.1, a table that has the added advantage of clarifying other oft-used concepts in past and current studies of legislative behavior, this study among them.

As the table illustrates, the term *specialist* applies to someone who has (1) concentrated on a fairly narrow policy domain and thereby (2) acquired ex-pertise within it — the lower-left cell of the table. As the table also illustrates, nothing compels the legislator to concentrate narrowly — that is, to develop a specialty. Some participate on a wide range of issues; the trade-off is that what they gain in breadth of activity (and perhaps in visibility) they lose in depth of knowledge on any given issue. In Capitol Hill parlance, such legislators are *generalists*. This term is more often applied to senators than to House mem-bers because senators are fewer in number, their energies are divided among a greater number of committees, and by virtue of their larger and more diverse constituencies, senators are motivated to participate on a wider range of issues. At the same time, however, members who concentrate narrowly are not immediately anointed "specialists." Personal expertise comes with time, study, and experience in an area. Members who have not yet acquired expertise in the relevant domain of the legislative profession are, like artists and craftspeople, labeled apprentices. The fact that the lower-right cell is empty, in turn, follows from the assumption that the individual member's time and resources are sufficiently scarce that he cannot devote significant attention to all issues that come before his committee, much less his chamber.

It bears noting that the terms *specialist* and *expert* are simply descriptive, reflecting observations about the behavior and/or attributes of particular members. Nothing is implied here about the factors, sociological or otherwise, that might generate a particular description. Moreover, the categories *specialist, apprentice,* or *generalist* pertain at the fairly general level of analysis. A person is a specialist or an apprentice within a particular policy area or jurisdiction, which invariably includes multiple issues and action on various bills. My objective in this study, however, is to identify and explain the highly variable participation of members across specific bills, not aggregate behavioral patterns that appear across more or less broad committee jurisdictions. It is seldom possible to say with accuracy that a member is a specialist on a bill. It is possible, however, to impute to a member and his enterprise expertise relating to a given bill. The sources of experience and expertise relevant to particular pieces of legislation thus figure prominently in my theory of participation, but for reasons that should now be clear, I will avoid using the terms *specialist* or *specialization.*

Participation in Committees: The Data

For most committees in both chambers, the records available on decision making in committee and subcommittee are remarkably rich. This is especially true for the official markup stage of the process.

PARTICIPATION IN MARKUP

Committee files contain the verbatim transcripts of each markup session, recorded by a professional stenographer; detailed minutes of the same meetings, compiled from notes taken during the markup by the committee clerk or an executive secretary; and original copies of bills (or working drafts of bills), amendments, insertions, and reports that are referred to in the course of the markup debate.

From these records, one can construct a nearly exhaustive account of each member's participation during the markup of each bill, at both the subcommittee and the full-committee stage. I did that for a saturation sample of bills from each of the three committees: twenty-one from House Agriculture (97th Congress), seventeen from Education and Labor (97th Congress), and twenty for Energy and Commerce (98th Congress). Taken together, these samples constituted about half of the bills that saw any kind of markup action in the committees during the two-year congress. In choosing the sample, I included bills from the various subcommittees in rough proportion to the number that members reported for full-committee action, but I generally excluded bills for which the legislative markup at both the full committee and subcommittee was merely perfunctory.[5] In the end, the sample reflected a mix of major and minor bills (somewhat weighted in favor of the former), spanned diverse areas of domestic policy, and included several bills that raised issues of foreign policy and international trade.

I collected from these records data on the markup behavior of every committee member in whose office I was also able to arrange an interview. This was possible for over 80 percent of the representatives who were committee members for the full session.[6] The data reflect participation in five markup activities, described here in rough order of the time and effort that each entails.

Showing Up

Attendance at markups is, by and large, a precondition for more serious involvement in the committee's decision making at this stage and normally indicates minimal attentiveness to the bill under consideration. In certain situations, moreover, attendance — or, rather, nonattendance — can have noteworthy consequences. House quorum requirements stipulate that a majority of committee members must be present for the purposes of reporting out a bill; the failure or refusal of members to attend can thus delay action. Should several members of the majority be absent, for instance, the minority can simply slip into the anteroom, leaving one member behind to challenge the presence of a quorum. Referred to as a disappearing quorum, this tactic was commonly used on the House floor during the the late 1800s, until Speaker Reed instituted measures to nullify its effectiveness. But the tactic is still avail-

5. This sampling strategy likewise excludes bills that did not reach markup. Successful efforts at premarkup obstruction thus fall outside the scope of the study, important though they are. In other words, I cannot here investigate (non)participation in nondecisions.

6. Thus the samples come very close to including the full population of members on each committee, but in any case, care was taken to ensure that the samples were stratified along the lines of both seniority and party. See Appendix A.

able in committee, and markup records reveal that it was employed by the minority to delay action on three bills in the sample. In one case, an Education and Labor bill to establish a commission on domestic voluntary service, the Republicans employed a disappearing quorum to delay action for three weeks at the end of a session. By the time the committee finally reported the bill (by a vote of twenty-two to three), the session was nearly over, and the Rules Committee never considered Education and Labor's request for floor consideration.

The minority's potential to employ such tactics is a credible threat because the majority party requires exceptional attendance to constitute a quorum on its own. As table 2.2 shows, members are credited with having attended if they make so much as a momentary appearance at the markup, and many do just that. Even so, the official rates of absenteeism range from 20 to 30 percent in full committee, 25 to 35 percent in subcommittee — worse than one would expect for a typical university seminar!

Voting Early and Often

Our knowledge of members' voting decisions on the chamber floor is now extensive, but the same cannot be said for voting in congressional committees. To date, there have been very few studies of members' voting decisions at this stage.[7] At least two features distinguish voting in committee, both of which are relevant to legislative participation.

First, although roll call votes are important for deciding some of the most controversial issues before a committee, the personal participation of committee members in such votes is far less common than on the floor. As table 2.2 also shows, committee members are on hand to participate in formal roll calls for fewer than two votes out of three on average; on the House floor, by comparison, members participate in nine votes out of ten. In the jurisdictionally narrower subcommittees, the voting participation actually proves worse, not better.

There are no doubt several reasons for such patterns. One is that committee votes are far less visible than floor votes, and subcommittee votes are less visible still. For both prefloor stages, votes are rarely reported by the national news media, and none of the various groups that report voting records and voting participation on the floor do so for the committee stage. Hence, missing

---

7. Two books have been published that use committee roll-call data to map the coalitional patterns in House committees (Parker and Parker 1985; Unekis and Rieselbach, 1984), but little work has been published that explores the determinants of individual voting decisions in committee. For one important exception, see Wright 1990.

Table 2.2   Congress at Work? Congressmen in (and Absent from) Committees

	Agriculture (%)	Education and Labor (%)	Energy and Commerce (%)
Attendance			
Full committee	79.5	71.4	76.3
Subcommittee	73.6	68.8	66.9
Voting (excluding proxies)			
Full committee	45.2	36.6	45.1
Subcommittee	42.4	34.0	39.5
Participated in markup debate			
Full committee	41.2	34.7	31.9
Subcommittee	60.0	34.7	42.2
Offered amendment or motion			
Full committee	18.5	15.4	20.3
Subcommittee	40.8	23.4	38.8
Engaged in agenda action			
Full committee	5.8	9.3	3.5
Subcommittee	13.8	19.2	11.2

Source: Committee and subcommittee markup records for dense samples of bills and members. House Agriculture Committee (97th Congress), Education and Labor (97th Congress), and Energy and Commerce (98th Congress).

a vote in committee is far less likely to incite charges of legislative irresponsibility from some constituent, journalist, good government group, or prospective challenger.

Another reason members were infrequently on hand to vote in committee derives from the third distinguishing feature of voting at the committee stage: the procedural permissibility of proxy voting. Before the Republican reforms of 1995 that banished the practice, House rules gave committees local option with respect to proxy voting, and almost every committee exercised it.[8] Thus, as table 2.2 also shows, when members were not on hand to cast their votes in committee or subcommittee markup, they frequently relinquished their proxy to a colleague to vote on their behalf. In theory, then, the majoritarian nature of formal voting could be preserved even in the face of significant absenteeism. Interviews with congressional staffers suggest, however, that that cannot

8. However, Republican Senate majorities, inaugurated in 1981 and 1995, did not ban proxy voting in committee, such that it has remained a common practice throughout the postwar era.

be safely assumed. Members frequently relinquished their proxies with little knowledge of what issues would come up in the course of the markup and with no well-developed view of how they might vote in any case. Specific instructions were rare. One four-year veteran of the Education and Labor Committee staff told me that he could recall only a handful of times when a member had communicated an explicit instruction. Other staffers reported a similar indifference on the part of their bosses regarding how their proxies would be used:

> On the big votes, the ones that are going to be close, you try to be there. Most of the time (when a member gives up his proxy), it's some issue that he doesn't care much about.
>
> A lot of these bills just aren't a high priority for him. He'll give his proxy to [the subcommittee chair] and leave it to him to do with it whatever he wants.
>
> If he can't be there, he figures he just ought to leave it to [the ranking minority member's] discretion.

Neither is it the case that the members always select like-minded colleagues to cast their votes. Regardless of seniority, region, or ideology, the clear tendency is to give one's proxy to the committee or subcommittee ranking member of one's party. In fact, it sometimes happens that ranking members cast proxies that they do not actually have. For instance, the following exchange was called to my attention by one of the clerks for House Education and Labor, who found the incident humorous because it revealed what "everybody already knew," namely, that Committee Chair Perkins "was always casting proxies he didn't have," and that "he often didn't have any idea how the member would vote."

> *Chairman:* I am going to vote Mr. Andrews' aye by proxy.
> *Clerk:* He is right here, and he has already voted.
> *Chairman:* I did not hear him vote.
> *Clerk:* He votes no. [laughter]
> *Mr. Andrews:* Mr. Chairman, I will change my vote to aye. [laughter][9]

For the period of this study, in sum, proxy voting was common in committee; indeed, taking personal votes and proxy votes together, voting participation in committee was almost as high as voting participation on the floor. But the interview evidence suggests that the proxy procedure is not an effective mechanism for preserving the authority of the absent. If anything, it is more

9. Unpublished transcript of the House Committee on Education and Labor, June 9, 1981, p. 55. The context of the incident and the laughter "by both sides" was recalled for me by one of the clerks of the committee.

likely to augment the authority of those who are present and active. In practice, committee proxy provisions give rise to something like a system of weighted voting, whereby the individuals already well positioned to affect committee outcomes are endowed with enhanced voting authority as well. It was a relatively common occurrence for a minority of members present and voting in committee, wielding the proxies of their absent colleagues, to defeat a sitting majority.

Participating in the Markup Debate

Once they move beyond the activities of attending and voting, committee members' participation begins to drop off quickly for most bills, as the data summarized in table 2.2 reveal. This should not be surprising. Participation in the markup dialogue requires a good bit more of the member. With rare exceptions, speaking during a markup requires that the member be familiar with at least some of the issues or have formulated at least a few legitimate questions, if not well-developed positions or proposals to advocate before colleagues.

Participation in the markup debate can be substantively important in several respects. By raising or redefining issues or by taking and defending specific positions, participants in the markup debate can give expression to the views and interests of citizens in their district. Indeed, the markup transcripts are replete with arguments of this kind, even on a committee such as Education and Labor where constituency concerns are thought to carry relatively little weight. For instance, one member who represented a predominantly Hispanic district in southern California criticized the discriminatory implications of an immigration bill before the committee. Another member defended an increase in funds for summer youth training programs, noting that teenage unemployment in his Chicago district had reached all-time highs. Commenting on a bill that would provide matching funds to train displaced workers in the defense industry, a Connecticut representative summed up his interest thus: "When we get to formulas [for matching funds] — I have been here long enough to know what the impact would be on Connecticut were your amendment to be adopted."

And while show-horse behavior may turn up more often in public markup than in actions behind the scenes, comments such as those cited are not easily reduced to self-serving position taking. Unlike many committee hearings and most action on the House floor, committee markups are rarely covered by C-SPAN cameras; the transcripts of markups are not published; and the markup audience, for the most part, tends to comprise mostly legislative staffers, agency officials, interest-group representatives, and other relatively sophisticated observers of these proceedings. Little purpose is served by plying the audience of the committee markup (at least relative to most other forums on Capitol Hill) with fatuous rhetoric.

Finally, the sometimes lengthy committee debates often serve the purpose of providing policy-related information or specific cues to partisans of the active members. Alternatively, when the proposal does not cut neatly along partisan or ideological lines, the evaluations of diverse participants in a debate enables the interested but less expert members of the committee to make informed choices (Krehbiel 1991).

Working on Amendments and Engaging in Procedural Maneuvers

Most of the dramatic action in a committee markup occurs as members offer motions of various kinds. Some of these are procedural in nature, and at times they have important consequences for the course of the deliberations. Points of order, quorum calls, motions to report, and requests for recorded votes fall into this category. By themselves, such motions do not require much effort, but they often indicate that a member or his staff has been active in planning legislative strategy; it is rare for a member who engages in such procedural maneuvering not to be a prominent participant in the markup debate. Still, the more common and more consequential motions are amendments to the markup vehicle. If successful, an amendment can significantly alter one or more provisions in the bill. And even if unsuccessful, an amendment still serves the purpose of placing a specific alternative before the committee, thereby bringing certain features of the markup vehicle into sharper relief.

Depending on the scope of the amendment, however, amending activity tends to be labor-intensive, if not for the member, then for his staff. Staffers observed that the process of developing a single amendment often spanned several weeks. For instance, one staffer described an amendment that his boss offered to a conservation bill before the Agriculture Committee: "The idea came from a guy in our state's wildlife and conservation service, and [my boss] told me to look into it. So I got hold of the right guy over at ASCS to see what the administration might think of it. I called CRS. Then I called a couple of the farm groups — the Farm Bureau, American Farmland Trust. They made a couple of good suggestions. Then I took it to committee staff, who floated it on the Republican side. Once they signed off, I talked to the department again. Then I went back to my boss. Then I took it to leg[islative] counsel to get the thing drafted. By the time we got to markup . . . I probably had given it a week's worth of work."

Of course, not all amendments are alike, either in their potential effect on the bill being marked up or in the amount of effort they require. Ideally, it would be useful to isolate the relative scope of each. The best that I could do in this regard, however, was to classify amendments according to whether they (1) would make technical or grammatical changes in the legislation or were clearly characterized as being minor and noncontroversial, or (2) entailed substantive changes in the bill. Regardless of the type of amendment, however, only a few members will attempt to amend any particular bill that comes up in full committee. Table 2.2 shows the percentage of members who offered any kind of amendment or procedural motion at any time during the markup of the bills in the three committee samples. While amending activity is more common in the smaller and more specialized subcommittee context, at neither the full- nor the subcommittee stage do half the members take any kind of amending or procedural action.

Setting the Markup Agenda

The final type of behavioral data to be analyzed here involves actions that members take to shape the markup agenda or otherwise frame the alternatives that the committee will consider. Such actions typically occur as the legislative vehicle is drafted, usually under the supervision or authority of the subcommittee or full-committee chair. In this respect, then, the formal and informal modes of participation converge at the high end: members' role in the behind-the-scenes drafting process predetermines whether they have a significant role in the formal markup (even if they are ultimately unable to attend). An alternative means by which a member can refocus the committee's agenda is to offer an amendment as a substitute to the markup vehicle or to some significant portion of it. Unlike when controversial action occurs on the House floor, there are no restrictive rules or other procedural mechanisms available to the committee or subcommittee chair to prevent amendments from being offered. The minority can and often does draft its own alternative and see that alternative considered during formal markup. I thus credited a member with markup agenda action either if he was a principal author of the markup vehicle, as revealed in the markup record or in interviews with committee staff, or if he offered a major substitute amendment. (See Appendix B.)

Without a doubt, such actions are extraordinarily important for the markup deliberations that ensue. As E. E. Schattschneider put it, "the definition of the alternatives is the supreme instrument of power" (1960, 68), and this conclusion has been confirmed by a long line of empirical and theoretical scholars. It was also confirmed by the respondents in this study. One Education and Labor staffer observed: "The [legislative vehicle] sets the terms of debate, and that's half the game. Is there going to be a public jobs title or not? Is the program going to be administered by local governments or by PICs [private industry councils]? What sort of formula do we use? You try and settle those things first, or at least figure out what the alternatives are. Once you get to markup, it's usually too late to bring up new options."

As the data reported in table 2.2 reveal, however, few individuals can be credited with significant agenda action. In the typical case, only three or four members are involved in defining the nature and scope of the problem that a bill will address and the boundaries of the proposed solution. The role of most participants in committee markups is largely reactive: they support, criticize, or try to amend a legislative vehicle that was produced elsewhere, perhaps through processes from which they have been excluded.

A PARTICIPATION SCALE

Taken together, then, the data on these five activities constitute an almost complete account of the role that each member plays in the markup of each bill that comes before the panel. Depending on one's purpose, one may wish to examine the causes and consequences of each separately. At times in the analysis to come, in fact, I will do just that. But for most purposes of this study, I will have need of a more economical measure. The one I will employ here is an eight-point scale of the participation of member i on bill j, constructed from a Guttman scale analysis of the five activities, two of which I have divided into subdivisions to retain more information.

0   Engaged in none of the activities.
1   Attended one or more markups.
2   Voted in one or more recorded roll calls (proxies excluded).
3   Spoke during markup, minor participant in the discussion.
4   Spoke during markup, major participant in the discussion.
5   Offered minor or technical amendment or procedural motion.
6   Offered one or more substantive amendments.
7   Engaged in agenda action.

The characteristics of this scale and the analysis that produced it are discussed more fully in Appendix C, but two points call for emphasis here. First, although the separation of each activity into dichotomies causes some loss of information about the degree to which individual members engage in an activity, the loss is not great. The measurement of agenda action was dichotomous to begin with. And by far the preponderance of bills was marked up in a single meeting and saw no more than a single roll call vote; the measurement of these two activities thus proved to be essentially dichotomous. Second, the rank order of the activities generated by the scale analysis was identical for each committee and conforms to the ordering I laid out regarding the relative degree of time and effort that each requires. At one end of the scale, a member needs little more than a pulse and a few minutes of time to get credit for markup attendance; at the other, for serious involvement in drafting a complete bill or a substitute amendment, a member has to mobilize his enterprise to the full. On the basis of both the impressions culled from the interviews and the hierarchical nature of the Guttman scales, it thus seems reasonable to order members' markup participation along a single dimension, ranging from activity that requires very little time and effort at the low end to activities that require a major effort at the high end.

PARTICIPATION BEHIND THE SCENES

Like participation in the official committee markups, informal participation covers a wide range of specific activities, each of which is potentially important for which views and interests get represented and the legislative provisions that are ultimately adopted. We have already noted one particular way in which action behind the scenes is important. By playing a major role in the drafting process, a member helps define the markup agenda. But short of full-blown authorship, members can be involved in other ways and varying degrees in a panel's informal deliberations. Often a bill entrepreneur will consult with the members he thinks might be especially interested or might be important for building a majority coalition. Committee staff members suggested that this is often the case on major pieces of legislation, which sometimes require several days of staff meetings, during which objections may be aired and particular provisions renegotiated. To the extent that this occurs, involvement in behind-the-scenes negotiations can be an alternative and less risky means of affecting some particular provision than offering amendments during a subsequent markup. As the legislative assistant to an Agriculture backbencher observed: "Getting what you want in the chairman's mark is really important. It's almost always harder to put something in once the thing has gone to markup. Then everybody's watching, they're asking themselves 'What will this do?' 'Why the change?' If you get it in the original bill, it's just one of two dozen other things in there, and it stays there unless somebody decides to make a fight out of it."

Beyond the negotiations over particular provisions, members and their staff can engage in other important behind-the-scenes activities as well. Planning party strategy, negotiating with the administration, soliciting proxies, lobbying other members on the committee, or negotiating amendments with outside groups — these activities have an important role in the legislative drama that takes place off the public stage.

Unlike formal markup activity, however, none of the behind-the-scenes activities described here are officially recorded. Neither do they include only those activities in which a member participates in person. Prior to and outside of markups, most of the deliberations take place at a staff level, with representatives participating through their agents. To assess the degree to which members participated in this informal, often indirect fashion, I conducted tape-recorded interviews with the committee and subcommittee staff members who had principal responsibility for staffing each bill in my sample. In the course of a semistructured interview about each bill's development, I sought to (1) identify the committee members who helped shape the original legislative vehicle, and explore the role that each played, (2) discuss the involvement of members in subsequent premarkup deliberations, and (3) identify the legislative assistants with whom the committee and subcommittee staff interacted during committee consideration of the bill. In 88 percent of the cases, I managed to obtain interviews with at least two staffers, one (or more) who staffed the bill on the majority side and one (or more) from the minority side. For 29 percent of the bills, I also interviewed both a majority committee staffer and a majority subcommittee staffer. (The minority on these three committees did not have distinct subcommittee staffs.)

The transcripts of those interviews were then coded with the following index to reflect the involvement of each member's enterprise in the behind-the-scenes deliberations on each bill:

> 0   Negligible. No mention of member's enterprise in any behind-the-scenes capacity
> 1   Minor. Member's enterprise cited as exhibiting support or opposition for, or interest in, some aspect of the bill, but reference to behind-the-scenes activity occurs rarely and only in passing.
> 2   Moderate. Member's enterprise mentioned as actively pushing one specific point of view or provision or as being party to a key compromise, but not as participating frequently in the behind-the-scenes deliberations.
> 3   Major. Member's enterprise central to most informal negotiations, compromises, staff meetings, and the like. Perhaps had some role in drafting provisions of markup vehicle, but not as principal author.
> 4   A Principal Author. Member's enterprise clearly responsible for the shape of the original vehicle, as well as crucial in all subsequent negotiations, compromises, staff meetings, and the like.

The staffers' responses provide an indicator of the informal participation of each member's enterprise on each bill in the sample, and participation was assessed by different staffers with different partisan loyalties and institutional locations. (For tests of the interstaffer and intercoder reliability of this measure, see Appendix C.) How widespread is participation behind the scenes? As is evident from table 2.3, the simple answer is, not very. Staffers' recollections

Table 2.3   Legislative Action Offstage: Informal Participation in Committee Decision Making

	Agriculture (%)	Education and Labor (%)	Energy and Commerce (%)
Informal participation			
Negligible	73.5	79.9	81.2
Minor role	12.8	9.1	11.7
Moderate role	7.0	5.7	3.9
Principal author	6.8	5.3	3.2

Source: Interviews with committee and subcommittee staff.
Note: The number of observations of member *i* on bill *j*, by committee, was as follows: Agriculture, 672; Education and Labor, 493; Energy and Commerce, 660. (See Appendix C.)

undoubtedly truncate the scale at the lower end; minor or fleeting discussions with a particular member's office are not likely to register in a staffer's legislative memory. Still, it appears clear from the table that participation in deliberations behind the scenes is the province of a very few players.

No doubt several reasons combine to produce this general pattern, but two bear mentioning here. The first is that much of the work that goes on in the premarkup deliberations is highly specialized, often esoteric. The principal players at this stage are thus usually committee and subcommittee staff members, some of whom have worked in the relevant area for several years. Still others may have been hired for their particular expertise, gained from experience in a related agency, think tank, state government, or private industry. Most committee backbenchers, in contrast, can seldom allocate more than a single legislative assistant (L.A.) to cover the range of often unrelated issues that come up before a committee on which they serve. That assistant is generally young and rarely has much specialized training; and the breadth of the responsibilities forces him to be a legislative generalist, trying to learn the language of telecommunications policy one week, of natural-gas marketing the next. The frustrations that such responsibilities generate for the typical L.A. were a frequent refrain during the interviews. Legislative assistants often described bills as "extremely complex," "over my head," "intricate," or "impenetrable." Several noted that bills were often finished before they could "get up to speed." Another lamented, "Just once, I wish I could devote the time to an issue that it really deserves." Reflecting on the 1981 Omnibus Farm Bill, an agriculture staffer observed: "You have to go through one farm bill before you have any idea what's going on. The first time through, you're just an observer. . . . Unfortunately, the next one doesn't come along for four or five years, and most (L.A.s) are long gone by then."

A second reason for the limited scope of informal participation is the exclusive nature of the informal communications network. Unlike the formal markup, where parliamentary rules are in force, behind-the-scenes deliberations provide no institutionalized opportunities for participation. Unless the backbencher's staff is vigilant, in fact, much of the behind-the-scenes action may be over and many of the deals struck before she learns that the informal bargaining process has begun. Committee membership, in short, provides entry into the committee hearings and official business meetings, but admission to the behind-the-scenes game is not automatic, save for ranking committee and subcommittee members.

The Efficient Committee

In a book on the House Committee on Foreign Affairs published three decades ago, Holbert Carroll distinguishes between what he called the "formal" and the "efficient" parts of congressional committees. The formal part, according to Carroll, consists of the committee chair and the party majority — the coalition that, according to a parliamentary theory of collective responsibility, at least, was endowed with the authority to act. The efficient part, by contrast, "consists of a core of members, usually only a handful of men representing both political parties. These men actively participate in the hearings, propose the amendments, and shape the legislation. They write parts of the committee's report, or at least take the time to slant it to their satisfaction. . . . Probably less than 10 members of the 32-member Committee on Foreign Affairs, for example, persistently and actively participate in the deliberations of the group" (Carroll 1966, quoted in Kozak and McCartney, 1981, 122–23).

Bearing in mind the activities that together constitute committee members' participation, we are now in position to identify the efficient committees — to map the bill-specific behavior patterns that constitute the real, rather than reified, division of labor in three jurisdictions. Table 2.4 summarizes those patterns for the fifty-eight bills in the three-committee sample. For the purposes of the table, I counted as active a member who was a major participant in either the subcommittee or full-committee markup debate or who was rated by either the majority or minority staff as having played a "moderate" role in negotiations behind the scenes. The categorization is probably more inclusive than the one implied by Carroll's characterization of Foreign Affairs participants. Even so, the table indicates that his generalization about House Foreign Affairs would be a bit generous for the three committees whose behavioral patterns are summarized here.

For instance, in only two of the seventeen Education and Labor bills did as

Table 2.4   The *"Efficient"* Committee: Active Members on Committee Bills

Number of members active on bill (Subcommittee or full committee)	Number/Percentage of Bills		
	Agriculture	Education and Labor	Energy and Commerce
Fewer than 5	1 (5%)	1 (6%)	1 (5%)
5–9	9 (43)	13 (76)	10 (50)
10–14	8 (38)	1 (6)	4 (20)
15 or more	3 (14)	2 (12)	5 (25)

Note: Cell entries are based on dense samples of committee members and bills. A member was counted as active if he or she was an active participant in either the subcommittee or committee markup debate or was at least moderately active in negotiations behind the scenes. The sample of members, by committee, was as follows: Agriculture, 32; Education and Labor, 29; Energy and Commerce, 33.

many as a third of the members either author or coauthor an amendment during markup or push a particular provision either in markup or in negotiations behind the scenes. One contained the committee's recommendations for the 1981 Omnibus Reconciliation Act — a bill that was to become one of the most sweeping pieces of domestic legislation since World War II. As the Democrat-controlled committee reported, Education and Labor's titles in that act would have cut authorization of programs within its jurisdiction by more than a third. The other was the Job Training Partnership Act (JTPA) — the replacement to the expiring Comprehensive Employment and Training Act (CETA) and perhaps the most important domestic initiative to emerge from Reagan's first term.

The selectivity of participation becomes increasingly evident in the case of less important bills. In fewer than 20 percent of the cases was a third or more of the Education and Labor membership active at any point during committee consideration. The patterns are particularly striking when compared with Fenno's descriptions of participation on Education and Labor in *Congressmen in Committees*. Fenno's respondents described patterns of selective participation in certain committees, but Education and Labor was not one of them. The committee "places no restrictions on participation so that its members can be free to pursue their interest in good public policy," or as one of Fenno's Education and Labor respondents observed, "Everybody gets in the swim in full committee" (1973a, 102). However accurate such observations may have been in the early seventies, they no longer hold for the same committee in the postreform House.

Similar if somewhat less dramatic evidence of nonparticipation is evident in the other cases as well. In only about half of the bills before the other two committees were a third or more of the members active. And even though the sample of bills in each committee was weighted in favor of major pieces of legislation, in only ten of the fifty-seven bills from three committees did a majority of the committee do much more than show up and vote.

In fact, on several bills in each committee, as few as four or five members were at all active, and only two or three were engaged in the substantive negotiations. None of these were nationally prominent or otherwise major pieces of legislation, but neither were they routine or trivial. One such bill in Energy and Commerce, for instance, was the Secondary Mortgage Market Enhancement Act, a bill that would significantly increase the capital available to finance housing by increasing the participation of the private sector in the secondary market for home mortgages. According to both the Democratic and Republican staff, Subcommittee Chair Tim Wirth was the only committee member involved in defining and resolving the principal issues. Wirth and his staff bargained with representatives of the housing and real estate industry over the bill's provisions with relative impunity, at least insofar as his committee colleagues were concerned. When I asked one subcommittee staffer which members were involved in the deliberations on this bill, he replied, "Wirth, just Wirth. We touched base with Dingell's staff, but Dingell wasn't even all that involved." One of Dingell's staff members observed: "To be quite honest, the members felt the bill was a good thing if it helped housing. They broadly wanted to have a bill so that they could say they supported a bill. But there was nobody who knew anything about the nitty-gritty of the bill, much less defend any piece of it. Wirth was the only one coming in and raising any concerns, and no one could really take him on."

Similar accounts appeared during interviews with the staff of the other two committees. For instance, one staffer recounted how the cotton provisions of the Omnibus Farm Bill were drafted by the staffs of four southern Democrats, noting that the other members "couldn't care less." Likewise, on an Education and Labor bill regulating state and local public pensions worth billions of dollars, both parties' staffers described the negotiations as basically a two-person game. Summarizing deliberations that spanned three congresses, one of them observed: "It was Frank Thompson and John Erlenborn [in the previous congress], and then it was Burton and Erlenborn, and now it's Clay and Erlenborn, and that is the sum total of the people who have been involved. Everyone else was involved on a much, much more peripheral basis."

The behavioral patterns summarized here reveal that the standing committees of Congress are not really standing committees; in most cases most of the committee members are standing somewhere else. By far the prevailing pattern is one in which the majority of members do not participate and pay little attention to those who do. Neither is it the case, as Carroll suggests, that there is some "core" of members that "persistently and actively participate in the deliberations of the group." Participation varies not only from bill to bill but dramatically from member to member. If there is a core, it consists of at most five of the thirty-two members in the House Agriculture sample, two of the twenty-nine members of Education and Labor, and one of the thirty-two Commerce members. Only those eight could be described as being persistently and actively involved in their committee's legislative business.

With perhaps a very few exceptions, members reveal no stable pattern of behavior across bills; hence no typology of lawmakers' "legislative styles" will fit the variations in the data. (For one attempt to employ such a typology, see Barber 1965.) For individual members, in fact, the pattern is to get engaged in only about a third of the bills that come before their committee, and in fewer than half of the bills that come before their more narrowly focused and specialized subcommittees. But a good deal of variation remains from member to member regarding the scope and degree of participation in the bills that arise within a committee's jurisdiction. For instance, one Education and Labor Democrat had a median markup score of zero — for over half of the seventeen bills, he attended neither a subcommittee nor a full-committee markup. Yet for three other bills, only one of which was reported from his subcommittees, he was clearly involved in a major way, offering and passing a total of sixteen substantive amendments during markup and playing a key role during behind-the-scenes negotiations. One junior member, in contrast, had a median markup score of two, reflecting a nearly perfect record of attendance and voting, but he sat silently in the markups of fifteen of the seventeen bills and did not offer an amendment during the entire congress.

Conclusion

For at least a century, students of Congress have quite rightly assumed that the identity of those responsible for legislating in a particular domain might have some bearing on the sorts of policies that get produced. Thus have legislative scholars paid considerable attention to the division of labor thought to be institutionalized in the congressional committee and subcommittee system. On the basis of the findings presented in this chapter, I would however suggest that those formal divisions are modified in practice, sometimes radically so, by individual members' choices about how they will spend their legislative time and energy. For any given bill before any given committee or subcommittee, only a small subset of the nominal members become players in the legislative game, with the size and composition of that subset changing from bill to bill.

By themselves, of course, these patterns do not tell us that the legislative deliberations in Congress are systematically minoritarian, that the self-selected subsets of participants necessarily subvert the general will of their parent assembly. But speaking from experience, I would say that neither can the parent assume that its children, in doing what they want to do, are doing what their parent would have them do. The issues one must take up are ones to which we will turn in later chapters, issues that have been sharply delineated in recent work on legislative organization.[10] As Krehbiel (1991) argues, for instance, it matters a great deal whether the chamber's presumed "specialists" are reasonably heterogeneous — that is, whether they represent roughly the distribution of preferences in the chamber. The patterns described here, however, reveal that the informative members the chamber chooses to appoint are not necessarily the members who choose to participate. To put it somewhat differently, the committees that are informationally efficient (in Krehbiel's sense) are not necessarily the efficient committees (in Carroll's sense). Understanding both the decisions to participate and the positions that the *participants* ultimately choose should thus provide a natural and important advancement in the study of legislative majoritarianism.

10. Among the most prominent works are those of Cox and McCubbins 1993; Kiewiet and McCubbins 1991; Krehbiel 1991; Rohde 1991; Shepsle and Weingast 1987a; and Weingast and Marshall 1988. For critiques and extensions of this diverse body of scholarship, see the essays in Shepsle and Weingast 1995.

3

Participation and Purpose

It is not every new member that comes to his seat with serious purposes of honest, earnest, and duteous work. There are numerous tricks and subterfuges, soon learned and easily used, by means of which the most idle and self-indulgent members may readily make such show of exemplary diligence as will quite satisfy, if it does not positively delight, constituents in Buncombe. — Woodrow Wilson, *Congressional Government*

The virtues and vices of the congressional committee system have been elaborated by students of the institution, as well as legislators themselves, for well over a century. On the negative side, Kenneth Shepsle observes, "there is the folk wisdom that defines a camel as a horse built by a committee and an elephant as a mouse designed by one; there is the Wilsonian concern with the veto power of small groups; and there is the modern reformer's concern with the biases inherent in committees that are unrepresentative of the parent body" (1978, 3). At the same time, the reputed virtues of the committee system are also numerous. This is where the "duteous work" of the member can be done in service to the chamber (Wilson 1956 [1885], 60). "On the other side of the ledger," Shepsle continues, are the claims that committees "benefit from and encourage the division and specialization of labor; they are repositories of expertise within their specialized jurisdictions; . . . and they are more expeditious and efficient in the molding of detailed proposals than the larger parent chamber."

It is probably safe to say that, on the whole, students of Congress have been more likely to emphasize the vices than the virtues,[1] but few have argued with

1. In particular, a substantial body of literature within political science and economics has emphasized the role of the committee system in overproducing distributive benefits and underproducing public goods. For a review of and a recent challenge to this line of scholarship, see Krehbiel 1991.

Richard Fenno's observation that "the only way such a large body can function is to divide into highly specialized and independent committees" (Fenno 1973b, 282). Even in the aftermath of the centralizing reforms of the 104th Congress, committees and their organizational supplements — party task forces — remain central to the legislative labor of the House and Senate.

The Puzzle of Participation

If the chamber benefits from the specialized labors of its committees, however, there are good reasons to doubt that the public good(s) of the institution will motivate individual members to engage in what Wilson refers to as "honest, earnest, and duteous work." The first follows from the simple illogic of collective action. As Mancur Olson (1965) has argued with respect to the participation of private citizens in political organizations, individuals who share some common purpose will not automatically participate in efforts to achieve that purpose, for they realize that their marginal contribution will be indiscernible, and in any case, they can enjoy whatever public good is produced whether they've participated in producing it or not. Hence the individual who does participate may be the least, not the most, rational. So too in Congress. The timeliness, expertise, and efficiency with which Congress makes policy decisions — that is, the reputed consequences of the member's duteous committee work — are all public goods. Why would a member participate in their production? Why not free ride? Why not let Representative Schmuck do it?

This question becomes even more perplexing when one considers the possibility that not only may members not be harmed, but they may even be helped by uninformed or ill-informed collective (non)decisions. Morris Fiorina argues, for instance, that members have a strong incentive to tolerate, perhaps even initiate, laws that are vague, misguided, or difficult to implement, so that the member can subsequently intervene in the federal establishment on behalf of her frustrated constituents. To the latter's complaints, Fiorina argues, the representative "lends a sympathetic ear, piously denounces the evils of bureaucracy, intervenes in the latter's decisions, and rides a grateful electorate to ever more impressive electoral showings" (1989, 46–47). And even should the actions of Congress and not the bureaucracy attract the antipathy of one's constituency, it is now well established that members are just as pious in their denunciation of their own institution as they are of the other. Members frequently and effectively run *for* Congress by running *against* Congress, including those who have been members of the institution for many years (Fenno 1975; 1978). And even when disdain for the institution does harm incumbents (as apparently occurred in 1994), it is not at all clear why individual members would compensate by contributing their time and energy to a search for collective remedies when the benefits accrue to all regardless of effort. Constituency service and district casework, in contrast, appear to be stronger competitors for the member's time and staff attention (Fenno 1978; Cain, Ferejohn, and Fiorina 1987).[2]

To summarize, the specialized work of individual members undoubtedly enhances the value of the chamber's ultimate legislative products, an outcome from which all members benefit, as Keith Krehbiel has persuasively argued (1991). Still, it is not immediately obvious why members (sometimes) participate in the labors of legislation. The problematic nature of collective action thus suggests an important insight into why we do not see more general involvement by members on a wider range of matters than we do.

But if such an account gives us some insight into why participation is frequently two-thirds empty, it does not say anything specific about why it may be one-third full, nor why it is mostly full on some issues, mostly empty on others. In the last chapter I demonstrated that few members participate in most matters before their panels, but also that most members play important roles in at least a few matters. Often enough, the reason a member neglects some issue before one panel is that he is tending to some other issue before another panel, not leaving his fellows to carry the legislative load while he carries his clubs around the Army-Navy Golf Course.[3] Indeed, among the robust behavioral regularities of the contemporary Congress is that members go to great lengths to acquire their preferred committee assignments; that they covet most those committees whose legislative responsibilities are greatest; and that they exert pressure on party leaders to increase the number of panels and seats — all this so that members can have even more, and more varied, opportunities to do committee drudgery! This is peculiar behavior indeed.

We are thus faced with the puzzle of legislative participation. Whatever

2. The centralization of committee assignment, promotion, and other powers in the Office of Speaker Gingrich suggests, however, that the Republican reforms of the 104th Congress may create greater institutional leverage with regard to members' execution of the leaders' objectives, at least for the majority party. For further discussion of such implications, see Chapter 8.

3. In fact, a systematic survey conducted by the House Commission on Administrative Review demonstrated that when Congress is in session, the average work day of the typical House member is eleven hours. In short, the choice that most members make is not between being a diligent legislator and being a legislative laggard; rather, it is a choice about how the long hours of the legislative day will be divided among competing activities. See O'Donnell, 1981.

labor the institution might divide and assign, members are under no obligation to do it—and they might actually lose by doing it. Viewed in this light, the question becomes not so much why members participate as little as they do, but why they participate at all. What is it that gets members out of bed in the morning and into the committee rooms? Of what use to a member are her legislative labors?

With little need of qualification, one can review the recent literature on Congress and conclude that these questions are rarely asked, much less answered. While scattered studies have described the variability of participation, theoretical work on the subject has extended little beyond general references to the norms of hard work, specialization, and apprenticeship that are thought to have structured participation in a previous era. With these norms now considered all but dead, the literature has curiously little to say about who participates, to what extent, and why—questions that students of both organizational behavior (Cohen, March, and Olsen, for example) and mass behavior (Rosenstone and Hansen 1994; Verba and Nie 1972) take to be profoundly important.

In this chapter, I begin to fill the gap. I start by revisiting the sociological account of participation norms that has governed most discussions of the subject to date. Adapting Kenneth Shepsle's work on committee assignments (1978), I then develop a theory of purposive behavior in an institutional context, with the aim of understanding the choices different members in different institutional forums make about participation. The various forums in which legislative decisions are typically made (subcommittee, committee, floor) present the member with a set of possible ways she might use her time and other resources to pursue her interests, akin to a set of legislative investment opportunities. Which she chooses and which she forgoes will depend on her estimates of their relevance to her several purposes and thus the likely political returns of each; the nature and quality of the investment options available to her by virtue of her institutional positions; the legislative resources she has to invest relative to her potential competitors; and the information and transaction costs that she will likely bear—calculations whose outcome will vary from member to member and bill to bill.

Legislative Participation and the Sociology of Congress

For the most part, one must go back to a literature now several decades old to find any sustained attention to matters of legislative participation. Cast in the sociological theory of groups that prevailed in congressional research at the time, however, the principal emphasis of that literature was on the careful description of the norms, roles, or folkways that characterized the "group life" of the Congress and enabled it to perform its functions, not on what might be an *individual decision* to participate.[4]

One of the major works of this genre, for instance, was Fenno's magisterial study of the House Appropriations Committee (1962; 1966). Crucial to the functioning of that group, Fenno argued, was "a fairly consistent set of norms, widely agreed upon and widely followed by the members," along with "control mechanisms (i.e., socialization and sanctioning mechanisms) capable of maintaining reasonable conformity to norms" (1962, 310). Among the most important, Fenno suggested, were the norms of "hard work" and "specialization." That is, members were expected to concentrate on a narrow range of subject matter, commit significant amounts of time and energy to its study, and thereby master its details and complexities. In his classic study of the Senate published at about the same time, Donald Matthews (1960), in turn, emphasized the importance of almost identical norms — what he labeled "folkways" — in the U.S. Senate: "The great bulk of the Senate's work is highly detailed, dull, and politically unrewarding. According to the folkways of the Senate, it is to those tasks that a senator *ought* to devote a major share of his time, energy, and thought. Those who follow this rule are the senators most respected by their colleagues. Those who do not carry their share of the legislative burden or who appear to subordinate this responsibility to a quest for publicity and personal advancement are held in disdain" (Matthews 1960, 94–95, emphasis in original).

According to this view, it was the prescriptive norms or folkways of the group, sustained by the promise of peer approval and the implied threat of peer repudiation, that solved the free-rider problem of the organization. Members contributed to the "detailed, dull, and politically unrewarding" legislative work because they were expected to, and violating the expectations of the group would render one "ineffective" (Fenno 1962; 1966; Matthews 1960).

Other norms — better labeled *pro*scriptive than *pre*scriptive — reflected group expectations regarding when members should *not* participate, when

---

4. Most of the norms revealed by interviews of the period had much to do with participation; but no attempts were made to consolidate the participation-related observations into a more general account of individual decisions to participate. The norms were treated more or less discretely when studied in any depth, or if they were taken together, the author was more likely to focus on abstract questions of "group life" or "integration" than to develop an individual-level behavioral theory. More generally, the problematic issues of behavioral theory were circumvented through functionalist logic (the institution cannot function if members do not specialize; therefore, members will specialize so that the institution can function).

they were unwelcome as players in the legislative game. For instance, the complement of the specialization norm was the norm of deference.[5] If members were to concentrate on matters within their own panel's jurisdiction, they needed to leave the decisions on other committees or subcommittees to the expert discretion of their counterparts. "It's a matter of 'if you respect my work, I'll respect yours,' " according to one of Fenno's Appropriations respondents. "It's frowned upon if you offer an amendment in the full committee when you aren't a member of the subcommittee," according to another (Fenno 1973a, 95). The most noteworthy of the restrictive norms, however, was that of apprenticeship, a period during which newcomers were to "be seen and not heard" by their senior colleagues. "The differentiation between senior and junior members is the broadest definition of who shall and who shall not participate" (Fenno 1962, 318; see also Fenno 1966). As Matthews observed, "The new senator is expected to keep his mouth shut, not to take the lead in floor fights, to listen and learn." "The period of apprenticeship," Matthews concluded, "is very real and confining" (1960, 94–95).

Taken together, the set of prescriptive and proscriptive norms described by an earlier generation of scholars reflected a sociological theory about the everyday actions of members regarding when they should and when they should not participate in the deliberations of their chamber. To what extent is it still possible to repair to such explanations?

The only answer one might construct from recent work on congressional change is an emphatic *not much*. Research conducted over the last two decades consistently attests to the disappearance of House norms. Writing in 1975, Herbert Asher concluded from interviews with House freshmen that "the need for a lengthy and inactive apprenticeship no longer seems to be accepted" (1975, 233). Less than a decade later, Ornstein concluded that the incentive for freshmen to serve an apprenticeship no longer existed: " 'Those

5. Closely related to the norm of deference, so much so that the two terms are sometimes used interchangeably, is the norm of reciprocity. The distinction at the heart of this study — between positions and participation, between revealed preferences and revealed intensities — renders the distinction between these two norms clearer. *Reciprocity* refers to the trading of votes or positions — the members of my committee support the proposals of another committee, with the implicit agreement that those committee members will support my committee's proposals. *Deference,* though, refers to the cooperative agreement that members of one committee will not interfere in the business of another. To state it somewhat differently, deference is to members' revealed intensities what reciprocity is to members' revealed preferences. As I discuss more directly in later chapters, however, I believe that the observed patterns of deference have been largely misunderstood; they reflect not so much conventions on mutual noninterference as the rational calculations of individuals regarding when to participate and when to abdicate.

who stand and wait' get no more or better internal rewards than those who do not" (Ornstein 1981, 369).

More recent and more comprehensive descriptions have extended the line into the present day, pronouncing flatly that the older norms are dead. "The apprenticeship norm has disappeared in both chambers," Steven Smith (1989) summarily concludes. So too with other norms thought to have governed behavior in the past. Smith finds evidence of what he takes to be the "demise" of the committee deference and specialization norms (1989, 139–45). In her historical analysis of the Senate, Sinclair likewise finds that the norms of apprenticeship, specialization, and hard work have given way to a "new Senate style" "predicated upon high rates of activity in multiple arenas and across a broad range of issues" (1989, 101).

In sum, whatever explanatory value one might have attributed to participation norms in some earlier era, little remains in the postreform Congress. Such accounts, numerous scholars have testified, are simply dated. I will argue here, however, that those accounts are not so much dated as wrong. For reasons that I will elaborate in the analysis to come, the prescriptive norms described in past scholarship *never were* major determinants of member behavior. The merits of this revisionist view, of course, can be assessed only against the backdrop of the alternative theory of participation that I have to offer — the focus of this chapter and the next — and the empirical analysis that supports that theory, the focus of the ensuing three chapters.

Pursuing One's Interests

More than most of us, House members enjoy considerable latitude in what they do on the job. If peer pressures do not now constrain them much, neither do the requirements of organizational superiors. Legislators are members of what the sociologists call a free profession, in the sense that they individually set their own schedules and decide the topics (among those on or near the legislative agenda) of their attention (Bauer, Pool, and Dexter 1963, 409). How then do members make choices, day by day, issue by issue, regarding what (if anything) to work on as a legislator? Why does a member get out of bed and (some days and not others) go into the committee rooms? Why does she ignore the activity on the floor for weeks, then spend several days there tirelessly promoting some legislative proposal?

Members and their aides do not themselves easily answer these questions. When I asked one staffer why her boss got so involved in a bill then before the House Subcommittee on Select Education, she noted, "One of Murphy's staffers told me about the bill early on, and the congressman expressed an interest.

So we just jumped in." Another staffer noted, "I don't know that we really [budget our time]. . . . We just sort of react to things as they come up. [Congressman X] will say, 'This is something we need to go after,' and it's pointless to tell him that I've got sixteen other things going on. Some of them just fall by the wayside." Other staffers characterized priority setting within the enterprise as a process constantly in motion and mostly decentralized; the member or the relevant legislative assistant makes rough calculations about whether a particular issue is, as one staffer put it, "worth our time."

But what factors affect calculations about whether an issue is worth the time? I begin with the premise that legislators are purposive actors, that the subjectively assessed relevance of an issue to the member's interests is at the heart of such calculations. This account of legislative participation, then, replaces the language of sociology with the language of economics.[6] Individuals act to pursue their interests, not promote the functioning of the group.

At the same time, I take a fairly broad view of the sorts of considerations to be subsumed under the rubric of interest — considerations that are not reducible to an inelastic concept of individual "self-interest," at least as it has been commonly formulated by rational-choice theorists of legislative behavior. Rather, I have in mind here more an ordinary meaning — to wit, what a member is "interested in." While members are undoubtedly interested in issues relevant to their constituencies, there is good reason to doubt that they are sufficient to produce the patterns of collective effort described in Chapter 2. One may happily invoke the abstract notion of utility, in other words, but only by unpacking the substantive meaning of utility to individual politicians will we be able to understand their behavior.

Specifically, I explore the potential behavioral importance of three distinct types of interest: (1) enhancing the likelihood of reelection or, more generally, servicing one's constituencies (see Smith and Deering 1984, 85); (2) pursuing one's personal policy interests or ideological commitments; and (3) prosecuting the president's agenda or, to use the language of the Washington Beltway, "carrying water for the administration."[7]

6. Theories of legislative behavior that include some form of this assumption have rapidly gained currency over the past two decades. For an early review of the importance of economic theory to the study of legislative behavior, see Ferejohn and Fiorina 1975. Eulau in his excellent essay (1984) also discusses the different shades of meaning among concepts of the motivational psychology of legislators. Given my purposes here, however, I employ few of the fine distinctions that he illuminates. I will use the term *interests* interchangeably with such other closely related words as *goals, purposes, objectives,* and *motivations.*

7. The pilot study for this project (Hall 1987) originally explored the effect of a fourth category of interest — that of "making a mark" in a policy domain. Subsequent criticism

Representing Constituents' Interests

As I noted in the opening chapter, the influence of constituency on members' legislative behavior has been a problematic matter at least since the time that Mill wrote about the nature and practice of representative government in nineteenth-century England. In postwar America, the concern of legislative scholars with this question has become, if anything, overriding. This for two reasons. One is the set of normative questions with which Mill and his contemporaries wrestled, that government by consent requires a system of electoral accountability, whose purpose is to ensure responsiveness on the part of representatives to their constituents.[8] The second has more to do with behavioral than democratic theory. Whatever normative evaluations one might attach to the tendency, there are good reasons to expect that constituency considerations will figure prominently in the calculations of rational legislators. As David Mayhew has observed, "reelection underlies everything else" that individual members might want to accomplish, and members certainly believe that what they do in Congress affects how long they will stay there (Mayhew 1974, 16, 37–38). In short, one need not impute to legislative elites some adherence to democratic norms or perhaps some delegate "role orientation" (see Eulau et al. 1959) to predict that they will respond to constituency interests.

The research on constituency influence is now extensive — too extensive to review here — but two closely related elements characterize the bulk of it. The first is that constituency influence has been mainly defined in terms of the congruence between constituents' opinions and member's positions. Second, the extent of this congruence is best investigated by analyzing the effect of constituent opinion on members' roll call votes. The seminal work in this tradition is a 1963 article by Miller and Stokes, "Constituency Influence in Congress," in which the authors employ surveys of both members and district constituents to assess the degree of agreement between them. Since at least the early 1960s, constituency variables have been central to empirical and theoretical work on legislative voting. For instance, the three most important books on the subject — those by Fiorina (1974), Jackson (1974), and Kingdon (1989)

---

from colleagues and ensuing analysis of my own revealed, however, that this variable suffered from measurement problems that rendered the estimation of its effects highly problematic and the ensuing inferences thereby questionable. It is thus excluded from the analysis to come.

8. See David Mayhew's classic *Congress: The Electoral Connection* (1974) for a lucid discussion of electoral accountability and its importance in the contemporary Congress. For a more general treatment, see Pitkin 1967, chaps. 9–10.

—all place constituency at the center of their analysis. So too in the comparative study of legislatures. The magisterial study of representation in France by Converse and Pierce (1986), for instance, follows directly in this tradition. In short, most of what we now know about members' legislative responsiveness to constituents comes out of this important line of research.[9]

Still there is much that we do not know, indeed, that we have not studied. Whatever connection there might be between district opinions and member positions, there is an additional, qualitatively different, and perhaps more important way in which individual legislators respond to their constituents. The argument I advance here is two-pronged: to the extent that a member believes that her district has an interest in an issue that comes before her, the more involved in the legislative action she is likely to become. Constituency influence, in short, should operate not only on legislators' revealed preferences but on the intensities that they reveal in their decisions about when and to what extent they will participate in particular matters before their chamber. The relation between constituent interest and member participation is neither simple nor unconditional, however. In particular, several strategic considerations should enter into the constituency-conscious member's calculations.

THE NATURE OF CONSTITUENTS' INTERESTS

Of what electoral use are a member's legislative labors? However nervous members may be about casting a politically incorrect vote, it is not immediately obvious that they face similar constraints in allocating their legislative time and energy. Though one may not share the cynical opinion of either Congress members or constituents in the wry observation with which this chapter opened, Wilson is correct in implying that the member's day-to-day legislative efforts are considerably less visible to the district than the votes recorded on the floor and that the incentives for duteous work may consequently be slight.

At the same time, however, there are good reasons to believe that, ceteris paribus, constituency interest in an issue will matter to the representative's investment of legislative effort in it, Wilson notwithstanding. The crucial point is that in setting their legislative priorities, as in taking positions, rational, reelection-minded representatives should not concern themselves with the undifferentiated citizenry of Buncombe. Rarely are constituents consistently attentive to what their congressional delegates do, but some are attentive on

---

9. It is important to note that other scholars have studied nonlegislative activities in an effort to tap other dimensions of members' responsiveness to constituents. See especially Cain, Ferejohn, and Fiorina 1987, chap. 1; Fenno 1978; Johannes 1988; Parker 1986.

certain issues.[10] Even in districts that rank near the top in national dairy production, for instance, few constituents will know much of anything about either their representative's positions or her participation in drafting a dairy program. But the district dairy producers will know a great deal; indeed, through industry newsletters, local farm organizations, and various informal communication channels they can become very well informed about how vigorously the member pursues their interests (Hansen 1992). To varying degrees, the same principle applies to subconstituencies associated with other issues: textile producers on textile tariffs, labor union members on labor laws, educators on aid to education, and so on. Although the general district electorate may exhibit little awareness of an issue, in short, some subset may care deeply about it and attach high benefits or costs to the outcome.[11]

This conceptual point has an important corollary in members' perceptions, as Richard Fenno has explored in his study of House members in their districts (1978; see also Kingdon 1989, 31–45.) The constituency that a member will represent, Fenno rightly remarks, is the constituency that he or she sees. To Fenno's analysis of concentric circles of constituencies — geographic, reelective, primary, and personal — I would simply add that the constituency that the member sees as she goes about her Washington work depends on the issue she has before her. To draw on Fenno's later work (1986), the context in which a member acts is crucial for understanding her legislative behavior. And the issue sets the context for how a member thinks about her constituency at the moment that she is deciding whether and to what extent she will participate (see also Kingdon 1989, 35–38). The legislative director of one Louisiana member, reflecting on both sugar price supports and legislation to decontrol natural gas, observed that his boss paid close attention to the interests of his district constituents, but the constituencies he described — sugar cane farmers in the first, natural gas companies in the second — were altogether different in the two cases. Likewise, when I spoke with another member about the relevance of the Job Training Partnership Act to his district, he spoke not of Fenno's concentric circles but of unemployed workers and the workforce

10. This section on the variable electoral importance of district subconstituencies draws heavily on Fiorina 1974, chap. 2. See also Arnold 1990; Kingdon 1989; and Fenno 1978.

11. R. Douglas Arnold (1990) has outlined the features of an issue to consider in estimating citizens' probable attention to it and hence the rational stake in it for the legislator seeking reelection. One such feature is citizens' perceptions about the incidence of costs and benefits associated with a proposal. Dairy price supports provide a classic example of a distributive issue, where the difference between expected benefits and costs is extremely high for the group immediately affected.

needs of specific district industries. In discussing his boss's involvement on a dairy bill before the House Agriculture Committee, one legislative staffer captured the point concisely: "To get to your question about the relevance of the bill to the district, the first thing I'd point out is that it's not the district that matters. It's only one very small part of the district — the dairy farmers. But insofar as dairy legislation is concerned, they are the district."

LEGISLATIVE PARTICIPATION AND THE ELECTORAL CONNECTION

For many, though certainly not all, issues that come before her, then, the member of Congress is apt to see only a subset of her geographic constituency, the citizens who are interested and thus attentive (or potentially attentive) to what she does. When the relevant subconstituency is large and/or intense, in turn, the member neglects its interests at some cost. The costs are of two complementary kinds. One is the electoral harm that the member might suffer from the conspicuous failure to help on matters that constituents feel strongly about. For these citizens, the "idle and self-indulgent" behavior attributed to representatives by Wilson is not likely to go unnoticed. Thus do members perennially confront the question "What have you done for me lately?" and worry that they lack an adequate answer. Indeed, Fiorina (1974) has argued that the unrequited constituent is apt to punish more than the requited is to reward.

The second and more important costs lie in opportunities forgone. The reelection-minded member may fear no political retribution for his legislative sloth, but neither can he expect any political reward. Particularly with matters to which a subconstituency is attentive and committed, the member has an unambiguous opportunity to parlay (usually invisible) Washington activities into something that someone will notice and appreciate. Indeed, the more attentive the members of a subconstituency are (or might become), the more likely the representative's actions on their behalf are to elicit both positive evaluations and electoral support.

This is a prominent theme in David Mayhew's *Congress: The Electoral Connection* (1974) and more generally in a long line of works on members' incentives to engage in distributive politics. Mayhew identifies three categories of activity through which members pursue reelection. The first two, advertising and position taking, are almost certainly magnified by the member's active participation on an issue that some constituents care about. To the extent that activity generates visibility, the member achieves an electoral payoff regardless of whether the actions have any ultimate effect on policy. But participation is even more important to Mayhew's third reelection-oriented activity, claiming credit. In contrast to advertising and position taking, credible claims of credit are not easy to generate. The most obvious difficulty is that credit cannot be claimed for benefits that have not been produced. And it is unlikely that those will materialize without the strong efforts of the district's advocate inside the legislature. Legislative pork, in other words, does not come to members who sit idly by; how much they get depends, among other things, on how hard they work for it. Free riding in this case is not an option.

Of course, the distributive benefits that districts might want and legislators might seek are not limited to earmarked projects — that is, classic pork. Tariffs on textile imports provide economic protection to workers and businesses in several states; so, too, are there unevenly distributed benefits associated with feed grain subsidies, inland waterway projects, weapons procurement decisions, mass transit programs, and natural gas deregulation, to name only a few. In the legislative effort to produce nontrivial changes in such larger policy areas, the member may well estimate that the investment of her own office may have little effect at the margin. But even when this is true, Mayhew suggests, the member has a strong incentive to claim credit far in excess of her marginal contribution. Active participation is what makes the claim to credit credible. To use the language of R. Douglas Arnold (1990), it is what renders "traceable" to her some outcome that the member expects her constituents to like.[12] The aide to one junior member of House Energy and Commerce discussed an amendment that his boss offered during reauthorization of the Clean Air Act: "We knew that our role was going to be pretty limited. Dingell and Waxman were the big boys, fighting the big fights, and they would get most of the attention. Our niche was acid rain. That was what our people cared most about, so we drafted the amendment and pushed it for all it was worth." Another staffer discussed his boss's authorship of a measure to limit executive use of grain embargoes as a foreign policy tool: "Lots of people were interested in it, not just in our district. But we jumped in first and busted our butts on it. We drafted the thing; [Y] introduced it and pushed it all the way through. . . . When he met with farmers back in the district, it didn't hurt to have it referred to as the [Y] bill."

To the member aiming for reelection, then, the favorable reactions of constituents to her legislative efforts on matters that they care about count as powerful and important signals, positive reinforcement for the investments of scarce time and resources she has made. Moreover, such reactions provide a

12. As Arnold (1990) also observes, members may desire traceability for outcomes they expect to be popular, but they may also want to avoid traceability and thus culpability for outcomes that they expect to be unpopular. Such incentives incline members to consider certain strategic options, which I discuss below.

strong incentive for her to look for other opportunities to parlay her legislative work into electoral support. "Less important than whether constituents actually care," Fiorina observes, "is whether the representative thinks they can be made to care" (1974, 33). Thus Mayhew observes that "credit claiming is highly important to congressmen with the consequence that much of congressional life is a relentless search for opportunities to engage in it" (1974, 53).[13]

To summarize, there exists no strong theoretical basis for expecting that the interests of the constituency — where *constituency* is defined as some objective, undifferentiated, geographically circumscribed mass of voters — are what drive the calculations of reelection-minded legislators. In this respect, Wilson's cynical observations are right. But they are wrong in their implication that members can without cost abdicate their legislative responsibilities on matters that affect the interests of subconstituencies who care or might be made to care. They cannot.

STRATEGIC CONSIDERATIONS

The general hypothesis to which we are led, then, is that, ceteris paribus, the intensities that members reveal in their Washington work should reflect the revealed intensities of their subconstituencies at home. But having advanced this hypothesis as a broad claim, we must quickly complicate it. As Fiorina has said of the relationship between constituents' attitudes and legislators' roll call votes, "We should hardly expect our answer to be a mathematical relationship invariant in time" (1974, 24). We require careful arguments, Fiorina admonishes students of roll call voting, regarding precisely what we expect to find and when we expect to find it. So too in the analysis of members' participation decisions. In particular, several strategic considerations relevant to reelection seeking warrant our attention here.

First, efforts on behalf of constituents are not very valuable if they are not visible. Members, of course, can and do take pains to achieve visibility; such are the rites of advertising, position taking, and credit claiming, which ever-larger Capitol Hill press operations are organized to perform (see Cook 1989). But activities that are publicly observable (perhaps recordable) enhance the visibility of the members' efforts and hence the political marketability of such claims. The electoral incentive to participate is different in different legislative

---

13. This point is also evident in Bauer, Pool and Dexter's study of legislative decision making on foreign trade: "Voters seldom know just what they want. Mostly they want evidence that [their representative] is concerned with their problem and is addressing himself effectively to it." (1963, 423).

forums, however. Electorally strategic behavior, as Mayhew (1974) argues, includes taking the right positions (in recorded roll calls or public speeches, for example) or otherwise engaging in symbolic activity, and the opportunities to do so are greater during the open markup (or floor debate) than during the considerable (but typically more important) legislative activity that goes on behind the scenes. One senior Agriculture staffer observed, for instance, that the markup of a major farm relief bill in House Agriculture was staged solely for the benefit of midwestern farm groups: "No one on the committee, not even [the author], thought it would go anywhere." Similarly, a junior Democrat summarized the "political realities" that he had just communicated to his staff in a meeting on his "game plan" for the coming year: "We've got to make up in visibility what we can't [provide] in action. We may not like it. But it's a fact of life. Politically, we've got to keep telling these people that we care. I'd much rather deal in substance, but we can't always do it. We've got to show them that we're sensitive to every bullshit problem that comes along."

The electoral connection, in short, provides theoretical grounding for what I will refer to as the Show Horse Hypothesis: Members should not allocate effort on the basis of constituents' interests without regard to the legislative forum of their actions; specifically, constituents' interests should affect members' formal participation more than their informal participation.[14]

The second strategic consideration is the flip side of the first. If members are seeking public opportunities to reap credit, they should shun public forums where they are likely to incur blame, a tendency I will refer to here as the Blame Avoidance Hypothesis. Specifically, there are two conditions under which we should expect member participation to go down as constituency interest goes up. The first occurs when constituents likely to be attentive to the issue at hand reveal preferences that are heterogeneous and hence at odds with one another. When such intradistrict conflict occurs, the member is faced with the prospect that by advancing the interests of one segment of the electorate,

---

14. The hypothesis does not imply, however, that the coefficient on constituency interests for informal participation should be zero, for two reasons. First, as explained in Chapter 2, formal and informal participation are not unrelated. Legislators or their staff members frequently need to engage in informal intelligence gathering and negotiations with the legislative principals behind the scenes during markup (if they wish to offer a bootless but constituent-pleasing amendment, for instance). Second, the markup has greater visibility than behind-the-scenes deliberations only to a degree. In particular, representatives of organized groups (say, dairy industry lobbyists) are themselves usually involved in informal deliberations and are thus aware of and able to report (to district dairy farmers, in this case) who is actively advancing their interests and who is not.

she will alienate another. She may, of course, still wish to become active — say, if one segment is a more important part of her reelection constituency. But the returns will diminish at the margin to the extent that the other segment is alienated.[15]

An additional and probably more common condition under which participation should diminish as constituency interest goes up occurs when the preferences of constituents conflict with the personal policy preferences of the member. As studies of voting decisions reveal, members sometimes disagree with constituents; on occasion they may even vote against the wishes of an electorally relevant constituency, so long as they do not generate a string of such votes.[16] A wrongheaded vote is one thing; however, actively promoting a proposal that some interested and attentive constituency opposes involves a good deal more risk. The staffer to one senior Republican on House Education and Labor observed:

> [Z] comes from a fairly conservative district, but there is some unionism, so he can get hurt by being conservative on labor matters. So this is a potential negative of this assignment. That is, he may not get involved on some issues even though they may be important to "the district." Like on Fair Labor Standards; that was very important to the district. But a lot of congressmen will "take a walk." You have to understand that congressmen play two roles. One is to be a representative, to represent the district; the other is to use their own judgment — taking a policy position and pushing it. On the labor issues, these come in conflict. [Z] may have strong views but will lie low anyway.

How frequently do members face such a dilemma? Unfortunately, issue-by-issue data on members' policy positions are not available for the cases under study here, so I cannot say for sure. But the logic of partisan strategy gives rise to a prediction testable using the available data. Consider, for instance, the likely calculations of a majority party leader in search of a winning coalition. From her point of view, issues that evoke a conflict of policy preferences between the majority rank and file and their constituents simply will not be

15. This condition, however, turns out to be more theoretically interesting than empirically prevalent. Even for districts that are quite heterogeneous, members do not frequently perceive electorally relevant conflict on specific issues that come before their committees. The original interview schedule contained a question that asked staffers to designate bills in the sample for which there was significant intradistrict conflict. Several dozen interviews failed to identify more than a single case, and I subsequently dropped the question from the schedule.

16. See Kingdon on the relevance of such member-district conflict (pp. 38–41) to members' voting decisions and the potential electoral consequences of a "string of votes" inconsistent with constituents' wishes (pp. 41–43.)

strong candidates for agenda space. Thus cross-pressured, member defections are apt to be high, increasing the chance that the majority leadership will suffer an embarrassing defeat. To the extent that defections are kept low, on the other hand, the leadership will have compromised the electoral positions of its own party's membership. What, then, is a strategically savvy leader to do? Avoid issues that cross-pressure her party's rank and file, of course, but do just the opposite insofar as opposition members are concerned! The reelection-minded minority member either defects to the majority side or sticks with the minority position and incurs electoral harm. But even if she chooses the latter course, the Blame Avoidance Hypothesis suggests that her marginal propensity to invest time and resources in the legislative fight will be, relative to the majority member, considerably less. The agenda power of the majority gives rise, then, to a specific and testable formulation of the Blame Avoidance Hypothesis: ceteris paribus, the behavioral effect of constituency interest in an issue should be diminished by minority party status.

A related set of considerations derive from the special circumstances of the electorally marginal member. Ceteris paribus, we should expect that marginal members will allocate more time and staff to their districts, hence less time and staff to their Washington work. Thus Fenno finds that members representing insecure seats spend most of their time solidifying their electoral base: "So long as they are in the expansionist stage of their constituency careers, House members will be especially attentive to their home base. They will pursue the goal of reelection with single-minded intensity and will allocate their resources disproportionately to that end. Building a reelection constituency at home and providing continuous access to as much of that constituency as possible requires time and energy. Inevitably, these are resources that might otherwise be allocated to efforts in Washington" (Fenno 1978, 215).[17]

Beyond the Electoral Connection

Until this point the economic logic of this discussion has been fairly conventional. Legislative participation is interest-driven, that is, motivated by

17. In this work, I assume that members' reelection incentives derive from the interests of citizens, firms, and groups within their districts — what Brooks Jackson (1988) has referred to as members' "constitutional constituencies." But Jackson argues that for several decades members have grown increasingly sensitive to their "cash constituencies," that is, the political action committees and other campaign benefactors within and beyond the district. In the study of members' voting decisions, however, this assertion finds little support (see Grenzke 1989). But do members, in setting their legislative priorities and allocating their time, respond to cash as well as constitutional constituencies? I

the member's self-interest — whatever is "in her interest" — a view that brings electoral considerations squarely into focus. The assumption that members are constituency-minded, in short, strikes me as it has struck political economists, as the best place to start in modeling legislative behavior.

But it does not follow that it is the best place to stop. If members are optimizers, nothing in economic theory says that certain goals and not others determine the expected utility of economically rational actors. Indeed, these are matters to which economic theory does not speak. The attachment to the reelection assumption, rather, has been a matter of modeling ease or elegance, not of theory. To move from the abstract world of optimization theory to the enterprise of generating testable predictions about legislative behavior, one must imbue the concept of utility with some substantive meaning (Fiorina 1974, 35). One must be able to assert, on prior empirical grounds, something about the particular goals or interests of individual legislators. Given that those interests are subjective and unobservable; given further that the connection between interests and observable behavior is a problematic matter about which one must theorize; and given further that no empirical methodology for measuring the subjective interests of legislators has been readily available, the legislative scholar is thus faced with no easy task.

Although altogether understandable, however, following the path of least mathematical resistance should not be permanently tolerated when there are good reasons to think that doing so limits our theoretical grasp of the phenomenon under study. Such is the case here. Some of what the reelection-seeking assumption purchases in tractability and elegance it pays for in relative irrelevance. Or to put it somewhat differently, we have good reasons to believe that the assumption about the member-as-reelection-seeker upon which most economic models build strips away "essential aspects of the situation under study" (Fiorina 1975, 37).[18] How does one know, in advance of a well-devel-

---

believe that there are good theoretical reasons to think that they do. Unfortunately, the scope and nature of the data here do not permit the systematic investigation of this important question, but the basic model I have developed permits extension precisely along these lines. See Hall and Wayman 1990 and Hall 1994a for an elaboration of how such research should proceed. From the exploratory work I have done on this question, I would also note that the addition of variables measuring the investment of moneyed interests in a legislator's enterprise does not affect appreciably the coefficients on variables in the basic model. Again, see Hall and Wayman 1990.

18. In making this claim, I am not indicting formal models as inevitably and distressingly "unrealistic." All models simplify; that is what we want them to do. But in all modeling there is a tension between simplicity, which is a virtue, and the simplistic, which is a vice. In this case, the simplifying assumption that members are mindlessly constituency-minded is simplistic. For one positive model that thoughtfully addresses this tension, see Fiorina 1974.

oped theory, what those "essential aspects" are? In no appropriately positivist manner, I readily admit. But neither are we wandering in an epistemological wilderness. Two things may guide us.

One is the observation of what the conventional premise appears not to explain, what anomalies it appears not to fully resolve. The earlier discussion about the electoral payoffs of show horse behavior, for instance, leaves one somewhat puzzled by the considerable legislative effort that members sometimes expend in behind-the-scenes or closed-session deliberations; in long, hard fights to win largely invisible victories; in developing expertise in a complex or technical policy area — in short, in the onerous work of "getting into the mix" and building a coalition. Indeed, Mayhew (1974) suggests that the electoral payoff for winning a legislative fight may not be very much greater than that for waging it. Members can advertise and posture without investing much time or effort; and they can frequently generate credible credit claims without "busting their butts," as one staffer put it. But bust they do, at least on some issues. Members sometimes expend effort, then, at levels where the law of diminishing marginal returns should have taken over, at least insofar as reelection is concerned. And while investment in such entrepreneurial efforts is typically limited to a few members on any given bill, Arnold (1990) has convincingly argued that it is crucial to successful coalition building in Congress.[19]

The second and more important source of guidance is the rich inductive literature on member motivations. It may be, as Fiorina observes, that "those who read standard philosophy of science texts literally might blanch at the suggestion that empirical research may suggest theory rather than vice versa. But certainly," he adds, "one would be foolish to ignore empirical findings when formulating one's theories" (1975, 2). What do the empirical findings suggest on the nature of legislator motivations? The most important work on this topic is Richard Fenno's *Congressmen in Committees,* an interview-based study that explored members' reasons for seeking particular committee assignments and the general purposes that they believed their committee work served. Fenno concluded that members are motivated by the goals of procuring reelection, influence within the House, and good public policy and sug-

19. Arnold's excellent account of the logic of congressional action presupposes that "coalition leaders" for an issue will emerge and that they will "invest their scarce time and precious resources in mobilizing support for proposals" (1990, 8). However, he self-consciously limits his theoretical focus to exclude member decisions to make such investments (though he speculates in a single footnote that such behavior is legislatively altruistic (1990, 8). In this sense, the behavioral theory I advance complements Arnold's account of coalition building. Coalition leadership or, more generally, entrepreneurial activity is simply a special case of participation.

gests that "all congressmen probably hold all three goals" in different mixes (1973a, 1). Fenno's own subsequent work has reinforced the validity of this view, as have various inductive studies conducted over the past two decades.[20] Such work provides the point of departure here. Whether a multidimensional model of member motivations is warranted, or whether, alternatively, the single-minded reelection-seeking assumption does not strip away too much will be a matter for the data to decide.

Legislative Participation and Personal Policy Interests

In this section, I explore the possible relevance of members' personal policy interests to their participation — what Fenno generally refers to as the goal of good public policy. This goal has received a mere fraction of the attention that students of legislative behavior have given to electoral self-interest.[21] Still, good if somewhat scattered evidence indicates that members' personal policy interests may be related to their investment of legislative time and effort. For instance, although Fenno's interviews focused on members' purposes for seeking particular committee assignments rather than on their postassignment behavior, the general connections between the two are suggested by several of his respondents (1973a, 10–11):

> I'm the most issue-oriented guy you'd ever want to meet. I know there won't be a Wagner Act with my name on it during my first term. But if I can get a few of my ideas in I'll be satisfied. Legislating in Washington, for the district and in the public interest — that's what interests me the most. Serving your constituency — that's a noble effort, too. But, frankly, I consider any time spent in Washington with a constituent as time wasted that I could have spent doing more important things.

> I had an interest in world problems and wanted to make some contribution.

20. Fenno concludes in *Home Style:* "Most members of Congress develop, over time, a mix of personal goals. . . . All want reelection in the abstract, but not all will pay any price to achieve it; nor will all pay the same price. This complex view of House member goals is, we think, a realistic view. And it is the job of an empirical political science to describe and explain the various mixes of goals, and the conditions under which they are adopted or altered" (1978, 221). See also Kingdon 1989; Strahan 1989; Sinclair 1983a.

21. Students of roll call voting behavior have paid considerable attention to the importance of members' personal ideology; indeed, a debate currently rages among political economists over the relative importance of (electoral) self-interest and ideology in legislative roll call decisions (see, e.g., Kalt and Zupan 1984; Peltzman 1984). Beyond the interview-based study of Kingdon 1989, however, conventional methodologies have permitted scholars to say little about the importance of members' personal ideology in their roll call voting. See Jackson and Kingdon 1992.

I think foreign policy is the most important problem there is. So why fool around with anything else?

In his study of members' "home styles," Fenno also finds that members' policy interests lead them to allocate fewer of their resources to the district and more to Washington work as they advance in their careers. Having studied thirteen bills in three Senate committees, Price observed that legislative activism was related to liberal members' belief in federal action as an effective instrument for social betterment (Price 1972; see also Perkins 1980.) And while his work focused primarily on members' voting decisions, Kingdon observed that "most members have their conceptions of good public policy, and act partly to carry that conception into being" (1989, 248).

Exploratory interviews that I conducted with members and their staffs confirmed the view that the value members attach to an issue often derives from certain personal policy interests that they bring to their committee work. Those interviews also provide some insights into the conditions under which such interests will be evoked. One prominent theme concerned the connections between specific issues on the committee agenda and the work that had preoccupied members before they entered politics.[22] When I asked one senior Republican about his priorities on House Education and Labor, he mentioned, without prompting, both electoral and policy considerations and traced the latter to interests rooted in his professional background. "First, you look at how it affects your district. What legislation would be beneficial to your constituents. Second, there's personal interests. I'm a former school superintendent, so I'm going to be involved in education matters. Even within education, I have some real pets. If you're talking about the training of administrators, that's something I'd be interested in. If you're talking about recruiting teachers, that's something I'd be interested in. If you're talking about school lunch or child nutrition, the same. Because that's something I feel strongly about."

Similar themes emerged in open-ended discussions with members of other committees that are not so well known for attracting ideologues or policy advocates. For instance, an aide to a junior member of the House Agriculture Committee attributed his boss's active involvement in commodities exchange regulations to his experience as a commodities broker. Another Agriculture member mentioned his experience as a public advocate for the poor in discuss-

---

22. This theme is evident in the comments of Fenno's respondents as well. In particular, he traces the interests of members of the Education and Labor to "precongressional involvement in the two fields." He likewise summarizes the interests of Foreign Affairs members as reflecting a "combination of personal interest, prior experience, and policy commitment" (1973a, 11).

ing his interest in international hunger relief and domestic nutrition issues. And a member of the House Commerce Committee observed that "it was only natural" that he get involved in the fight over oil and gas deregulation, given his background as a consumer advocate.

Still other respondents suggested the importance of policy interests unrelated to prior employment or professional background. Many of these reflected policy commitments traceable to personal experiences or important events in their political education. The aide to one member explained his boss's interest in educational policy: "Postsecondary ed. is something he feels strongly about, especially student loans and educational opportunity issues. They're important to the district — middle-class constituents worrying about how they're going to afford college for their kids. But it's also important to him because he never went to college [when he was young]; he got a law degree at the age of forty-five. So he cares a lot about increasing financial opportunities to go back to school for adults — housewives, part-timers who are becoming a larger part of the college population."

Other members revealed similar reasons for assigning issues a relatively high priority in the competition for their time:

> I have my staff do a lot of [constituency service] so that I can feel free to work on some of the things that I care about . . . problems that I think get too little attention, [where] I think I can make a difference. Some are issues that get lots of congressmen interested . . . like retraining displaced workers, JTPA [Job Training Partnership Act]. But others are small potatoes, no national attention, no constituency. For me, it's poverty and health care on Indian reservations. Also Indian education. The poverty there is Third World . . . [I've seen the] alcoholism, diabetes, malnutrition. Violence. Suicides. You can't go there and not be affected.

The policy interests of other members were closely related to their group identifications, a theme that has long been important in the study of political attitudes and behavior at the mass level but has been largely ignored in the study of Congress. In particular, several interviews provided new and different evidence about the legislative importance of members' race, ethnicity, and gender.[23] The staffer to one black member of House Education and Labor

23. This evidence, admittedly preliminary, is new in the sense that almost all studies of race, ethnicity, gender, and representation have focused on members' legislative voting, not their setting of priorities. It is different in suggesting that minority attributes may be very important for understanding members' legislative behavior; in the case of members' race, at least, this is not a conclusion that is strongly supported by the literature on race and roll call votes. For the clearest statement of this view, see Swain 1993. See Hall and

explained how members' identification with an underrepresented group affected their policy priorities: "A lot of these congressmen see themselves as having not only a district constituency but also a national constituency, especially women and minorities. For [K], it's the black community. For instance, he was floor manager of the voting rights legislation in the 97th Congress, and he's been very active with respect to EEO, very responsive to women's groups and civil rights groups [outside] the district." Another staffer to a black representative commented: "One of the things he cares most about is improving the life chances within the black community, and he doesn't care whether they're from Watts or Washington. . . . Equality to him is now mostly a matter of jobs, economics, opportunity. . . . We've got a long way to go, and he wants to do something about that."

Interview evidence from other sources suggests that the policy interests of women in Congress are likewise affected by their identification with a group that extends well beyond the boundaries of their districts. Barbara Mikulski, a member of the House Energy and Commerce Committee, commented to a reporter during the period of this study: "Because there are so few women in Congress, we have a responsibility for representing American women as congressmen at large." Similarly, Republican Representative Claudine Schneider noted that, although she did not initially run for Congress as "a champion of women," she soon took on that role: "I now feel I have a greater responsibility beyond my district concerning women" (Cohadas 1983, 784).

In sum, the preliminary evidence suggests that members harbor policy interests that affect their choice of legislative priorities and are not reducible to rational calculations regarding electoral self-interest. At the same time, members' personal interests derive from and are associated with very different factors — professional background, personal experiences, group identifications — and the relevance of any one of these to a member's behavior depends on her subjective perceptions of the issue at hand.[24]

Heflin 1995 for an alternative analysis, one that finds clear evidence of the importance of members' racial and ethnic identities.

24. Keith Krehbiel (1991) has argued that members are assigned to committees in part on the basis of occupational or other related background. Such background makes them "low cost specialists," in that they will be more likely to begin with and easily expand the policy-relevant expertise that will help the chamber to produce informed majoritarian choices. The argument here is a very different one. Prior interest or professional background in an area may render a member a relatively "low-cost" specialist, but the lower cost accrues to the member, not the chamber. The implications of the theory of participation elaborated here for theories of legislative organization and, in particular, the connec-

Prosecuting the President's Agenda

The two categories of member interests discussed thus far are adapted from previous, mostly inductive work on purposive behavior in Congress (for example, Fenno 1973a; Mayhew 1974). The third derives from similarly inductive work by Kingdon (1989) as well as some preliminary soaking and poking of my own. Under certain conditions, members will invest legislative time and energy to "prosecute the President's agenda," as one staffer put it. Several spoke of Republican members "carrying water for the administration" or serving as "point man" for President Reagan. One Republican member described three of his colleagues as "administration loyalists," whose designated role was to obstruct, delay, or dilute proposals that the administration opposed. A Democratic committee staffer, in turn, derided two of those same members as "White House puppets."[25]

Why do some members act as agents of the administration? Under what conditions can we expect that purpose to matter to the participation decisions of partisans in Congress?

One possibility is that the revealed interests of partisans in promoting the administration's agenda may be related to — indeed, may simply be an indirect means of achieving — other purposes already discussed. For instance, members of the president's party have an electoral interest in seeing that his legislative program is based on sound policy principles (that is, if enacted, it is likely to produce the desired results) and is legislatively successful (thereby showing that the president has the ability to lead). The electoral stake they have in his program is especially high if they expect retrospective voters to reward or punish the president's party because of the performance of the administration (see, for example, Fiorina 1981) or they otherwise anticipate coattail effects in forthcoming elections. At the same time, however, the expected electoral payoffs from efforts on behalf of the president are at once less tangible and less certain than those associated with serving an attentive district constituency. While the party and president may benefit in some diffuse way from the member's efforts, the benefits in party support may vary from district to district. For any individual member acting as administration agent, in any case, such benefits may well be swamped by other election-relevant factors. Moreover,

---

tion between members' policy interests and their participation will be taken up in the concluding chapter.

25. Note that Waldman (1995) characterizes Representative William Ford (a Michigan Democrat) as carrying President Clinton's water in ushering the latter's national service bill through both the Education and Labor Committee and the House.

if the president's program subsequently proves unpopular, the member has through her legislative efforts ensured that an unpopular program will be that much more traceable to her. And even should the member confidently anticipate some partisan electoral gain, that gain is itself a collective good from which she would benefit whether she contributed to its production or not.

The electoral basis for acting as an administration agent, then, does not appear to be particularly strong. What relationship might there be between the president's agenda and the personal policy interests of committee partisans? The possible connections here appear more plausible. During the period under analysis here, Republicans were certainly more likely than Democrats to share the policy positions of the Reagan White House. At the same time, it is not generally the case that Republicans' personal policy interests (the issues that members considered most important) are uniform or identical to presidential priorities. As one Republican committee staffer observed, "Stockman had his agenda; we had ours." Even when the White House objectives and the partisan committee member's objectives do coincide, why should the revealed intensities of the president incline the sympathetic member to be any more aggressive than she otherwise would?

The answer lies, I believe, in two different kinds of benefits that administration loyalists might anticipate. One kind is the additional bargaining leverage that the legislative actor acquires from her standing as administration agent. As we have already noted, minority members have more reason than majority members to doubt that their legislative investments will pay off with a tangible effect on the final legislation. When the bargaining weight of the White House is behind her, however, a member can hope for enhanced efficacy; if she cares about producing good outcomes and not simply taking good positions, the value of her participation stands to increase. The member sympathetic to the party's agenda on policy grounds, in short, should be willing to reallocate time and resources from an issue that she might actually care more about to an issue she cherishes less, in anticipation of greater political success.

The second kind of expected benefit that can incite members to go beyond the call of duty in service to the administration was characterized by one staffer as the "rewards of loyalty"; another referred to it as the administration's "cost of doing business on Capitol Hill." Chief legislator he may be, but the president simply has no parliamentary right to participate in the legislature. For his preferences to have much effect on the collective deliberations there, he requires agents to introduce his legislation, articulate his positions, offer and defend his amendments, and execute parliamentary strategy. Political scientists focus most of their scholarly attention on winning friends on formal roll call votes, yet that is only one (sometimes small) part of a labor-intensive White House strategy that has as its more proximate objective the mobilization of legislative supporters to act on the president's behalf. That presidents might do something to inspire such behavior is thus an important though somewhat obvious observation. For services rendered, administration agents may require particular provisions to be included in the administration's bargaining position, public praise or attributions of credit from the president, and the like. Or members may simply retain the credit for use in acquiring some future legislative or nonlegislative benefit. The agent's commission might well come in the form of district benefits that the administration is able to dispense to the committee loyalist. Prosecuting the president's agenda, then, would have a tangible, electorally relevant payoff. But in any case, both presidents and legislative partisans realize that the White House has substantial selective benefits with which it can reward loyalists willing to invest their office in serving the administration's policy agenda, either in promoting what the administration favors or by diluting or obstructing what it does not.[26]

In general, members of the president's party will sometimes have special incentives to work as legislative agents of the administration. But it is not the case that all members of the president's party will have an equal incentive to carry water for the administration on all issues. Those most strongly predisposed to back the president's policy or ideology should have the strongest incentives. Their opportunity costs in terms of pursuing their own policy interests will simply be lower when the two coincide, and, from the point of view of the administration, the costs of doing business will be cheaper. A conservative White House might enlist the help of a moderate Education and Labor member for some "bribe price," but other things being equal, the White House can win commitment of greater time and resources at a lower price from partisans who share the president's policy preferences. Furthermore, the willingness within the administration to pay for the services of sympathetic legislators should be directly related to how high an issue is on its own list of legislative priorities. For a member to foresee some benefit from carrying the administration's water, the administration must want the water badly.

Participation and Purpose

As I have developed the account thus far, each member makes decisions about how to invest her efforts and those of her enterprise without regard to

26. An analogous argument applies to members' incentives for carrying water for the party leadership of their chamber. Such incentives were barely apparent in the period of Democratic control of the House studied here. In the aftermath of the 1994 Republican

the collective purposes or the expectations of her colleagues. In this view, members are individual optimizers. But the particular, individual interests that figure into their estimates of expected utility — indeed, the substantive interests that give the concept of utility any meaning — are several, not single, and the relevance of those interests varies predictably across issues and contexts. Several implications of this view for our understanding of legislative participation warrant emphasis.

First, little is gained by treating goals or interests as attributes of individual legislators, a tendency that runs deep in discussions of congressional committees. For instance, while Fenno suggests that all members of Congress hold all three of the goals he identifies "in different mixes," he classifies members according to a "dominant" or "primary" goal in a relatively stable "goal hierarchy" (Fenno 1973a, 5, 7). This approach, in turn, has given rise in committee studies since Fennos to classify legislators and committees according to their motivational attributes or goal "orientations" (see, for example, Smith and Deering 1984; Hinckley 1975). Other scholars who maintain some notion of mixed motives view them as being ordered and assume that reelection is the first concern of the member and that other other goals become important only when reelection is reasonably assured (Fiorina 1974; Shepsle 1978, 65–66; Arnold 1979). The foregoing analysis suggests a somewhat different conceptualization of member motivations. Every member, I believe, wants reelection or good public policy in the abstract, but insofar as we are interested in members' legislative decisions, that is somewhat beside the point. What matters is the relevance of one or another kind of interest in the calculation of the behavioral moment, which depends in turn on the issue being considered. The behavioral effect of any abstract purpose, in other words, is contingent on the object of legislative action, subjectively perceived by the actor. Whether and to what extent individual members exhibit "single-minded" behavior and whether a particular goal can be used to characterize a committee of individuals are questions one can answer only after investigating those individuals' choices across an appropriately chosen sample of issues.

A second and related implication is that any particular issue may prove relevant to several abstract purposes simultaneously, and at the margin the (variable) relevance of each goal should make a difference in the member's behavior. By way of contrast, consider the very different nature of the mem-

---

takeover of the House and the centralization of power in the new majority leadership, a great many members would have intra-institutional incentives to carry water for their party's leadership within the House. I explore the implications of such institutional changes for understanding legislative participation in Chapter 8.

ber's voting decision. Where an issue is salient to a member's constituents (and the signal from the constituency is unambiguous), the good delegate votes with the constituency, and that is that. If, as typically happens, the member's own policy preferences coincide with the district's, it matters little for the voting decision (Kingdon 1989). The member cannot vote any louder, longer, or more often because she is doubly convinced of her position. Of course, the member's policy views may in some sense "reinforce" a decision prompted by constituents' interests, but except in special circumstances this distinction yields no behavioral difference. Thus can modelers of the voting decision assume that members act "as if" they are good delegates and lose very little in predictive power. That members' legislative investment decisions are matters of varying *degree,* in contrast, makes simple prediction considerably more problematic. The relevance of a bill to any of the member's interests is likely to inspire greater activity, and the confluence of two or more should incline her to participate all the more.

Unpacking Utility

The empirical difficulties to be overcome in the systematic investigation of purposive behavior, however, are several and significant. One may abstractly theorize about utility maximization, for instance, but it is then necessary to unpack what utility means in the concrete practice of members' behavioral decisions. As I have noted, Fenno's classic *Congressmen in Committees* breaks important ground on this subject. But in the study of individual behavior, goals as Fenno conceptualizes them are not the psychological phenomena of interest. The difference lies in the level of analysis. Fenno and his scholarly progeny ask why members sought assignment to committees with more or less large, more or less heterogeneous jurisdictions. Posing the question in that way elicits general, sometimes mixed and qualified answers. Such answers certainly help us to understand something about assignment seeking (though even here Fenno's own characterizations of members' committee-relevant goals are consistently mixed), but as I have emphasized, they provide only the most general clues about individual behavior in the ensuing post-assignment legislative choice.[27]

The general conceptual point I want to emphasize is not so much that goals

---

27. Thus Fenno characterizes committees according to their members' "modal" goal tendencies and otherwise describes committee members' behavioral patterns in light of the secondary or tertiary goals that service on the committee might serve (1973, chap. 1, passim).

as general attributes are tough to measure; rather, "goals" thus conceived may not be what we want to get at (or may not even exist). The language of members' goals at best implies only the central tendencies that we (or members themselves) impute to some unspecified set of potential choices. Whether some abstract goal makes a difference in a member's behavior depends on the matter to be acted on. A member may be a personally committed environmentalist, but if the issues before her panel involve Social Security cuts or district pork, she is more likely to behave like a constituency-minded delegate — not because of any change of conviction but because the agenda of issues evokes a different kind of calculation. Even an intense desire to promote environmental radicalism will remain latent and unfulfilled, awaiting opportunities in other forums.

I would thus suggest that the concept of members' goals as abstract attributes should be forsaken. Members have no simple, generally applicable motivational map that they introspectively consult. Rather, members define what we refer to as goals as they make concrete behavioral choices regarding particular issues (see also Shepsle 1978, 43). Our analysis, then, must be focused on the relevance of specific issues to members' (single or several) interests. Abstract assumptions about utility maximization, general descriptions of members' "primary" or "secondary" goals, characterizations of members in terms of their attributes or personalities — none of these can we expect to do satisfactory theoretical work.

MEASURING MEMBERS' INTERESTS

The foregoing discussion suggests two principles that should guide us in measuring members' interests. Given that calculations of interest are individual and subjective, the ideal measurement strategy should enable us to tap members' perceptions rather than simply impute interests to them. Second, interests are issue-specific, such that measurement must be at the level of the member-issue, not the level of the member or even the member-(sub)committee.

To these two principles I add a third, namely, that it is not so much the member per se, but the member's enterprise that acts in the legislative deliberations of Congress. Salisbury and Shepsle (1981a, 1981b) correctly emphasize that in the contemporary Congress, members are akin to leaders of organized enterprises, which include not only the principal or CEO but numerous staff members who serve as their agents. Indeed, it is often one of the member's legislative assistants or the legislative director, not the member herself, who screens issues, alerts her to various legislative opportunities, briefs her on the "upside" opportunities and the "downside" risks, and otherwise helps determine the priorities of the office. Information the staff provide to their boss thus becomes an important basis for her perceptions of particular bills. The boss's reactions to staffers' recommendations, in turn, form the basis of staff perceptions of how the boss perceives her interests.

None of this is to say that members are somehow ciphers, as institutional critics sometimes charge. On the contrary, the agent's impulse to learn and then faithfully represent her principal's interests is exceedingly strong in the legislative context. Perhaps the first and most important job of the new legislative assistant is to absorb as much information as possible about the member's district and the member's policy interests. To unwittingly recommend some action that the boss recognizes as politically dangerous, for instance, is the surest way to lose credibility within the enterprise. To act in a way that ultimately causes electoral harm, legislative embarrassment, or a violation of the representative's policy interests is the surest way to lose one's job. In an attempt to anticipate and correctly represent their boss's interests, legislative staffers employ a number of information sources, including past speeches and statements; consultations with the legislative director, administrative assistant, or other staffers; and of course consultations with the member herself.[28]

Bearing these guidelines in mind, I employed a measurement strategy to tap members' interests that was based on interviews with the legislative aides who handled each of the committee issues in my samples. (See also Appendix C.) The first portion of the interview was highly structured in nature, relying on pretested survey instruments. The remainder of the interview ranged from semistructured to unstructured. Throughout, several steps were taken to ensure the reliability and validity of staffer responses.

First, I took special care to identify and interview the personal staffers who would be best qualified to provide the required information, typically the legislative assistant (L.A.) in charge of the issues in my sample. My response rate for this category of respondent was nearly perfect, at 98 percent, producing interviews with well over one hundred personal staffers (see Appendix E). Second, I designed the interview schedule to exploit information that staffers were likely to have and willing to communicate. As I had done with the committee staff interviews, I tried to enhance this willingness by giving each staffer a written guarantee of anonymity.

28. See Salisbury and Shepsle (1981a, 1981b). My interviews with staff members also consistently revealed that the principal provides periodic signals to her agents within the enterprise that reveal both her preferences and her intensities. Indeed, the interactions between members and their staff have to do far more often with recommendations for action or inaction — whether to give a speech, offer an amendment, engage colleagues, introduce or cosponsor legislation, send or sign a "dear colleague" letter — than they do with how the member should vote.

Potentially the most serious problem with this measurement strategy derives from the necessity of conducting all interviews after action had been completed on the bills in each committee sample. The danger thus exists that staffers' perceptions of their boss's bill-specific interests may be contaminated by the level of involvement that the member displayed (and the staffer observed). To the extent that such revisionism occurred, any relationship I might subsequently uncover between the interview-based interest variables and member participation would be artificially inflated.

Though I had no means to completely avoid this danger, I took considerable pains to minimize it. First, I carefully avoided questions that asked the staffer to speculate directly about her boss's participation until the end of the interview. Neither in arranging the interview nor during the administration of the interview instruments did I make any mention of my interest in participation on committees. I avoided evoking the respondent's recollections of what her boss had done and simply focused on the relevance of specific bills to different interests.

Second, I attempted to identify and interview a second staffer who was familiar with the member as a person and a politician and knew well the diverse interests within the district but was not involved in the day-to-day business of legislative negotiations or markups. This effort led me to conduct interviews with the member's administrative assistant, legislative director, or both in just over 20 percent of the cases and produced more than one thousand interstaffer response comparisons for which one of the respondents was not a participant-observer in the committee action. The coefficient for interstaffer agreement exceeded .74 for every committee, averaging .77 across the observations of all three. More important, the relation I estimated between members' participation and the ratings of the L.A.s was virtually indistinguishable from the analogous estimates based on the ratings of the administrative assistants or legislative directors.

Finally, I exploited the opportunity provided by one office to administer the interview instruments independently to the member and the staff, using a sample of bills that cut across the member's major committee assignments and thus involved several different staffers. The high member-staffer agreement scores, discussed more fully in Appendix E, provided additional assurance of the interview instrument's validity.[29] The interview schedule, then, was de-

29. To reassure the still-skeptical reader, I would simply note that the model of floor participation estimated in Chapter 7 relies on objective measures of members' several interests, and yet I reach conclusions similar to those regarding participation and purpose at the committee level.

signed to obtain information regarding the relevance of each committee bill to the various interests of each committee member.

Interests Within the District

The early part of the interviews with members' legislative aides centered on the administration of a structured two-page survey instrument (see Appendix E). The instrument listed each bill in the appropriate committee sample, along with a two- to three-sentence description distilled from committee documents. Staffers were asked to rate each bill solely according to its importance to their boss's district, using four categories listed on the form: major, moderate, minor, and negligible. This proved to be a straightforward exercise, which virtually every respondent completed without hesitation. As they filled out the form (or when subsequently prompted), in fact, staffers discussed at length how a given bill would affect the district and more specifically key constituencies within it. Most of the bills in each sample, in fact, dealt with already existing programs and thus affected already existing constituencies. Working from constituents' mail, casework, interest group contacts, and a good (often personal) knowledge of the district, staffers were invariably able to give a much more detailed picture of how proposed legislation might affect the district than I asked for or could have acquired in the space of a thirty- to sixty-minute interview. That the staffers had sufficient knowledge to make the rankings I required, however, was not in doubt.

The Policy Interests of the Member

Indicators of each member's personal policy interest in each committee issue were obtained in a similar fashion. This point was raised second in the interview sequence.[30] I stressed that I was seeking the respondent's perceptions of how personally interested the member was in this issue, independent of whether it affected the district; I was asking staffers to think as if their boss did not represent a district. Using a form otherwise identical to the one described earlier, I asked each staffer to assess how closely each bill related to the boss's personal policy interests or ideological commitments. Once again, staffers exhibited little trouble filling out the form, and their general comments provided good evidence that they were interpreting the form as I intended. When they did not spontaneously comment, I pushed the respondents to discuss the member's issue-specific policy interests after they had completed the form. The

30. In cases where I interviewed more than one staffer for a single member, I reversed the order of the district and policy survey instruments. I found no evidence that the order of questions affected the results.

nature of staffers' comments made clear that they were not confounding district and policy interests; indeed, many commented on how the member's district and policy interests were in concert on some issues and were clearly distinct in others.

Prosecuting the President's Agenda

Recall the theoretical basis for hypothesizing when members of the president's party will have an interest in promoting matters on the administration's agenda, independent of the electoral or policy interests they might have in common. This interest is conditional; it depends on the member's ideological predisposition to support the president's positions on matters within the purview of the relevant committee. Hence the measurement strategy for this variable was broken down into two parts. Interviews with committee and subcommittee staffers were used to determine first which bills had high priority (coded 0/1) on the administration's agenda and second how committed the aides' boss was to the administration's agenda in the relevant policy domain. I coded their answers using a four-point scale analogous to that for members' district and policy interests. For both questions, the unhesitating responses, the high level of interstaffer agreement, and the detailed explanations that frequently followed confirmed that the questions were validly measuring the interest, as I intended.

Issues and Interests in Congressional Committees: A Preliminary Look

The nature of the data thus described, we are now in position to examine the patterns of member interest in the issues that came before each of the three committees. These patterns for the first two types of member interests (district and policy) are summarized in table 3.1 and support two observations about the nature and variability of members' interests that I have made thus far. First, even though congressional committees tend to be disproportionately populated with "interesteds" (Shepsle 1978), the descriptive statistics show that interest in the issues before one's own jurisdiction-specific, frequently self-selected committee is often low, if not altogether negligible![31] Even the committee with the most narrow, most homogeneous, and most constituency-oriented jurisdiction (Agriculture) is sufficiently diverse in its membership and

31. A predominance of interest-intensity outliers on a panel, in any case, does not necessarily imply the existence of a preference bias on the panel (Hall and Grofman 1990).

agenda that the fit of committee issues to members' interests is far from perfect. The typical member on all three panels had no significant district interest in more than 40 percent of the bills under consideration; yet the bills were sufficiently distinctive that, unlike the huge majority of bills dropped into the House hopper, they actually lived to see markup action. So too with the fit between committee agendas and members' policy interests. The typical member on all three panels had no significant policy interest in more than 45 percent of the bills that saw markup action.

While the variation across issues within committees is striking, however, some evidence in table 3.1 suggests that, as Fenno (1973a) says, not all committee jurisdictions are alike and hence not all evoke the same patterns of interests. As the committee's reputation would suggest, for House Agriculture the relevance of issues to members' constituency is relatively high: almost 60 percent of the bills rated by Agriculture respondents fell into the "major" or "moderate" category for district relevance. By contrast, only 44 percent of the bills were so categorized by Education and Labor respondents, with Energy and Commerce falling between those two. Though the patterns are less distinct, the Agriculture Committee members' policy interests appear to be less commonly evoked by comparison with the other two committees; almost 30 percent of the responses classify the relevance of Agriculture bills to their members' policy interests as negligible. Still, even these overall contrasts between what is reputed to be a classic "constituency committee" on the one hand and a classic "policy committee" on the other are slim. More noteworthy is that if Agriculture issues are somewhat more likely to evoke committee members' constituency interests, and Education and Labor issues slightly more likely to evoke members' policy interests, Energy and Commerce exhibits high levels of interest along both dimensions. Not for nothing is Energy and Commerce a highly coveted committee assignment. Given the breadth and salience of its jurisdiction, it is more likely to bring forth legislation that evokes district and/or policy interests among its members.

Table 3.2 provides a summary of House Republicans' interest in prosecuting the president's agenda during Republican president Ronald Reagan's first term. Of course, one should not expect the ratios for this type of interest to be as high as for the other two, given that this variable is not simply a function of the members' priorities and ideological predispositions but of the president's as well. Moreover, in the early 1980s, the majority in the House (and hence in the respective House committees) had a party affiliation opposite that of the president, and as a consequence the issues that progressed to committee markup were dominated more by Democratic leaders than by the Republican White House (especially after the Reagan/Stockman Budget Reconciliation Bill passed

Table 3.1   Members' Bill-Specific District and Policy Interests

	Agriculture (%)	Education and Labor (%)	Energy and Commerce (%)
District interest			
Major	32.3	21.9	25.1
Moderate	25.9	22.3	28.9
Minor	19.2	27.0	27.8
Negligible	22.5	28.8	18.2
Policy interest			
Major	28.8	32.5	32.4
Moderate	25.6	21.3	23.2
Minor	16.2	28.0	26.9
Negligible	29.5	18.3	17.4

Note: Cell entries are based on staffers' ratings of their boss's district and policy interests in dense samples of bills considered before each committee. The number of observations, by committee, was as follows: Agriculture, 672; Education and Labor, 493; Energy and Commerce, 654. (See Appendix D.)

Table 3.2   Minority Members' Interest in Prosecuting the President's Agenda

	Agriculture (%)	Education and Labor (%)	Energy and Commerce (%)
Major	7.6	4.8	5.2
Moderate	10.5	4.8	7.9
Minor	3.2	0.0	4.1
Negligible	78.7	90.4	82.8

Note: Cell entries are based on staffers' ratings of their boss's commitment to the president's agenda within the respective policy domains and are based on dense samples of bills considered before each committee. The number of observations, by committee, was as follows: Agriculture, 315; Education and Labor, 187; Energy and Commerce, 267. (See Appendix D.)

in the summer of 1981). Table 3.2 thus reveals that minority members seldom exhibited a strong interest in serving as agents of the administration.

Considering the different types of interests separately does not fully reveal members' interest in issues before their committees, however. That is, following the assumption about the subjective perception of issues, one should not expect all members of a committee to be interested (or uninterested) in a given issue for the same reason. Those of a caveat-emptor cast of mind, for instance, might be wholly indifferent on policy grounds to the issue of bovine growth hormone. But at the same time, they might become wholly infatuated with the

Table 3.3   Members' Interest in and Indifference to Committee Bills

	Agriculture	Education and Labor (%)	Energy and Commerce (%)
Major	40.6	40.4	41.1
Moderate	25.9	23.5	28.4
Minor	17.3	25.1	21.9
Negligible	16.2	11.0	8.6

Note: Cell entries are based on the highest level of any of three interests, as reflected in staffer's ratings of issues within the three respective committee domains. The number of observations, by committee, was as follows: Agriculture, 672; Education and Labor, 493; Energy and Commerce, 654. (See Appendix D.)

matter if they had dairy farmers in their district who cared about bovine growth (and death) a great deal. Table 3.3 summarizes the extent to which individual members were interested in an issue on any grounds, that is, where the intensity of their interest is categorized according to the highest threshold it meets on any of the three interest dimensions. As table 3.3 shows, the percentages of members who were more or less interested in an issue for any reason or set of reasons is consistently greater than appears in any of the earlier tables that report on separate interests separately. Across the three committees, the percentage of members exhibiting a major or moderate interest of some kind in the respective sets of issues was about two-thirds.

Conclusion

At the very least, the patterns evident in the tables in this chapter should undercut the reductionist premise that the interests of individual representatives nicely align along one dimension. More generally, two simple but important conclusions can be drawn at this stage of the investigation.

First, the common claim that committees are disproportionately composed of interested members may be fine as far as it goes, but it does not go far enough. One certainly should flinch from inferring that committee self-selection tendencies can be neatly connected to any categorical claim about committee bias, as many have claimed (Shepsle 1978; Weingast and Marshall 1988), and hence to any second-order hypotheses about committee decision-making tendencies, distributive or otherwise. Policy choices are made with respect to subjectively perceived issues or bills, not more or less homogeneous, objectively given jurisdictions. Moreover, the distributive hypothesis regarding committee bias turns on the assumption that self-selected committee members have reasonably clear and mutually compatible constituency interests,

interests that drive the ensuing collective choices of their panel. Tables 3.1 through 3.3 render that view difficult to sustain as a general claim, though at this stage of the analysis it remains possible that members act on the basis of constituency interests and no others.

Second and more specifically, the patterns of table 3.3 reinforce the view articulated in Chapter 2, namely, that we ought to expect that what Carroll (1966) called the "efficient" committee will be quite different from the nominal committee. On most issues that come before their very own, presumably self-selected panels, most members are simply not interested. Lest one assume carefully inculcated norms of "duteous work," credible threats of institutional sanctions, or, say, some enforceable precommitment for a distributive reward, hypotheses about why the uninterested many would be anything but indolent are difficult to derive.

4

Getting into the Game

I think you'll find it harder to explain why members don't participate in something than why they do. — House subcommittee staffer

Why do members participate in particular legislative matters before
them? The profound if partial answer of the last chapter was: Because they
want to. While strategic considerations sometimes come into play, what legislators want is to advance one or more of several interests they think relevant to
the matter at hand. The equally profound point of this chapter is that legislators cannot always do what they want. Simply put, not all members are
equally able to pursue their objectives on each of the issues that more or less
concern them. Each member must make rough calculations of his enterprise's
ability to play as well as his interest in the game. Thus the distinction between
"intensities" and "revealed intensities" comes more sharply into focus in the
pages to come. Two members may be equally interested in an issue (for similar
or different reasons), but the intensity that they reveal through their legislative
involvement is a function not only of interest but of the size and quality of their
staff-support system, the positions they hold, and the procedural prerogatives
that provide more or less easy entry into particular legislative games.

We thus begin this chapter by exploring the variable costs of the resource-
constrained enterprise as it considers entering the legislative mix on specific
issues. Without straining the economic metaphors too much, the barriers to
entry can be characterized under two conceptual rubrics: information costs
and transaction costs. Of course, these are only analytically distinct; in the

blur of legislative practice they often slide into one another. But as I will use it here, the term *information costs* refers to the time and effort required for the enterprise to acquire, assimilate, and apply the issue-specific policy information needed to identify and fully develop interest-serving positions or proposals.[1] The relevant *transaction costs,* in turn, include the time and effort required to communicate with other actors (both on and beyond the committee) to credibly convey policy-relevant information, negotiate compromises or trades of various sorts with other key players, mobilize committee sympathizers who may otherwise be inattentive, or anticipate the reactions of the opposition and implement strategies to counter them.

In sum, the enterprise has much to do when it is active on even one bill, let alone on the several bills under consideration by the member's committees at any given time. Of course, not all information and transaction costs must be paid on every issue, and in any case I have no means to measure each of the particular cost components that the enterprise roughly and subjectively estimates in deciding how it will order its legislative priorities, even across issues on a single panel. However, I begin with a simple but fundamentally important premise that the costs of participation are typically nontrivial and, more important, that members are not equally endowed with the legislative resources to pay them. In this chapter I will explore the set of factors likely to structure those costs and the member's capacity to pay, as those factors are estimated inside the enterprise.

A Seat at the Subcommittee Table

In the aftermath of the "Subcommittee Bill of Rights" and other reforms passed during the mid-1970s, sweeping statements regarding the legislative autonomy of House subcommittees became commonplace. Numerous students of the institution emphasized its radical decentralization, such that the century-old Wilsonian lamentation that Congress is governed by committee was updated to the more current claim that Congress is governed by subcommittee (Davidson 1981; Hardin, Shepsle, and Weingast 1983; Dodd and Oppenheimer 1993).

Such generalizations regarding subcommittee power, I believe, have been badly overblown, all the more so in light of the centralizing reforms enacted in

---

1. In this respect, I follow Krehbiel's practice in *Information and Legislative Organization* of equating *information* with policy expertise — that is, information about the connections between alternative policies that the collective might adopt and the real-world consequences that particular actors want to produce.

the mid-1990s (Aldrich and Rohde 1996). Subcommittee action remains but one stage in a sequential legislative process in which actors beyond the panel play a significant role, either through direct intervention (say, amending what the subcommittee reports) or through clear communication, the consequence of which is that subcommittee members anticipate how others will react to alternative proposals they might put forth (Hall and Evans 1990). Nonetheless, subcommittees enjoy a number of comparative legislative advantages, including at least a weak agenda power over bills within their jurisdictions and certain strategic advantages associated with moving first, deciding when to move, and deciding on and implementing strategies at subsequent stages of the legislative process (Shepsle and Weingast 1987a). These factors do not automatically render them institutionally *powerful* on issues within their domain. That was not the case before the 1995 reforms and is less true after. But they do enhance the opportunities of individual members to *participate,* the behavioral focus of this book.

In particular, subcommittee members usually enjoy the opportunity of first review, which is often the *only* opportunity for review. Should the collective decision of the subcommittee be not to consider or report a bill to the full committee, seldom will the bill go farther. For instance, more than 1,500 bills were referred to the full House committees under study here, but only 179 saw any markup action, and all but two dozen began in subcommittee. Most bills died a subcommittee death. Of the bills that ultimately see any markup action, moreover, most are drafted behind the subcommittee scenes, such that subcommittee members have greater access to this very early but very important stage of the bill-construction process.

Because the subcommittee is the typical location for both the first informal and the first formal considerations, then, subcommittee members have the advantage of moving first. Members on the lookout for viable proposals to advance a desirable policy objective or for amendments that offer them a chance to claim credit for advancing the interests of some district or group constituency are first in position to do so. Indeed, many of the ideas for amendments come directly out of the hearing process or informal discussions with groups interested in the measure (who frequently dominate the hearing witness list). Valuable opportunities also exist at the subcommittee markup stage for legislative opponents, who have an opportunity at this early stage to obstruct, dilute, or damage the bill at hand.

In short, one need not invoke some grand generalization or, indeed, say anything about subcommittee power, to assert noncontroversially that subcommittees tend to be the first and one of the most important tables around which particular legislative games get played. The member of the subcommittee with jurisdiction, then, enjoys a seat at an informal bargaining table from which most others are excluded.

Subcommittee Membership: The Informational Advantage

One of the most important assets that derives from the preferential position that subcommittee members hold is the additional information they tend to possess about specific subcommittee bills.[2] As we noted above, the vast majority of legislative hearings in the House are held at the subcommittee level. Subcommittee members have the formal right to participate in questioning witnesses at those hearings. But of what use to a member is special access to legislative hearings? Not much, it might seem, given that rarely more than a member or two is present and paying attention at any particular moment in a typical hearing.

The key point here is that attendance need not always be by the member himself; more often than not the representative appears for only a portion of even the most important hearing, if at all. Numerous legislative assistants assigned to staff their boss's subcommittee business noted that they prepared for almost every hearing. Several L.A.s speculated that their boss often did not decide whether to participate in a hearing until after he had reviewed the relevant briefing materials prepared by the L.A. Frequently the boss had explicitly asked for such material, scheduled time to attend, and then never showed up, presumably kept away by some other claim on his time. In preparing for or attending such hearings, the staffers for the subcommittee member acquire an informational advantage. Although one staff member remarked that most hearings are "staged for public consumption," she quickly added that the information that is generated "just through the process of scheduling a hearing, soliciting witnesses, reading, writing memos, getting the CBO estimates or whatever [is] very important . . . if you want anything to happen."

If subcommittee members start with a comparative informational advantage, they should rationally capitalize on it. Thus do members assigned to a subcommittee invariably appoint one from among their small corps of legislative assistants to cover meetings. Often a member will hire a particular staffer who can bring relevant experience to the enterprise. For instance, the L.A. for

2. Such participatory advantages are related in important ways to expertise and "specialization," concepts that have been reinvigorated in recent work on the nature of legislative organization by Krehbiel (1991). The implications of the individual-level behavioral theory outlined here for theories of organization will be more fully discussed in Chapter 9.

one member of the Commerce Health and Environment Subcommittee had recently completed a health-policy fellowship through which he studied and staffed health issues on Capitol Hill for almost a year. A staffer who covered both labor subcommittees for an Education and Labor member was a labor lawyer. The agriculture L.A.s for several Agriculture Committee members had already spent a year or more doing casework out of their boss's district offices, through which they became field-level experts on the implementation of particular programs that affected the district.

Whether the member's L.A. begins with considerable expertise or not, over time he acquires greater knowledge of the often related issues that come before the committee, so that when any given issue arises, the marginal costs in staff time of "getting up to speed" are simply lower than for the nonmember's L.A., who is more likely to be confronting a subcommittee issue de novo. Perhaps more important, the subcommittee member's L.A. generally knows how to acquire the information quickly. This latter point is in part a reflection of the closer connections between L.A.s and the subcommittee or committee staff assigned to cover the issues of a particular subcommittee. One senior staffer for a House Agriculture subcommittee commented that many members "may have sat through similar hearings before . . . but what matters is what's in *this* bill—how much will it cost, what difference will it make, does it stand a chance? . . . Besides, most members don't remember much—you have to explain some of the same things to them over and over. . . . The L.A. that may have staffed [the issue] the last time around has probably gone on to greener pastures. So we spend a lot of our time getting [the L.A.s] up to speed."

Thus do subcommittee members not only start with an informational advantage relative to nonmembers, but their enterprise tends to exhibit greater issue-relevant expertise and lines of access to cover the marginal information costs.

The magnitude of this advantage, I hasten to emphasize, can be easily overstated. Policy-relevant information on even narrow legislative issues is abundant, perhaps embarrassingly rich, on Capitol Hill. Interest groups of various ilks are more than happy to fax or mail information, meet with members or staff, suggest ideas, even provide the correct legislative language for a particular amendment—information that the typical L.A. often lacks. Moreover, on most any issue anyone might ever care about, there is likely to be a Congressional Research Service "issue brief" on file, a Government Accounting Office analysis, various administration reports, preprinted hearing testimony, or any number of studies or reports conducted by academics, think tanks, or policy analysts, both in and outside government. While neither member nor staffer is likely to accept such information uncritically, this wide variety of issue-specific material provides useful, sometimes heterogeneous signals to the enterprise that in turn enable it to act with a more informed view of how its preferences over outcomes comport with the proposal at hand. Policy-relevant information, in short, is rarely scarce.

However, familiarity with and access to such sources of information tend to be greater for the enterprises of subcommittee members than of nonmembers. More important, once policy-relevant information is acquired, it must be understood, assimilated, and then applied to the matter at hand, often under very tight time constraints. Subcommittee enterprises need not give up as much in the way of beneficial activities elsewhere to pursue actively their interests on a particular subcommittee bill. In sum, they can do much more in the legislative game than read informative signals and then cast their vote.

SUBCOMMITTEE MEMBERSHIP: THE TRANSACTIONAL ADVANTAGE

The premise of the foregoing discussion was a simple one. In order to enter the mix on a particular bill, one must know something about the programs and policies that the bill purports to address. Whether a member is playing to win or simply to lay claim to credit, his proposals and arguments must be credible to his audience.

The premise of this section, in turn, is that there is much more to acting credibly in a legislative game than deploying policy-relevant information. "Practical politics," Henry Adams once wrote, "consists in ignoring facts" (1903 [1918], 373). More than a bit cynical, I would say, but I take from the spirit of Adams' epigram (and a bit of my own research) that practical legislative politics involves something more than facts. Having the policy analysis right or the experts on your side may not hurt, but it is seldom enough.[3]

What matters as much, perhaps more, is the ability to pay the transaction costs of communicating and negotiating with other players (or potential players) regarding the particular matter at hand. Here, too, information comes into play, but it is a different kind of information than the policy- or program-related material I have emphasized thus far. It is better labeled political intelligence than policy expertise.

The simple point is that save for the symbolic gestures of pure show horsemanship, a congressional enterprise cannot act alone on a particular bill. To suggest even a single proposal be included in the markup vehicle, the member's

---

3. Numerous cases that explore the legislative use of policy analysis and other policy-relevant information reinforce, sometimes disturbingly, how often Adams' epigram approximates the truth. See Malbin 1979; Reid 1980. At the same time, however, numerous works point to the importance of such information in the policy process on Capitol Hill. See Derthick and Quirk 1985; Kingdon 1984; Whiteman 1985.

enterprise simply wastes its time if it does not, as one staffer put it, "pave the way." An aide to a moderate Commerce Democrat described the work involved in offering a single amendment to a major bill:

> The first thing you've got to do is talk to the political people, [X] in our office, but also the district office as well. Is this something that will cause Mr. [X] problems back in the district? Or is it something that small businessmen will want? I usually have a pretty good guess, but you still want to talk to these groups, make them feel included. Then you've got to run the amendment by the subcommittee staff. Have they considered it? What do they think? What will [the full-committee chair] think? Sometimes you get names of other people to call, in this case, [P], who handles such things for the Chamber of Commerce, and also the guy at SBA. If you get that far, you have to get up with someone at leg. counsel to get the language right. If possible, you try to get it into the [subcommittee] chairman's mark. If not, then you've got to inform all of the other L.A.s of what you're doing; that way they'll know what's going on so their boss won't get caught off guard. Usually, I'll try to get hold of the agency people as well. . . . In this case, though, nobody seemed to care much but us. It was an important bill, and they had bigger fish to fry. . . . The amendment flew through on a voice vote.

An additional advantage of subcommittees' informal agenda control, then, is that subcommittee members are more likely to find themselves with lines of communication to various other players with a stake in their panel's jurisdiction. At this early stage, the subcommittee tends to hold a central place in a specific policy network that extends beyond the House and usually beyond the government. For gathering political intelligence and negotiating with other key actors, they are well positioned. Indeed, interest groups with which the enterprise finds it has a political affinity often become extensions of the enterprise, what Milbraith once referred to as "service bureaus" to the legislator (1963). This is no innocuous relationship. When members and group lobbyists have interests in common, the latter actively subsidize the transaction costs of the former — acting as an informal liaison with other members, committee staff, agencies, and other interested groups and otherwise gathering political intelligence that legislative players require. Given the resource constraints of the typical office, such subsidies help overcome an important barrier to a member's involvement in a matter both the group and the member care about (Hall and Wayman 1990; Hall 1994b).

To summarize, the congressional committee is a well-developed communications network through which interested parties interact (Price 1972), and the subcommittee member is "plugged in" in a way that the nonmember is not. Likewise, the subcommittee nonmember must overcome important procedural barriers to entry. The right to participate in the subcommittee hearing is not guaranteed, and the subcommittee nonmember enjoys no prerogative to vote, speak, raise points of order, or offer amendments during subcommittee markup. Whatever interests the nonmember might want to promote, he must do so behind the scenes or await the full-committee markup, should the bill be reported. His access to the informal deliberations, moreover, is not automatic: by comparison with the subcommittee member, the nonmember's staffers must go out of their way to find out what is being done and why, assess whether his participation is worth the time, and then act in a reasonably credible way. By the time of the full-committee markup, the agenda is often set, some of the central issues fully debated, and many of the legislative deals already made.

Subcommittee Leaders: Players with Extra Cards

If subcommittee members typically enjoy both lower information and lower transaction costs than their nonmember colleagues, the more important point is that not all subcommittee members are equal. The procedural prerogatives and the legislative capacity are substantially greater for the subcommittee chair and, to a lesser degree, the subcommittee ranking minority member.

As I have already suggested, the capacity and experience of the staff is crucial to a member's ability to acquire, assimilate, and deploy the issue-specific information needed to participate on particular bills. In this respect, the advantages of subcommittee leaders are greater still, significantly enhancing their ability to dominate the deliberations and negotiations on particular bills. The reforms of the 1970s guaranteed subcommittees their own budgets and staffs, but the principal beneficiaries of this endowment were the subcommittee chairs, not the membership at large. And while many of these advantages were diminished in the mid-1990s in favor of centralizing budget and staff control in the hands of House committee leaders, in practice, the staff advantages of subcommittee leaders relative to subcommittee backbenchers remained significant.

To a lesser extent, the same holds on the minority side as well. For example, staff budget allocated to the House Education and Labor minority in the 1980s was, as on most committees, relatively thin. The policy adopted by the ranking minority member at the time (and continued by his successors) was that the minority staff would be at the disposal of the ranking subcommittee leaders as needed. Hence, while all minority staffers were technically listed as adjuncts to the full committee, each subcommittee ranking minority member had at least one staff member assigned to him de facto almost all of the time. When I asked an aide to the ranking minority member of one Education and Labor subcommittee why her boss chose to head up the subcommittee he did, she responded, "There simply wasn't anything left if he wanted to be a ranking member. You take what you can get. . . . As a [ranking member] you get a legislative associate on the committee staff, so there is that incentive to go ahead and take the ranking position that is available. [Q] started to play a role in things right away."

Beyond whatever personal staff they might want to deploy for their panel's business, then, subcommittee leaders benefit from additional staff, assigned specifically to the subcommittee's jurisdiction, who are generally hired for their knowledge of the jurisdiction and their political experience in the relevant policy domain. Many are semi-permanent attachments to the committee, carried over from the staffs of previous subcommittee or committee leaders. Others are "promoted" L.A.s, who have worked on the issues at hand for several terms as their boss worked his way up to a leadership position. Still others come from administration positions in one of the agencies over which the subcommittee has jurisdiction. Whatever their background, in short, subcommittee staffers are much less likely to be newcomers to the policies and politics of the subcommittee than is the typical member's L.A.

Perhaps more important, holding a leadership position places the member and his staff at the epicenter of the communications network in which most important legislative interactions take place. The costs associated with, say, disseminating a proposal, eliciting reactions and recommendations, entertaining modifications or counter-proposals, building a coalition, or planning legislative strategy — in short, the marginal transaction costs associated with shaping legislation and building coalitions — are far less for the subcommittee leader than for other subcommittee members. And, of course, since most of these activities are handled by staff, subcommittee leaders not only face lower marginal transaction costs, but they enjoy greater resources with which to pay them.

The relative staff advantages of variously positioned committee members are captured for the three committees in table 4.1, the data for which are based on the number of staffers on the committee's payroll who were designated in interviews with the majority and minority chief counsels as legislative (as opposed to administrative) personnel. On the dual assumption that what matters to a member's enterprise is not simply staff quantity but quality and that staff quality is reflected at least roughly in the salaries staffers are paid, table 4.1 also summarizes data taken from the Office of the House Clerk on the salaries of the individuals designated in my interviews as committee legislative staff.

*Table 4.1   Distribution of Staff Resources: Number of Staffers and Staff Salary
Expenditures*

	Agriculture		Education and Labor		Energy and Commerce	
	Number of staff members	Staff salary budget ($)	Number of staff members	Staff salary budget ($)	Number of staff members	Staff salary budget ($)
Subcommittee						
Nonleaders (mean)	0	0	.2	6,300	0	0
Chairs (mean)	1.6	53,450	3.9	117,942	7.6	347,600
Ranking minority members (mean)	1.2	43,086	1.2	37,886	2.0	90,480
Chairs (total)	12.8	427,600	31.2	943,536	38.0	1,738,000
Ranking minority members (total)	9.6	344,688	9.6	303,088	10.0	452,400
Full committee						
Nonleaders (total)	0	0	0	0	0	0
Chairs (total)	5	245,600	15	510,800	25	1,348,000
Ranking minority members (total)	3	130,000	7	297,200	6	217,600

Source: U.S. Congress, Office of the House Clerk, 1982, 1984.
Note: Statistics are based on staff allocated from the respective committee or subcommittee budgets. Staff allocations from members' personal office budgets are not reflected here. Only individuals classified by subcommittee counsel as legislative staff members are included in the subcommittee statistics. Only individuals classified by full committee counsel as legislative staff members are included in the full-committee statistics.

As table 4.1 shows, the committee staff allocated to subcommittee non-members and subcommittee backbenchers is negligible. While the latter may hold a staff advantage relative to the former, that advantage is due to greater experience and access, not additional personnel. Rather, the enhanced legislative capacity within the subcommittee accrues to the formal leaders. On average, even subcommittee ranking minority members control enough staff salary to expand their capacity by one legislative specialist — in effect, double the personnel that the typical backbencher can allocate.

The variation among the leaders of the respective parties, however, is striking. As the institutionalized prerogatives of the majority allow, subcommittee chairs consistently enjoy more and better-paid staff than their ranking minority counterparts. This proved true without exception for the twenty-one legislative subcommittees under study here. The majority's exploitation of its prerogatives in this regard varies considerably across the three committees, however. Note that the party difference within committee is relatively small for House Agriculture, a committee whose member-to-member politics tend to be among the most bipartisan in the House. In contrast, the two committees with strong ideological and regional cleavages — Education and Labor, and Energy and Commerce — exhibit a majority-minority staff ratio of more than three to one. Ceteris paribus, such statistics suggest that minority subcommittee leaders should be less disadvantaged in their ability to participate on House Agriculture than on the other two committees.

More generally, table 4.1 reveals patterns that should imply important behavioral differences from member to member, depending on their positions. Indeed, numerous respondents stated matter-of-factly that a subcommittee staff allowance greatly enhanced the ability of the chairs and ranking minority members to get involved, if not take the lead, on issues before their panels. The chief counsel to one subcommittee chair said in a self-satisfied tone that "we get to as many issues as the staff can handle, plus a few." A minority Commerce staffer commented regarding his subcommittee staff contingent that "the three of us [staffers] can pretty much cover the waterfront" but added that some subcommittee issues "don't get the attention we'd like." Several respondents commented that their boss's participation was sometimes affected by the particular expertise that their subcommittee staff happened to bring to the enterprise.

> A lot of what happens around here is staff-initiated. Take our work on pension reform. I doubt that I would have ever paid much attention to it on my own. It's important, but it's just a complex topic. But [Q], the subcommittee counsel at the time, was an accountant . . . and he loved the stuff. So, he dug into it. The actuarial imbalance in most private and state pension systems is even worse than in Social Security, if you can believe that. He got fired up about it, and I got involved.

> A lot of what a congressman does depends on how good his staff is. You can't bring in a whole bunch of new people and get anywhere. [M] is very savvy. He helped Mr. [R] walk through the minefields. His major job was to help with the equal opportunity issues. He came to the committee from the EEOC director of legislative affairs. He had this as part of his background and had worked with the ACLU, the Washington lawyers, and [other groups]. Mr. [R] had been interested in equal employment issues, but he would not have been able to get as involved without [P].

Beyond the staff-dependent ability to pay the costs of participation, the subcommittee leaders enjoy certain procedural prerogatives that work to their participatory advantage as well. As noted above, for instance, hearings are scheduled and other relevant agenda decisions and nondecisions made at the subcommittee level, but here too, the procedural prerogatives that provide agenda power are, save in extraordinary circumstances, in the hands of the chair. Such prerogatives translate into two types of political advantage. First, if such work is likely to conflict with other business that the member finds important, the subcommittee leader is better able to adjust the timing of events to suit his objectives. Second, and more important, the chair can, on all but the most salient bills, simply decide not to act. Or, more strategically, he can postpone action indefinitely until the press of other legislative business makes action on a particular matter inopportune for everyone.

Full-Committee Leaders: Players with Extra Cards, Keepers of the Rules

The preceding arguments regarding the legislative capacity and institutional advantages of subcommittee leaders also hold for the full-committee chair and ranking member. The alleged growth of subcommittee government, most observers claimed, witnessed the concomitant decline in importance of the full-committee chair and, one might surmise, the ranking minority member. Perhaps so; this is not to say, however, that the advantages of these positions wholly evaporated. They did not.

Table 4.1 reveals that full-committee leaders enjoy staff resources far larger than those allocated to their subcommittee counterparts. For all three committees, the chair's staff budget was four or five times that of the typical subcommittee chair, and in each case the committee ranking minority member's staff budget was more than twice that of the ranking subcommittee members' average budget. And if anything, the committee leaders' advantages expanded in the mid-1990s, a change the importance of which, I suggest in Chapter 8, can be assessed only in the context of a general model of participation.

In any case, the staff at the disposal of the full-committee leader must be allocated across issues from all subcommittees, whereas the subcommittee staff is more narrowly focused on the issues within its own jurisdiction. Thus we find that the number of staff members and total staff salary allocated to subcommittee chairs exceed those of each of the respective full-committee chairs.[4]

Once bills have been reported out of subcommittee, full-committee leaders

---

4. This pattern was reversed in the 104th Congress, however. Such changes in patterns of staff allocation within committees is discussed in Chapter 8. The central point remains that the variability of allocations is central to understanding the comparative advantages of full-committee leaders, subcommittee leaders, and panel backbenchers.

have a clear procedural advantage in deciding when and sometimes whether subcommittee reports will be considered in full committee. There is, for instance, no staffer in committee analogous to the parliamentarian on the House floor; that role is played by the committee chair. Generally, procedural maneuvering is in itself an important form of participation (one partly evident in the markup participation measures discussed in Chapter 2), and in this respect, the committee chair has a great advantage, notwithstanding the majority-rule principle envisioned in the committee rules.

To take one important example, Energy and Commerce chair John Dingell delayed for several months bringing up a natural gas bill reported by the Synthetic and Fossil Fuels Subcommittee, fearing that full-committee proponents of deregulation had the votes to push through amendments that would benefit gas-producing states and hurt energy-consuming states such as Dingell's own state of Michigan. When Dingell finally convened a full-committee markup that November, one member walked over to him and boasted, "John, we've got the votes," to which Dingell replied, "Yeah, but I've got the gavel" (Maraniss 1983). Dingell soon demonstrated its value. When markup began, Dingell first allowed consideration of two amendments that served as test votes of whether his voting coalition was, in fact, a losing one. When he lost both (by narrow margins), Dingell simply gaveled the markup to a close. He did not bring up the bill again until April of the following year, after he and his allies from energy-consuming states had negotiated a substitute bill acceptable to a few swing voters yet less favorable to the gas industry. The committee (again, by a narrow vote) quickly reported the newly revised bill, over the vigorous objections of members from gas-producing states.

In sum, it is not clear from the statistics that the advantages of subcommittee leaders outstrip those of full-committee leaders, even in the allegedly weakened position that the latter held in the 1974–94 period. Both sets of leaders enjoy substantial staff subsidies, access to important lines of communication and negotiation, procedural prerogatives, and other advantages. The significance of these different institutional positions requires careful behavioral analysis. As students of reform have taught us, it is implausible to assume that a particular reform will have the effects intended.

Getting into the Side Game: The Behavioral Importance of Minority Status

Given the importance I have thus far attached to institutionally subsidized information and transaction costs, the impact of majority or minority status on committee participation warrants special attention. A party majority implies much more legislatively than 50 percent plus one. It enables one party and not the other to organize the chamber, write and interpret the rules of the game, and allocate most of the resources. At the committee as well as the chamber level, it is an interesting theoretical puzzle why a committee majority grants the committee minority as many resources as it does, given that House rules guarantee the minority only about a half a dozen staffers to cover clerical, administrative, and legislative work. Indeed, one could imagine the majority keeping minority subcommittee assignment rights to itself, perhaps denying the minority subcommittee seats altogether. Or, more plausibly, it might set subcommittee ratios much more favorable to the majority than it usually does, regardless of the party ratios in the parent committee or the parent chamber.

Interesting though such puzzles may be, the more relevant question here is how the institutional advantages held by the majority play out in the behavioral calculations of individual members. While minority leaders, both at full committee and subcommittee, enjoy greater resources to pay the costs of participation than do their backbench colleagues, their procedural prerogatives and other institutional subsidies clearly do not match those of majority committee leaders.

Minority members can be expected to face other barriers to participation. In particular, they have less access to and affinity with individuals with formal prerogatives (committee and subcommittee chairs) and have fewer staff resources at their disposal. In the drafting of the markup vehicle and other informal activities, these disadvantages should be especially serious. We should therefore expect that minority status should significantly depress informal participation. But given that minority members are more likely to have been excluded from the informal deliberations, they should be all the more likely to participate at formal markup. The minority's right to participate in markup is procedurally guaranteed, so the markup becomes their opportunity to react to and try to amend the majority vehicle. We should thus expect minority status to enhance formal participation.

Participation in a Sociological Key?

As I reviewed in the previous chapter, the study of legislative participation may be conspicuously absent from recent scholarship on legislative behavior, but this has not always been the the case. A prior generation of scholars whose empirical work focused on the postwar Congress paid considerable if somewhat general attention to legislative participation. Their mode of analysis, however, was sociological, not economic; their focus was thus on the prescriptive (and proscriptive) norms of the group, not the issue-specific choices of individual members.

While no longer in theoretical vogue, what value might we attribute to this alternative approach? Is it useful still? Alternatively, was it valid during its time but subsequently dated by growing individualism in the postreform Congress? If the optimization approach employed here is valid for the current legislative era, is it similarly time-bound in that it accounts poorly for behavior in earlier historical periods? The more general question, of course, is whether the theoretical clothing in which one wraps behavioral explanation depends on the historical season of the legislative world one sets out to explore. In political science as opposed to popular fashion, one hopes that the relative merit of alternative approaches is mostly a matter of careful reasoning and systematic investigation, not marketing-induced tastes or intellectual faddism.

In this section I thus elaborate how the alternative explanations differ and discuss how their competing hypotheses can be investigated. My two-pronged argument will be that the older sociological approach does little explanatory work in the contemporary era, as others have argued (see especially Sinclair 1989; Smith 1989). But my second point is fundamentally revisionist, namely, that the explanatory punch of sociological theory was never all that strong in the first place. To state the claim baldly, the widely reported transformation of the U.S. Congress over the past four decades may be more the artifact of our social-scientific categories than of underlying changes in the social order in which members legislate.

Reasons both general to sociological theory and specific to the sociology of Congress support this view. First is the suspicion that the prescriptive norms simply generalize and label the phenomena they purport to explain. For instance, it may well be that the institution cannot, in some sense, function without norms of specialization and hard work, but it does not automatically follow that such norms arise so that the institution can function. At the very least, it is necessary to explain how such behavioral regularities arise and how they are maintained in the face of individual incentives to violate them and a dearth of institutional mechanisms or individual incentives to punish violations (see Axelrod 1984).

With theoretical hindsight, then, it is somewhat hard to understand how those norms ever carried the explanatory weight that they presumably did in the prereform Congress. In this section, I will review three norms in greater detail, derive from them implications that differ from those of the optimization theory developed earlier, and elaborate several tests to assess the behavioral vitality of prescriptive norms, both before 1970 and now.

NEW PLAYERS IN THE GAME:
A RATIONAL-CHOICE PERSPECTIVE ON APPRENTICESHIP

Perhaps the most commonly invoked concept in the older sociology of Congress was that of apprenticeship. The freshman member was pressured by house norms to remain relatively passive in legislative affairs until he had undergone a significant period of apprenticeship (Matthews 1960; Fenno 1962, 1966, 1971). Freshmen were to be "seen and not heard," more or less, and the failure to observe this admonition was likely to provoke sanctions by more senior members. As noted, however, commentaries over the last two decades reveal that this norm has been dying off, and several recent analyses suggest that it is now quite dead.

When time permitted, I asked my respondents whether the prescriptive norm of apprenticeship showed any vitality. Included were several current and former members and numerous staffers whose matriculation on the Hill pre-dated the period of egalitarian reforms. The answers to my queries without exception corroborated the conjectures of other scholars who have plotted the demise of the norm. One member responded: "Yes, I think the apprenticeship norm has disappeared. That began disappearing when my class came to Congress. There were some forty to sixty new liberal Democrats that year. They came busting in, going to save the world, impatient. They changed the system here entirely. No one expects new members to keep quiet anymore." Senior staffers consistently offered similar observations regarding participation on their committees:

> No. In our case there is no tradition of preemption of anything by senior members . . . or for junior members to hold tight and to listen and learn. [Agriculture]
>
> Not on this committee. [Education and Labor]
>
> That's not true on this committee. [Energy and Commerce]
>
> That's one of Foley's favorite stories. When he was a freshman, the chair said that under normal circumstances, the senior members did the talking. If you had a point, then you got a senior member to make it. With the reforms, freshmen participate on this committee as much as anybody else. [Agriculture]
>
> Just the opposite. . . . We try to encourage freshmen to take a more active role. From the Republican point of view, we try to bring them in as much as possible. The thing is that we don't have that many members; we've got to utilize each one that we have. [Education and Labor]
>
> There is tremendous pressure on freshmen to make their mark. [Energy and Commerce]

If the scholarship of recent years and my own interviews are correct, the concept of apprenticeship appears destined for the dustbin of behavioral theory. Freshman status should no longer diminish a member's participation, either in committee decision making or on the floor.

I argue here precisely the reverse. The apprenticeship I wish to resuscitate is a different beast from the prescriptive norm of the older tradition. Apprenticeship has simply been viewed through the wrong theoretical lens. As an organizational norm of obsequiousness, socialized by the group and internalized by the member, apprenticeship does not restrain the newcomer's participation. Yet other features inherent in freshman status may diminish new members' ability to participate on an equal basis with more senior colleagues. Several important behavioral constraints on incoming members remain, even in the normless present. The new apprenticeship is rationally chosen rather than imposed by peers.[5]

First, freshmen consistently suffer from informational disadvantages analogous to those that frustrate the subcommittee nonmember. Relatively speaking, the freshman confronts each issue anew; he is less likely to be able to draw on prior legislative experience in an area. By contrast, even his sophomore colleagues will already have dealt with similar issues — read memoranda and experts' reports on the subject, sat through hearings, and observed the tensions and tradeoffs in deliberations on related topics. In short, the freshman member will tend to have inferior knowledge of the legislative background, substantive issues, and political possibilities associated with action on a particular issue.

The freshman's enterprise will also suffer a relative shortage of opportunities, networks, and resources to pay the marginal information and political transaction costs. At the very least, it takes time to learn the rules of procedure as they are practiced within the legislative forums in which the new member enjoys an official opportunity to participate. He and his staff will moreover begin with less developed relationships with other important actors in the relevant policy domains. In particular, relationships or connections with committee and subcommittee leaders are less likely to be well formed; so, too, with the relevant interest groups, bureaucrats, think tanks, and other actors on and beyond Capitol Hill.[6]

---

5. For a rational-choice perspective on norms other than those I examine here, see Weingast 1979, on whose insights I draw here.

6. This trend should hold to a lesser extent for members who have recently transferred onto a committee. Their familiarity with committee issues and networks will tend to be less than that of the returning member, but greater than that of the freshman. Transfers

According to my theory of rational apprenticeship, then, freshman status should significantly diminish a member's participation, both formal and informal. In this sense, reports of the death of apprenticeship are greatly exaggerated. This differs from the old kind of congressional apprenticeship, but its meaning is, I think, consistent with ordinary usage. An apprentice does not simply patiently wait and watch the master craftsman in deference to seniority and superior social status. Rather, he does so to learn, out of a recognition that he begins with little knowledge of how things are done and that it takes time to acquire the competence to produce something other than poor products or personal embarrassment. From the senior craftsman's point of view, in turn, were he to find an apprentice with a natural gift for the craft, would he slow the lad down, perhaps sanction him so that he does less than he is able? Absent a psychological theory that says organizational seniors necessarily possess weak egos or, worse yet, possess an irrational predilection to do more work rather than less, one ought to predict otherwise.

What we require, then, is not a repudiation of apprenticeship per se but a rejection of the sociological assumptions that have traditionally encumbered the concept. This argument I take to be a general one, not particular to the current period. Senior stalwarts may have proffered this-is-the-way-things-work lectures to incoming members. I have suggested why the newcomer would, then as now, act in ways consistent with such admonitions but not because of them. Then as now, freshmen had a relatively small and inexperienced staff. They had less opportunity than did experienced legislators to secure their preferred committee and subcommittee slots and otherwise suffered from the informational and transactional disadvantages described earlier. (The fit between institutional positions and legislative interests was correspondingly diminished.) To put the point in counterfactual form, if a newly elected member were subjected to the be-seen-and-not-heard socialization of the 1950s but endowed with the personal experience and political access, staff resources, and choice of panel assignments of most other backbenchers, the new member would not participate less.

To recast my claims in the hypothetical rather than the counterfactual, the empirically testable (ceteris paribus) propositions that follow are these. First, freshmen should participate less than nonfreshmen in the postreform period, even though scholars and participant-observers universally agree that the prescriptive norm of apprenticeship is dead. In the next two chapters, this propo-

---

(and their staffs) will also enjoy greater familiarity than the newly elected member with rules and procedures and various legislative practices.

sition will be tested in the context of a behavioral model. Second — and this is the acid test — I posit that the prereform freshman effect on participation should *not* be discernibly stronger than the postreform effect. The cooperative spirit of two anonymous staffers made this test feasible. In Chapter 6, I analyze comparable data on participation from House Education and Labor during one congress from the early 1960s (a decade before the democratizing reforms) and during one congress that took place a decade after the reforms.

Before concluding this section, it is important to note the ways in which the ceteris paribus assumption for testing the above hypotheses does not hold. Several factors related to freshman status confound the analysis of its importance. First, freshmen are less likely than nonfreshmen to have sought the committee they are on, at least as a top choice (Shepsle 1978). As we will see in the next chapter, this tends to be true in the subcommittee assignment process as well. It is thus less likely that the various areas of their panels' jurisdictions will include as many issues relevant to the first-termers' interests. One should therefore control for members' issue-specific interests — a move made possible by the elaboration and measurement of such interests described in the previous chapter.[7] Second, freshmen may participate less because they are more likely to come from marginal districts. The energy and attention of their enterprise is best allocated less to legislative work than to other, probably more profitable reelection-oriented activity — constituency relations, casework, trips to the district, fundraising, and the like (see Fenno 1978, 215–24). In order to properly test for the apprenticeship effect I have hypothesized, then, one must also control for electoral insecurity.

A RATIONAL-CHOICE PERSPECTIVE ON THE NORM OF SPECIALIZATION AND HARD WORK

While the puzzle of collective action was not yet central to the legislative scholarship at the time, we noted in Chapter 3 that the group norm of "specialization and hard work" could be construed as the political sociologist's solution to the free-rider problem. Members did dull and boring work because they were expected to. In service to their chamber, they were to concentrate on matters before the relatively narrow panels to which they were assigned and, in so doing, develop expertise.

According to the specialization norm, subcommittee members ought to attend to their business carefully, focusing their legislative attention consis-

---

7. This was not possible for the prereform analysis. I set up the comparative historical analysis, however, in a way that minimizes the potential for incorrect inferences about the nature of legislative apprenticeship.

tently on those particular domains. Unfortunately, this behavioral implication is similar to the implication — what I will refer to as rational specialization — that derives from optimization arguments elaborated to this point, namely, that subcommittee members will tend to be more willing and better able to pay participation costs within their domains than nonmembers. But if the sociological and rational choice views point in the same direction, they are not observationally equivalent. The prescriptive specialization norm suggests that whatever their other demands and interests, subcommittee members should consistently do the "duteous work" on legislative issues as they arise before their subcommittee. Optimization theory implies a weaker claim: that subcommittee members will be more likely than their nonmember colleagues to participate in forums where both are eligible participants, but that their participation will vary widely. No prediction follows that members will feel obligated to participate on even the "dull and boring" (that is, individually uninteresting) matters on the subcommittees to which they are assigned.

The implications of the two accounts thus involve matters not of direction but of degree. Still, two hypotheses enable us to disentangle the relative merits of the alternative theories. If the specialization prescription holds, subcommittee members should rarely shirk their responsibilities in subcommittee deliberations. The theory of choice advanced here, in contrast, presupposes that members make their participation decisions issue by issue and that those decisions will sometimes lead them to neglect a subcommittee matter in favor of some other activity where the expected utility is greater. Hence, subcommittee participation should be selective, not universal. Second, according to the prescriptive norm of specialization, members can be expected to work hard even on issues in which they are not interested. By contrast, the account provided here implies that members will be selective about their participation in subcommittee in a way that reflects their interests, rarely participating on issues where their interests are not evoked.

Finally, even if prescriptive specialization does not appear in the postreform period, was it important during an earlier, less individualistic, prereform era? The historical data should shed further light on the explanatory importance of this norm during a period presumed to be its behavioral heyday. Even if the norm is defunct now but was alive then, we should see a greater subcommittee membership effect in 1961–62 than in 1981–82. I hypothesize that we will not.

A NORM OF DEFERENCE, OR RATIONAL ABDICATION?

The current (or past) vitality of the norm of deference is more difficult to evaluate, owing in part to the greater ambiguity of its meaning in the older literature. Indeed, the conceptual boundaries between specialization and deference have not always been adequately laid: specialization is thought to generate expertise, and expertise ought to command deference.

Even more closely related to the norm of deference, so much so that the two terms are sometimes used interchangeably, is the norm of reciprocity. The distinction at the heart of this study, however — between positions and participation, between revealed preferences and revealed intensities — renders the distinction between these two concepts considerably clearer. The norm of reciprocity refers to an implicit agreement among members to support one another's positions on, say, a multimember logroll, even when certain of the actors disagree with the proposition before them. The norm of deference, by contrast, refers to an implicit cooperative agreement, internalized in the attitudes of the group, that members of one panel will not actively interfere in the business of the other. As Fenno's House Appropriations respondent put it: "It's frowned upon if you offer an amendment in full committee when you aren't a member of the subcommittee" (1973a, 95). To state the relation of the two somewhat differently, deference is to members' revealed intensities what reciprocity is to members' revealed preferences.

Thus clarified, the distinction between these two norms, and the theoretical basis for observable behavioral patterns consistent with them, turn out to be altogether different. Rejecting the sociologist's attachment to the power of group prescription, a long line of political economists have reasoned that collective choices based on reciprocity are inherently fragile.[8] The incentives to renege are often strong, and without an independent sovereign or set of external structural arrangements to enforce members' implicit or explicit promises, reciprocal agreements come unglued.

The optimization theory developed here implies, on the other hand, that behavior consistent with what political sociologists have referred to as deference is not particularly susceptible to such enforcement problems. The decision to vote contrary to one's true preferences on an issue is by definition costly, while the future compensation is uncertain. The decision not to participate actively on the same issue is (save for unusual circumstances) costly only in an opportunity-cost sense and only then to the extent that the next-best investment of one's resources is expected to be noticeably less profitable than the issue on which one takes a walk. In short, the behavioral patterns consistent with the old injunction "go along to get along" may appear, both in

---

8. Krehbiel 1988 and Shepsle and Weingast 1994 provide critical reviews of this scholarship. For specific efforts to address problems of coalitional fragility within a legislative assembly, see Aldrich 1991; Shepsle 1979; Shepsle and Weingast 1987a; Weingast 1989; Weingast and Marshall 1988; and the essays collected in Shepsle and Weingast 1995.

committee and on the floor. But I would suggest that such patterns reflect not a group norm of mutual noninterference but the rational calculations of individuals regarding when to participate and, more frequently, when to abdicate.

But how are we to assess empirically which of these explanations is the better? Again, if the sociological account is correct, it should be corroborated in conversations with participant-observers who should have learned the norm. It is not. Again, my interviews reinforce the findings of other scholars that attitudinal norms are not much in evidence in the socialized minds of members. When I offered the prescriptive definition of deference to one senior staffer, he replied: "If that's what you mean by deference, no one defers to anyone around here." Similarly, one Commerce member noted that there was "no expectation, none" that he refrain from participating on any issue, regardless of its jurisdictional origins or authorship. "If it's something you care about," he stated matter-of-factly, "you give it your best shot."

Beyond my own and others' interviews, there are more convincing means of testing whether the norm of deference has been inculcated in members, now or before. First, if subcommittee members do participate more than nonmembers, as I have hypothesized, the prescriptive norm of deference implies a stronger claim — namely, that nonmembers will rarely participate in full-committee deliberations, except perhaps for symbolic expressions of assent. Nonmember amendments to subcommittee bills should be altogether rare.

A second hypothesis that follows from the assumption of prescriptive deference is that subcommittee nonmembers who are interested in an issue will not participate anyway. Even if they are tempted, the implicit admonition not to interfere should restrain them. My optimization theory does not jibe with such a hypothesis. Rather, the greater the nonmember's interest in an issue, the likelier that he will expect the benefits of participation to outweigh the relatively high information and transaction costs. Under such conditions, the nonmember will not hesitate, out of regard for the social order, to enter the fray.

Third, subcommittee chairs might be expected to exhibit deference by not interfering in matters reported from subcommittees on which they do not sit. Of all committee members, they have the most to lose from undermining a socially constructed order in which they rank high and thereby enjoy special discretion in their domains. Chairmanship of a subcommittee that lacks jurisdiction on an issue should consequently have a negative effect on participation. Optimization theory, in contrast, predicts that these individuals will participate as their interests and opportunities allow, that is, no differently from the typical backbencher.

In broad terms, an explanatory framework built on prescriptive norms provides that some members (subcommittee specialists) who are not interested in an issue should participate nonetheless, while others who are interested (freshmen and interested subcommittee nonmembers) should suppress their inclination to do so. I hypothesize rather that participation is a matter of rational choice, subject to individual-specific constraints, not a product of group socialization.

Institutional Position and Egalitarianism in the House

House rules establish both in committee and on the floor the principle of one person, one vote. In this respect, legislative egalitarianism is institutionalized. In legislative politics as in electoral politics (despite *Baker* v. *Carr*), however, the actual practice of the political process is rarely egalitarian. As we have seen in this chapter, some members are institutionally richer in legislative resources. And in Congress, as in other arenas, riches may translate into political advantage. Subcommittee and full-committee chairs have agenda powers strong enough to affect whether and when an issue warrants consideration. Their position in the appropriate policy networks allows them to acquire information and transact business with other players at a lower cost, as is true to a lesser degree of minority leaders and subcommittee members in both parties.

A more pervasive and potentially more important theme of this chapter is the inequalities in the distribution of legislative staff who serve as assistants to, agents of, and sometimes surrogates for their bosses as the latter attempt to participate simultaneously in several different forums and attend to "the myriad personal requests from constituents" (Bauer et al. 1963, 408). If committees and subcommittees harbor political intelligence and expertise, the actual repository is more likely to be the mind (and files) of the staffer than the memory of the member. Committee and subcommittee chairs, and to a lesser degree their minority counterparts, have a clear advantage.

Of course, even with only "a modest staff" (Bauer et al. 1963, 408), the lowliest member whose interest in an issue is sufficiently intense will find none of the barriers to entry insurmountable. Still, given that numerous other games in which one may have a stake are being played simultaneously, it is no wonder members covet the panel assignments and formal institutional positions that expand the legislative capacity of their enterprise.

PART II

The Theory Tested

5

Players at Subcommittee Tables

The most important thing is getting a seat at the table. If you're on the subcommittee, you've got that. — Legislative assistant to House Commerce member

A frequent refrain of students of the institution, if not a salient feature of the textbook Congress (Shepsle 1989, 252–53), is that legislative deliberations in recent decades have been largely dominated by congressional subcommittees. The House, in particular, is said to be (in yet another invocation of Wilsonian language) the home of "subcommittee government." Whether this claim is more stylized fiction than stylized fact, however, has recently become a contested issue, one that is now at the center of an important debate in the theory of congressional organization and legislative majoritarianism. The House reforms of the mid-1990s to centralize legislative resources and prerogatives in the hands of party leaders and committee chairs should bring that debate into even sharper focus (Aldrich and Rohde 1996; Davidson 1996).

Engaging that debate directly, much less resolving it, is not the purpose here — my concern is with the legislative participation of individual members, not the distribution of power in a sequential process of collective choice.[1] But

---

1. As I suggest in Chapter 1, I believe the two to be related in important and theoretically specifiable ways; consequently, one motivation for studying participation is to better understand the behavioral basis of legislative power. Such matters are more where this study points than where it ends, however. I thus take them up in Chapter 8, where I discuss additional directions for and extensions of the study of legislative participation. See also Hall 1992; Hall and Evans 1990.

there is little doubt that subcommittees in the House provide most members with good opportunities to participate in, and so make a difference in, the chamber's deliberations. The process of legislative "governing" frequently *begins* even if it doesn't end with the actions taken on these panels. Put somewhat differently, this remains the stage at which much of the legislative labor occurs. It is where issues get their first proofing, and hence where the exercise of procedural or other legislative advantage, the anticipation of reactions, or the tactics of obstructionism may either alter the provisions or impede the progress of a bill through subsequent stages. And if issue-specific and hence outcome-relevant policy expertise is developed, it is mostly developed here.

Given its place and significance in a sequential legislative process, in short, it is especially important that a theory of participation do well at explaining members' behavior in subcommittee. But there are additional, analytical advantages that make it an appropriate place to begin the empirical evaluation of the account elaborated in the previous two chapters. In particular, it is well suited to disentangling the purposive from the institutional factors shaping members' legislative priorities. Membership on the subcommittee of jurisdiction, I have argued, carries with it a number of advantages, but self-selection also implies that subcommittee members are more likely than nonmembers to take a significant interest in issues within their panel's jurisdiction. As the next section demonstrates, the subcommittee assignment process is largely self-selective; indeed, there are strong reasons to believe that self-selection is far less constrained at this stage than are assignments to standing committees. Members' interests and their subcommittee positions are thus closely intertwined.

The subcommittee focus of this chapter thus has two analytical advantages. By first focusing our attention solely on similarly situated subcommittee members, we are able to assess more confidently the importance of purpose in their participation. Subcommittee membership is rendered a constant, not an institutional factor confounded with members' interests. Given that the assignment process has systematically censored many of the uninterested members from appearing as observations, moreover, the subcommittee stage presents us with a difficult, inherently conservative sample of observations with which to test the effects of member interests on behavior.

Self-Selection in the Subcommittee Assignment Process

In his seminal study of committee assignments in the House, Kenneth Shepsle argues that the assignment process exhibits what he terms an "interest-advocacy-accommodation syndrome" (1978). Members identify and aggressively pursue committee positions within the chamber that will best enable them to pursue their political interests. The party committees on the respective committees, in turn, do their best to accommodate member requests. Accommodation not only ingratiates the party leadership to as many members as possible; presumably it increases the reelectability of their rank-and-file, a goal that both the party leadership and its members share.

The accommodation of members' preferences for specific committee assignments in any given assignment sequence, however, is limited by "the sometimes competing goals and objectives of others and the formal rules that define the process" (1978, 5). Specifically, there are several significant constraints on unmitigated self-selection (Hall and Grofman 1990). First, House rules limit members to no more than two major committee assignments. Second, although the majority party leadership can and sometimes does modify the size of particular committees at the margin, the size is limited to a relatively small proportion of the House membership—typically less than 10 percent and never more than 15 percent. Hence, for most committees, unmitigated self-selection is limited by other members competing for scarce slots. Third, the respective party committees charged with making assignments frequently limit the number of members from a single state or zone allowed to sit on particular committees.

For the new member deciding which committees she will seek, the constraints are particularly acute. Returning members enjoy the presumption that they will retain the assignments they held in the previous congress, such that the newcomers must compete for available vacancies.[2] In ordering her initial assignment requests, then, the member must discount her sincere preferences by the likelihood of assignment. A wish list of Appropriations, Ways and Means, and Rules, for example, is probably not an optimal strategy for the typical newcomer. She has a relatively low probability of getting anything from such a list and at the same time will have failed to express a rank order that might help her secure one of her remaining and more realistic choices. According to Shepsle, nonfreshmen are also constrained, though in a different way. In deciding whether to give up a current assignment in order to transfer to a more preferred one, the senior member must discount the desirability of the committee by the costs of queue switching, that is, a loss in proximity to the top of the committee seniority ladder, and hence in the time and opportunities that make ascendance to a formal leadership position more likely.

Shepsle's account is directly relevant here in that, in general form, most of

2. For the minority, this right is limited by the availability of committee slots allocated to it by the majority.

what he says about the committee-assignment process holds for subcommittee assignments as well. It would, of course, be surprising if that were not true. If members purposively seek committees well-suited to the pursuit of their particular interests, we should hardly expect their calculations to change qualitatively when they move to the similar and often more important task of seeking specific subcommittees.

It does not follow that the nature of the institutional constraints is the same, however. In fact, they are structured quite differently. Assignment to subcommittees, far more than assignment to full committees, approaches unconstrained self-selection. Subcommittee assignments are not solicited from and then granted by some organizational authority. Rather, committee members meet at the beginning of each new congress in their respective party caucuses and select their subcommittee seats in a round-robin fashion, with each member making a first choice in order of seniority before the most senior member chooses her second. This process continues until all available subcommittee slots are filled. Yet even then the subcommittee sizes are frequently adjusted, sometimes dramatically, to meet member demand, especially among the majority contingent. For example, while the number of members on Education and Labor remained virtually constant (thirty-three plus or minus one) for the 97th through the 100th Congresses, the number on the Employment Opportunities Subcommittee fluctuated from ten to twenty to six to nine. Over the same period, membership on Energy and Commerce held at forty-two, while on the Energy and Power Subcommittee it fluctuated from twenty-two to eleven to fourteen to twenty-one. In each case, the membership on subcommittees during at least one congress exceeded 50 percent of the full-committee membership. Such patterns are common among subcommittees of all three committees under study here, as well as virtually every other significant committee in the House — from the time of the subcommittee reforms of the early 1970s to the Republican-controlled House of the mid-1990s.

The obvious consequence of this round-robin process is that there is no limit on the number of members from a state or zone that structures member assignments. Neither is there a significant constraint on the number of subcommittees to which a member can be assigned on any given committee; House rules impose ceilings on members' subcommittee assignments, but a member can allocate all to a single committee if she wishes. Third, no queue-switching costs constrain the movement of nonfreshmen members between subcommittees at the subcommittee level. Subcommittee rank is determined anew in each congress by the order in which members select their seats. Hence, to the extent that ascension to a subcommittee leadership position is affected by seniority, length of subcommittee service matters not. For instance, the rules of House

Education and Labor stipulated that "the majority party members of the committee shall have the right, in order of full-committee seniority, to bid for subcommittee chairmanships" (House Committee on Education and Labor 1983c, 5), and such bids were typically ratified by the committee's majority caucus.[3] With no subcommittee seniority credits carrying over from one congress to the next, in short, members can make the subcommittee selections that best suit their interests in light of the widely known forecasts of what issues are likely to arise on the subcommittee's agenda during the upcoming two years.

Thus does every majority member typically get assigned to her most preferred subcommittee, and frequently to her second and third as well. As one majority staffer to the Education and Labor Committee explained, the committee chair "generally lets anybody go on anything; it doesn't matter to him. We will commonly let a freshman go on whichever [subcommittee] he wants to, as many as he wants to." House Commerce staffers suggested that there was some unsatisfied demand for seats on two subcommittees, but one staffer summarized: "Everyone on our side always gets their first choice, but . . . trying to get on Health and Environment or Energy and Power in the second round can be tough. I know that a number of junior members had to go to their third choice. After that, some senior members will usually step aside if some junior guy really wants on a subcommittee [in the third round of bidding]."

The relatively unconstrained process of self-selection onto subcommittees operates for minority members as well, with one additional constraint. Unlike the committee majority, the subcommittee minority does not control the number of slots available on each subcommittee. Subcommittee sizes and party ratios are set by the majority, and these two variables determine the number of slots allotted to subcommittee minorities. In practice, however, the majority will sometimes increase subcommittee sizes at the request of the minority leadership. Thus did one minority staffer on Education and Labor note: "Subcommittee assignments weren't really a problem; everybody pretty much got what they wanted," a comment that was echoed by counterparts on the other committees.

The foregoing account of the subcommittee assignment process thus implies that the relationship between subcommittee membership and member interest in subcommittee-generated legislation should be strong and positive. And this

3. The tendency to ratify seniority-driven subcommittee chair selection has long held in other committees as well, though with some exceptions. In the aftermath of the 1995 House reforms, this tendency diminished, at least in the short run.

is precisely what we find. With considerable consistency across the panels of three jurisdictionally diverse committees, the interview data substantiate the interest-driven, self-selective nature of subcommittee assignments. Members of the subcommittee of jurisdiction exhibited a "major" interest — the highest rating — in approximately half of the observations, and they exhibited a "major" or "moderate" interest in about two out of three cases. In contrast, members who did not sit on the respective subcommittees of jurisdiction consistently cared less about those panels' proposals. In less than a third of the cases did members exhibit a major interest in bills that did not fall within their own subcommittees' purview.

Table 5.1 subjects the subcommittee self-selection hypothesis to systematic scrutiny. The first section of the table reports a difference-in-means test for the level of interest in subcommittee bills by subcommittee members and nonmembers, using a measure wherein each member is assigned the highest of her ratings on the three interest dimensions. For each committee, the hypothesis finds unequivocal support. Again, less distinction in the intensity of interests is evident between Education and Labor subcommittee members and nonmembers than for those on Agriculture and Energy and Commerce. Even so, we can reject the null hypothesis with 99 percent confidence. For the other two committees, the difference in means is even larger.

The ensuing sections of table 5.1 provide a more differentiated profile of subcommittee member and nonmember interests. The difference-in-means tests likewise exhibit patterns consistent with self-selection at the subcommittee level, but they also suggest several more specific tendencies that square with the nature of the issues within the respective committee jurisdictions. First, there is no reason to suspect a priori that members' bill-specific interest in prosecuting the president's agenda will comport with their subcommittee portfolios. The specific issues that the White House decides to emphasize are revealed seriatim, sometimes late in a session; if members have a strong inclination to carry water for the administration, information about how best to position themselves for subcommittee assignments often comes long after seat selections are made. Thus in the results of table 5.1 we find no systematic bias along this dimension in subcommittee members' interests.

The differences on the other two dimensions are stark by comparison. That Agriculture's jurisdiction is constituency-oriented has long been apparent in the structuring of most Agriculture subcommittees along regionally circumscribed commodity lines. This tendency finds clear support in table 5.1. The location of subcommittee members along the district-interest dimension is high — approximately two on a three-point scale — with a *t*-statistic such that we can reject the null with high confidence.

Table 5.1   Are Subcommittees Interest Outliers?

Interest in subcommittee bills	Agriculture	Education and Labor	Energy and Commerce
All dimensions			
Subcommittee member mean	2.23	1.98	2.29
Subcommittee nonmember mean	1.73	1.69	1.86
t-statistic for difference-in-means test	5.85***	2.84***	5.26***
Serving district interests			
Subcommittee member mean	1.98	1.44	1.79
Subcommittee nonmember mean	1.45	1.24	1.51
t-statistic for difference-in-means test	5.96***	1.87**	3.24***
Promoting personal policy interests			
Subcommittee member mean	1.83	1.83	2.09
Subcommittee nonmember mean	1.30	1.49	1.52
t-statistic for difference-in-means test	5.83***	3.27**	6.46***
Prosecuting the president's agenda			
Subcommittee member mean	.21	.05	.11
Subcommittee nonmember mean	.21	.10	.19
t-statistic for difference-in-means test	−.02	−1.19	−1.40

Source: Interviews with members' legislative and/or administrative assistants. (See Appendix C.)
*$p < .10$.   **$p < .05$.   ***$p < .01$.

Somewhat less distinctive are the respective levels of district interest for members on House Education and Labor, a committee that was included in Fenno's original comparative committee analysis (1973a) and typed as a classic "policy committee." The difference between subcommittee member and nonmember means shows that the diverse policy interests that lead members to select Education and Labor find expression in their subcommittee selection as well. Members of the reporting Education and Labor subcommittees on average found issues more relevant to their policy interests than to their district interests. The same pattern holds for Energy and Commerce, with neither committee reflecting a subcommittee-constituency connection nearly as strong as that of House Agriculture.

If table 5.1 suggests that, as Fenno said, the jurisdictions of different panels evoke different types of interest, perhaps the more noteworthy pattern is that these are relatively *modest* differences in central tendencies, tendencies that exhibit considerable variation on the panels of all three committees. While the district ratings are high on Agriculture panels, members of this classic constituency committee also exhibit high levels of personal policy interest that map

well onto their subcommittee assignment portfolios. Though the policy ratings are high on Education and Labor panels, members of that (reputed) policy
committee also exhibit high levels of district interest that map well onto their
subcommittee assignment portfolios. So too for Energy and Commerce. The
differences-in-means tests demonstrate that on both policy and district dimensions, subcommittee members of all three panels are more interested than their
nonmember colleagues.

Put somewhat differently, self-selection ensures that subcommittee members are interest-intensity outliers. Before concluding this section, however, it
is important to emphasize that the variable and overlapping nature of the
interests that drive subcommittee self-selection implies that one *cannot* thereby conclude that subcommittees are preference outliers, as some have asserted
(for example, Shepsle 1978; Shepsle and Weingast 1987a; Weingast and Marshall 1988). Even if the district interests of the subcommittee members were
inherently compatible, subcommittee members would not necessarily bring
compatible policy interests and ideological commitments to their subcommittee work. A digression from the behavioral analysis that preoccupies us here,
such considerations of representativeness and legislative organization will receive greater attention in the concluding chapters.

Who Plays the Subcommittee Game?

If, as Shepsle (1978) says, (constrained) self-selection operates in the
committee assignment process, the previous section demonstrates that self-
selection is even less inhibited as members seek positions on panels with more
specialized and distinctive jurisdictions. The fit between interest and position
is even more concrete and specific. Moreover, the subcommittee stage is
widely recognized as a central part of the legislative process, so that, in the
main, this is where the action is and where the interesteds sit.

As table 5.2 demonstrates, however, participation is far from universal even
in subcommittee. Recall, for instance, that a member is counted as attending a
subcommittee markup if she appears even momentarily during a deliberation
that often spans more than one meeting and sometimes spans several days.
Despite this generous coding, however, absenteeism was 24 percent in Agriculture subcommittee markups, 33 percent in Education and Labor subcommittees, and 20 percent in Commerce subcommittees. The simple and low-
cost act of voting was variably practiced, too. Despite the more self-selected
nature of their positions, subcommittee members commonly relinquish their
voting rights in unrestricted fashion to subcommittee colleagues. Hence members are on hand to cast their own votes in subcommittee markups in fewer
than a third of their roll call opportunities.

Table 5.2   *Congressmen in and Absent from Subcommittee*

	Agriculture (%)	Education and Labor (%)	Energy and Commerce (%)
Absenteeism	26	31	33
Voting by proxy or not voting	58	66	60

Source: Minutes and/or transcripts of subcommittee markup sessions. (See Appendix A.)
Note: Entries are based on summations for subcommittee member *i* on bill *j* marked up in the respective panels' subcommittees.

Table 5.3   *Selective Participation at an Early Stage: Players and Nonplayers in Subcommittee Games*

	Agriculture (%)	Education and Labor (%)	Energy and Commerce (%)
Players	55.9	46.8	46.3
Nonplayers	44.1	53.2	53.7

Source: Minutes and/or transcripts of subcommittee markup sessions and interviews with subcommittee staff. (See Appendixes B and C.)
Note: See text for definition of categories. The number of observations, by committees, was as follows: Agriculture, 247; Education and Labor, 149; Energy and Commerce, 218.

In table 5.3, I roughly classify subcommittee members into two categories, on the basis of the archival and interview data regarding their participation at the subcommittee stage: those who might reasonably be regarded as either "players" or "non-players" in the sample of subcommittee games analyzed here. Members are counted as players if they (1) were among the principal participants in the markup discussion, even if they took no responsibility for agenda, amending, or procedural action; or (2) they (or their staff) were mentioned by a single committee staffer as having played more than a minor role in behind-the-scenes negotiations. Applying this generous standard, I found that only 56 percent of the members of the reporting subcommittee could be counted as active players on particular Agriculture bills within their panels' jurisdictions, only 47 percent on Education and Labor, and only 46 percent on Energy and Commerce.

In sum, subcommittees are jurisdictionally the narrowest panels in the House. They have considerable legislative advantages that induce intrainstitutional attraction. And assignment to them approaches uninhibited self-selection as closely as one might reasonably expect. Even so, specialization and hard work are hardly universal. Rather, participation is highly selective. In approximately half the observations across three committees composed of very different subjurisdictions, members are passive observers as frequently as they are active players. Moreover, rarely is a subcommittee nonleader active when she is not obviously interested. The evidence thus weighs heavily against the sociological notion that specialization and hard work are group norms that carry broad behavioral meaning. Whether my rational-choice alternative is any better, however, remains to be seen.

A Model of Subcommittee Participation

So far as the subcommittee stage goes, we now have a data-rich, detailed description of who participates in the early stage of what previous scholars have labeled subcommittee "governing."

We are now in position to evaluate why. What induces subcommittee members to play leading roles on some issues, only to move into the audience (or leave the theater) on others. Why do they participate to the degree that they do? The relative invisibility of the subcommittee should presumably incline members to stay in bed, and out of the subcommittee rooms. Many indeed stay away much of the time.

Two important questions at the intersection of legislative behavior and legislative institutions await resolution. Given that members' institutional access to and level of interest in a particular subjurisdiction are closely related, how can one impute importance to a jurisdictionally defined division of labor without simultaneously evaluating the importance of individual purpose? Indeed, the selectivity of participation reveals that the official division of labor does not map onto the actual patterns of legislative labor very well. To the extent that they do correspond, the official divisions may be an artifact of purposive post-assignment behavior.

Second, are subcommittees something more than platforms for the reelection activities of advertising, position taking, and credit claiming (Mayhew 1974)? Put somewhat differently, are the expressions of other sorts of interests mere aliases for members' reelection-seeking instincts, rhetorical covers for members' electoral self-interest? Institutional critics and rational-choice reductionists have answered, with increasing frequency and decreasing hesitation, in the affirmative. But this important question is surely a matter for systematic empirical investigation, not cynical assertion or academic assumption. It seems quite possible that qualitatively different interests drive members' post-assignment behavior, even on the panels of committees that are usually characterized in one-dimensional terms. Despite their reputation as subsets of constituency-driven high-demanders (Weingast and Marshall 1988), we find that subcommittee members express both the extradistrict interests and the district interests that fall within their panels' jurisdictions.

A MULTIVARIATE MODEL

To systematically test such claims, one must embed the several related factors in a multivariate model of post-assignment participation. In this section, I thus translate the theory elaborated in Part 2 into mathematical form and analyze behavior at the subcommittee level. Given that subcommittee membership and the committee leadership position are constant at the subcommittee level, the model of subcommittee participation takes the following general form:

5.1
$$P_{ij} = \Phi(I_{ij}, IP_{ij}, S_{ij})$$

Where P_{ij} represents the participation of subcommittee member i on subcommittee bill j, with the observations pooled across subcommittees from each of the three respective committees. As described in Chapter 2, P_{ij} takes two forms — informal, behind-the-scenes participation and formal, markup participation; each will be analyzed separately.

I in equation 5.1 represents the vector of variables that capture the direct and conditional effects of subcommittee member i's interests in subcommittee issue j. Thus:

5.2
$$I_{ij} = \beta_1 D_{ij} + \beta_2(D_{ij}M_i) + \beta_3 EI_i + \beta_4 P_{ij} + \beta_5 PA_{ij}$$

Where D represents the district-related interest of i in j. M is a dichotomous variable that takes a value of one for members of the minority party and zero for the majority. Thus does the second term of equation 5.2 capture the interaction between district interest and minority status, the hypothesized effect of which is negative. EI represents the electoral insecurity of i, measured as one hundred minus the margin of victory in the most recent primary or general election, whichever is lower. (Hence, if a member ran unopposed in both the primary and general election, her lowest margin of victory would be one hundred and her electoral insecurity score zero.) P represents the policy interest or ideological commitments of member i for bill j. And PA represents the interest of member i in prosecuting the president's agenda on bill j.

IP in equation 5.1 represents a vector of variables that capture the relevant institutional positions of member i. Thus

5.3
$$IP_{ij} = \beta_6 CH_{ij} + \beta_7 RM_{ij} + \beta_8 M_i$$

Where CH_{ij} and RM_{ij} are zero/one variables that take a value of one if a member is either a chair or ranking minority member of the subcommittee with jurisdiction over j. As in equation 5.2, M_i is a zero/one variable that takes a value of one for members of the minority party.

Finally, S_{ij} in equation 5.1 represents a vector of variables reflecting member i's committee years of service and seniority-related status. Thus

5.4 $$S_{ij} = \beta_{10}CS_i + \beta_{11}F_i + \beta_{12}T_i + \beta_9 OC_{ij}$$

Where CS represents i's seniority on the committee.[4] F is a zero/one variable that takes a value of 1 if member i is in her first term as a House member. T is a zero/one variable that takes a value of 1 if a member is beyond her first term as a House member but in her first term as a transfer to the committee. OC_{ij} is a zero/one variable that takes a value of 1 for senior majority member i who chairs a subcommittee other than the one that has jurisdiction over bill j.

Combining the right-hand side of equations 5.2 through 5.4 and adding an intercept and error term, we have the fully specified equation of subcommittee participation, which I will proceed to estimate for both informal and formal participation on the panels of the three committees.

Constituency Influence in House Subcommittees

As I briefly discussed in Chapter 3, a huge literature in political science and economics is devoted to the importance of constituency influence on members' legislative behavior. That debate, I noted, has centered almost exclusively on the voting decisions of members on the chamber floor. Do members, in taking public and widely reported positions on the House floor, act as if they were district delegates and thus vote in an electorally correct fashion? Some evidence suggests that they often do, yet considerable evidence also suggests that they don't, at least not very often. Party, presidents, ideology, and interest groups are all contenders for influence on the member's vote. These factors are prominent in the member's "field of forces," to use Kingdon's language (1989). Constituents, though, are outside the Beltway, distant from members' Washington work, and for other reasons they may be inattentive or indifferent to the issue at hand. Members understand that they need court some constituencies, avoid clearly offensive votes, and take care not to develop

4. Recall that there is no such thing as seniority on House subcommittees; that is, other than leader status, there is no seniority queue that has any bearing on ascension within subcommittee ranks. The order in which members are listed on the subcommittee rolls is simply the order in which members select their subcommittees, as they do anew each congress, carrying over no property right or even any norm-based claim to a subcommittee assignment that they held in the previous congress.

a "string of votes" that might indicate that they have grown out of touch with their district (Kingdon 1989). Nonetheless, constituency influence is likely to be conditional, even at so public a stage.

This brief recapitulation provides the backdrop for interpreting the results of an altogether different form of legislative behavior at a different stage of the legislative process. To return to our earlier language, the question at issue is whether constituents affect not members' revealed preferences but their revealed intensities, as the latter become apparent in their participation decisions at the earliest stages of a sequential process. What can we say about the influence of constituency interests, as subjectively perceived within the member's enterprise, on these decisions?

Constituency Influence Absent Good Monitoring: Participation Behind the Subcommittee Scenes

Most of the negotiating over and drafting of the markup vehicle occurs behind the scenes, as does the preliminary legwork of building support, anticipating opposition, and developing parliamentary strategy. As numerous staffers noted, the importance of such activities is difficult to overstate. The resulting vehicle will often circumscribe the ensuing markup agenda and thus structure the actions or reactions that arise in that more public and accessible forum.

However important it may be in the legislative process, the informal negotiations are the least visible of legislative forums, rarely receiving attention even in the Washington publications that specialize in the coverage of legislative politics. If a member engages in shirking, this is the least dangerous place to do it, especially insofar as rank-and-file constituents are concerned. Monitoring the legislative agent behind the scenes is not simply costly, it can be very nearly impossible.

Table 5.4 reports the parameter estimates for the multivariate model of informal participation. For each committee, the first column provides the unstandardized coefficients; the second column reports the standard errors in parentheses. To make comparisons as meaningful as possible, each variable in each equation was first transformed to a zero to one scale. Hence each coefficient reported in table 5.4 estimates the effect of a change in the full range of the independent variable on the percentage change in subcommittee members' informal participation, ceteris paribus.[5]

---

5. That the dependent variable for both formal and informal participation is bounded and measured on a noninterval scale suggests that the equations would be more appropriately estimated with a maximum-likelihood estimator (MLE). I thus reestimated each

Inefficient though behind-the-scenes activity may be for displaying district attentiveness, the results of table 5.4 show that constituency interests matter there nonetheless. On this point, the evidence is clear across the panels of all three committees. The strongest effect appears in the subcommittees of House Agriculture, the jurisdictional locale that past research (Jones 1961; Shepsle 1978) and my preliminary evidence would predict. The behavioral difference between a subcommittee member whose constituency interest was negligible and one whose interest was major is an increase in participation along the behind-the-scenes scale of more than 20 percent, other things being equal. But the similarity as well as the difference in the district effects across the three committees warrant emphasis. Both on Education and Labor and on Energy and Commerce, the district coefficients are correct in sign and statistically significant. The magnitude of the effects appears nontrivial as well. A change in the value of district interest from negligible to major on bill j accounts for almost a 15 percent increase of member i on the informal participation scale. For all three committees, then, the constituency-influence hypothesis has passed its most difficult test — behind-the-scenes participation on subcommittees to which members have already self-selected, at least in part on the basis of jurisdictional relevance to constituency interests.

Other evidence consistently reinforces this finding and provides greater insight into the calculations of expected utility that underlie it. For instance, legislative assistants to House Agriculture members expressed specific worries about monitoring by constituents, noting that commodity groups and other organized interests were actively engaged in the early stages of the drafting process itself. Most of these groups, moreover, commanded strong local organizations within some significant subset of subcommittee members' districts. The associations of corn, wheat, dairy, livestock, sugar, peanuts, tobacco, cotton, and other agricultural producers could boast large concentrations of members in particular locales. Through newsletters, local chapter meetings, and national conventions, they enjoyed an impressive network for disseminating information about whether representatives from districts with particular commodity interests were genuinely working to promote them. To shirk "responsibility" for promoting commodity interests is to risk bad press in that

---

equation using ordered probit, a maximum-likelihood technique designed specifically for ordinal-level dependent variables. The statistical and substantive effects generated by the MLE demonstrated that the ordinary least-squares (OLS) results are robust. The coefficients' signs, their statistical significance, and — most important — the substantive inferences drawn from them were not appreciably affected by the choice of estimator. For a general argument that MLE is preferable to OLS under analytical conditions such as these, however, see King 1989.

Table 5.4 Participation Behind the Subcommittee Scenes: Multivariate Analyses

	Agriculture		Education and Labor		Energy and Commerce	
Intercept	.05	(.12)	−.02	(.09)	−.14**	(.05)
Bill-specific interests						
District	.21***	(.07)	.11*	(.07)	.11**	(.05)
Minority-district interaction	−.12	(.09)	−.02	(.04)	−.01	(.03)
Electoral insecurity	.02	(.05)	.09**	(.05)	.01	(.05)
Policy	.18***	(.05)	.33***	(.06)	.11***	(.04)
Prosecuting the president's agenda	.03	(.08)	.40***	(.19)	.20**	(.10)
Institutional position						
Subcommittee chair	.67***	(.10)	.60***	(.07)	.82***	(.06)
Ranking subcommittee member	.31***	(.08)	.29***	(.08)	.25***	(.06)
Minority party member	.20**	(.10)	.02	(.09)	.00	(.06)
Seniority/status						
Committee seniority	.01	(.13)	−.09	(.11)	.21**	(.09)
Freshman status	−.17**	(.08)	−.24**	(.08)	−.09*	(.06)
New transfer	−.20**	(.09)	—		−.11	(.10)
Chair, other subcommittee	.07	(.08)	.02	(.06)	.06	(.07)
Adjusted R²		.43		.62		.62

Source: Subcommittee markup records and interviews with subcommittee, committee, and personal staff.

Note: Parameter estimates are OLS coefficients. Standard errors appear in parentheses. Education and Labor had no new transfers in the congress under study here. The number of observations, by committee, was as follows: Agriculture, 240; Education and Labor, 158; Energy and Commerce, 214.

   *Statistically significant at .10, one-tailed test. **Statistically significant at .05, one-tailed test. ***Statistically significant at .01, one-tailed test.

electorally important information network. And the same information network can give credit to representatives who work hard, though without their having to claim it for themselves.[6]

   Though less frequently than their Agriculture counterparts, staffers handling Education and Labor or Energy and Commerce matters also noted that such monitoring takes place. Education and Labor Democrats emphasized the constituency basis of labor-union involvement in subcommittee deliberations, especially labor relations and employment opportunities legislation. For instance, one majority staffer for the Labor-Management Relations Subcommit-

6. Such incentives have been more generally elaborated in John Mark Hansen's excellent study of interest group access and legislative policy making (1992).

tee commented: "I feel like I work for the AFL-CIO." Others remarked on their interaction with educators and educational groups in the district. Both majority and minority Energy and Commerce staffers spoke of their "constant contact" with local industries in early deliberations over environment, energy, and trade. Of course, numerous other groups in the political environs of these two committees were involved in monitoring and lobbying at the early stage of bill drafting and negotiation, but far fewer had the strong constituency base to condition their influence (as Kingdon 1989 has shown it to in another context). This factor may help explain why Agriculture appears more affected by constituency interests than the other committees. Not only are the issues under Agriculture's jurisdiction more likely to evoke constituency concerns, but as John Mark Hansen (1992) has demonstrated, agricultural constituency politics is institutionalized in a federated system of agricultural groups that maintain a substantial and permanent organizational presence both in members' districts and on Capitol Hill.

Constituency Influence in Public Markups

What differences appear in the behavior of members and their staffers as the action moves from backrooms and informal conferences to public subcommittee markup? Specifically, are members who are strategically seeking reelection more attentive to their districts in public than in nonpublic forums? As I have noted, in public forums reelection-enhancing advertising, politically correct position-taking, and legislative actions that lend credibility to subsequent credit-claiming should be more prevalent (in accordance with the Show Horse Hypothesis derived in Chapter 3).

Table 5.5 reports the analogous coefficient estimates for members' formal subcommittee participation, as measured by the record-based participation scale developed in Chapter 2. The results suggest that constituents' interests exert a particularly strong effect on subcommittee markup participation, a finding that holds across the subcommittee samples of all three committees. Again, that influence appears especially powerful on House Agriculture. Not only are members of different committees mindful of constituency interests; it appears that they look for strategic opportunities to claim credit in public.

I hasten to reiterate, however, that the constituency-minded activity during subcommittee markup should not be assumed superfluous. Show horses do not simply play to the cameras while doing little to make a legislative difference. No doubt some of this goes on, especially in the ritual speech making at the beginning of markup. However, the point here is that the public forum has the benefit of allowing members to at once promote — through their votes, arguments, amendments, obstructionism — constituency interests and be seen

Table 5.5   Participation in Subcommittee Markups: Multivariate Analyses

	Agriculture		Education and Labor		Energy and Commerce	
Intercept	.04	(.12)	−.08	(.10)	−.03	(.08)
Bill-specific interests						
District	.42***	(.08)	.22***	(.08)	.13**	(.07)
Minority-district interaction	−.16*	(.11)	−.39*	(.25)	−.26**	(.13)
Electoral insecurity	.01	(.05)	.03	(.07)	−.10*	(.07)
Policy	.11**	(.06)	.47***	(.08)	.18***	(.07)
Prosecuting the president's agenda	.12*	(.09)	.20	(.32)	.17*	(.13)
Institutional position						
Subcommittee chair	.45***	(.11)	.51***	(.09)	.63***	(.08)
Ranking subcommittee member	.05	(.09)	.49***	(.10)	.19**	(.09)
Minority party member	.28**	(.12)	.04	(.09)	.19***	(.06)
Seniority/status						
Committee seniority	.14	(.15)	.13	(.14)	.51***	(.13)
Freshman status	−.24***	(.09)	−.21**	(.11)	−.11*	(.09)
New transfer	−.30***	(.11)		—	−.19*	(.15)
Chair, other subcommittee	.07	(.09)	.12*	(.07)	−.07	(.10)
Adjusted R²		.33		.70		.35

Source: Subcommittee markup records and interviews with subcommittee, committee, and personal staff.

Note: Entries are OLS coefficients. Standard errors appear in parentheses. Education and Labor had no new transfers in the 97th Congress. The number of observations, by committee, was as follows: Agriculture, 240; Education and Labor, 97; Energy and Commerce, 214.

*Statistically significant at .10, one-tailed test. **Statistically significant at .05, one-tailed test. ***Statistically significant at .01, one-tailed test.

doing so. Credit-claiming thus becomes credible, but for most members right-fully so.

MAJORITY STRATEGY AND CONSTITUENCY REPRESENTATION AMONG THE MINORITY

The results reported in table 5.5 enable us to make some other, albeit more tentative inferences about strategic behavior and the conditional nature of constituency effects. In Chapter 3, I argued that because the majority party has greater control over the agenda of the panels, we should expect bills favoring interests within the minority members' constituencies to find less agenda space. Indeed, the strategically minded panel chair should avoid issues that either because of intradistrict conflicts or incongruities between constituents' opinions and majority members' personal preferences, are likely to cross-pressure majority party members of the panel. At the same time, the panel chair should relish issues that create just such cross-pressures for her minority colleagues. In the face of such cross-pressures, the reelection-minded minority member either defects to the majority side or sticks with the minority position and incurs electoral harm. But even if she chooses the latter course, according to the Blame Avoidance Hypothesis, she should have much less propensity than the majority member to invest time and resources in the legislative fight.

A comparison of tables 5.4 and 5.5 provides evidence of such strategic behavior. The minority-district interaction is consistently correct in sign (negative) for all three committees across both models. Moreover, the interaction is both large and statistically significant for participation in subcommittee markup. At this stage, at least, minority status negatively affects the influence that district interests have on individual members' participation in subcommittee markup — clear support for the Blame Avoidance Hypothesis.

However, the asymmetric effects with respect to formal and informal participation warrant closer attention. While the supporting evidence is strong with respect to formal participation, the effects are statistically insignificant for behind-the-scenes participation in all three committees. One obvious reason for this asymmetry follows from the Show Horse Hypothesis. The incentive to pursue constituency interests being already low because informal participation is not public, there is simply less constituency-driven action to be diminished by minority status. At the same time, the more public nature of the markup is likely to make the risk-averse minority member all the more nervous about incurring blame, thereby diminishing her willingness to take the lead. In this respect, the asymmetric results regarding the interaction between the minority and the district only further corroborate the Show Horse Hypothesis.

In sum, the majority should structure the agenda in a way that maximizes the opportunities for majority member credit-claiming while minimizing such opportunities for the minority. And this is exactly what we find. This finding, in turn, provides a subtle but potentially significant insight into the way in which majority agenda power (coupled with majority unity) can structure the strategic options available to the minority when legislation moves into a forum where formal parliamentary procedures and egalitarian voting mechanisms should protect minority members' legislative leverage. The Blame Avoidance Hypothesis and the mechanisms that drive it can shed further light on two subjects to which scholars have paid growing attention: the importance of agenda powers on the one hand and majority party strategy on the other (Cox and McCubbins 1993). Behind the subcommittee scenes, that place of dubious repute, is in fact where majority party agenda setters can develop strategies that favor their members at subsequent legislative stages.

ELECTORAL INSECURITY AND SUBCOMMITTEE PARTICIPATION

Finally, we find little support in tables 5.4 and 5.5 for the hypothesis derived from the work of Fenno on House members' home styles that members from marginal districts "will allocate their resources disproportionately to [their reelection] end" (1978, 215). "Inevitably," Fenno argues, "these are resources that might otherwise be allocated to efforts in Washington." If anything, the results of table 5.4 suggest that the opposite is closer to the truth: marginality has a positive effect on members' behind-the-scenes participation for the subcommittees of all three committees, with the coefficient for Education and Labor statistically significant at the .05 level (in this instance, applying a two-tailed test). It is also positive for two of the three committees in the analysis of formal subcommittee participation. Only in the case of Energy and Commerce subcommittee markup activity is the coefficient negative, substantively nontrivial, and statistically significant (at the .10 level). At best, these results can be interpreted only as inconclusive with respect to the conventional claim about electoral insecurity and legislative work.

Beyond the Electoral Connection in House Subcommittees

A central theme of Chapter 3 was that a rational choice reductionism that imputes a simple, single, single-minded interest in reelection to members of Congress is a dubious assumption on which to build good behavioral theory. I provided preliminary empirical evidence and theoretical elaboration regarding the likely importance of two additional interests in the expected utility calculations of members as they select their subcommittees, set their priorities, and allocate their resources: their personal policy interests or ideological commitments and their commitments to prosecute the agenda of a president of their own party.

The results of tables 5.4 and 5.5 provide compelling evidence that this differentiated account of member interests is important to understanding their participation at the earliest and perhaps most important stages of a sequential legislative process. Since this general inference will be a major theme of the remaining chapters, implying a number of significant implications for matters of representation and legislative organization, it is important that we consider it here with some care.

MEMBERS WITH POLICY-MINDED MINDS OF THEIR OWN

With the possible exception of House Agriculture, the effect of constituents' interests on members' decision making in subcommittee was not overwhelming and was partly contingent on the legislative forum under consideration. To gain a comparative perspective on members' constituency-mindedness, let us now examine the coefficients on the other two types of member interest.

In the agenda-relevant and other important action behind the subcommittee scenes, members' policy interests have a striking and statistically significant effect. This finding holds even for House Agriculture subcommittees, which have long been notorious as forums for unadulterated distributive politics. The coefficient on the policy variable, in fact, is almost as large as its (identically measured) constituency counterpart. For Energy and Commerce, the coefficients for the policy and constituency variables are identical. And for Education and Labor, the coefficient on the former is thrice the size of the latter.

The results of table 5.5 provide additional evidence that members' policy interests affect their participation decisions. The markup participation analyzed there provides a more difficult test of this hypothesis, however. Again, the tendency for constituency-minded behavior to increase in public forums should prove especially evident on House Agriculture panels, given the nature of their jurisdictions and the strong lines of communication between local constituencies and Washington groups that monitor what the subcommittee does. In this respect, we have in Agriculture subcommittee markups something of a limiting case. If we find that members' policy interests make an independent behavioral difference in a public forum where constituency interests are notoriously potent, then we are on strong argumentative ground that these effects should generalize, perhaps with greater punch, to other jurisdictions and decision-making forums.

According to the results reported in table 5.5, behavior in Agriculture subcommittee markups passes this test. As predicted, the constituency coefficient is by far the larger of the two, but we can also conclude that the greater the personal policy interest that members bring to an issue, the more active they will be as players in the early innings of the game.

In the other two committees, the coefficients on the policy interest variable are statistically significant and actually exceed the estimates of the constituency effects. On Education and Labor, the difference between negligible and major interest in a bill accounts for movement halfway along the formal participation scale. To provide a more tangible sense of importance, this is roughly equivalent to the behavioral difference associated with being a subcommittee leader rather than a typical backbencher. In Energy and Commerce subcommittees, a like change in members' policy interests moves the purposive member 18 percent along the participation scale, a coefficient that is also greater than the corresponding one for constituency influence. Again, this holds despite the more attractive opportunities for show horse behavior in this forum.

Members of Congress, it seems, do have policy minds of their own. They allocate their legislative time and resources in order to pursue their personal policy and ideological agendas, independent of district interests and other important constraints on their behavior.

PROSECUTING THE PRESIDENT'S AGENDA

Tables 5.4 and 5.5 also provide statistical insight into the third interest at work in decisions to participate for legislators whose party affiliation is the same as the president's—what I have labeled prosecuting the president's agenda. Recall from Chapter 3 that the precise nature of the interest at work here is not easy to unpack. Whether it reflects a more basic desire to "make a mark" (the likelihood of which is enhanced when presidential leverage is on your side) or to better realize one's immediate or long-range progressive ambitions within one's party organization, we cannot say with the data available here. Nonetheless, the multivariate results are consistent in suggesting that, separately or in concert, such interests do affect the participation decisions of members of the president's party.

For participation behind the scenes in subcommittee, this effect was particularly strong among minority members on Education and Labor or Energy and Commerce; the effect was correct in sign but slight on House Agriculture. By comparison with the other two interests, however, the coefficient on this one is not easy to interpret, except in the context of a particular president's jurisdiction-specific agendas. The results from three very different jurisdictions provide insights into the way that presidential efforts mobilize partisans in committee.

In the congress under study here, virtually the entire range of programs under the jurisdiction of Education and Labor became the target of a frontal assault. President Reagan's Office of Management and Budget (OMB) director David Stockman, himself a former member of the House Budget Committee, engineered the passage early in the 97th Congress of the Gramm-Latta budget resolution, which among other things required draconian cuts in the domestic programs within Education and Labor's purview. Committee records reveal that the Democrats at first refused to comply with the injunction that they report cutback levels to the Budget Committee, as the budget resolution required. When told that the Budget Committee would do the dirty work for them, however, Education and Labor Democrats chose instead to come up with cuts in closed party caucus, which served for the remainder of the congress as the committee's de facto budget subcommittee.

Out of that caucus emerged a sophisticated package of insincere cuts, most notably, a massive scaleback of the expensive but universally popular Impact Aid Program, which subsidized the public education of children who lived on or near military bases. Technically, this proposal enabled the committee majority to claim that it had met the spending ceilings imposed by the Budget Resolution. But politically, the Democrats knew full well that cuts in a such a popular program would never survive subsequent stages of reconciliation. When faced with the Democratic Caucus's package in open markup, however, the Republicans, led by ranking minority member and Reagan lieutenant John Ashbrook (from Ohio), loudly protested, publicizing to the Budget Committee that the Democrats' cuts were mostly bogus. Their protests did not fall on deaf ears. Again, the Budget Committee repudiated the Education and Labor package for noncompliance.

The committee Democrats thus went back into caucus to develop a package of more serious cuts. Records of this closed caucus reveal the Democrats' genuine angst. Several likened the situation to being "forced to kill our children," an apt metaphor, for several of the endangered programs had been fathered by sitting members of the committee. In fact, one subcommittee chairman refused to bloody his hands and simply sat back as the caucus decided where to cut programs under his own panel's jurisdiction, then voted against them in the caucus vote.

Formally excluded from the "budget subcommittee" deliberations, conservative committee Republicans did not sit idle. They caucused as well, with several key players developing a specific set of cuts that would fulfill the Gramm-Latta requirements in the spirit of the president's conservative agenda. They were thus prepared to offer a multititled amendment as a substitute for the Democratic caucus package.

These efforts are important insofar as they illustrate the degree to which certain members of the president's party mobilized on behalf of his agenda, in such a way that the president's positions and priorities regarding a wide range of programs were vigorously represented at the earliest stages of the legislative process. At the subcommittee stage that representation did not take the form of voting; indeed, given the exclusivity of majority's markup of the budget packages, no official votes on presidential proposals were held. Rather, it came in the form of public criticism during open forum, the development of specific counterproposals, and behind-the-scenes negotiations with other legislative actors — colleagues in the Senate as well as the legislative liaison to OMB and the White House.

To turn briefly to the other two committees, we find differences in the importance of the interest in prosecuting the president's agenda. In contrast to Education and Labor members, few Agriculture Republicans were willing to pick up the president's mantle: prosecuting the proposed Stockman cutbacks in agricultural programs would have been akin to falling on one's sword as far as the constituency was concerned. Except for the Food Stamp Program, budget cuts were informally negotiated in a bipartisan manner, because the specific programs targeted for cuts affected districts represented by members of both parties. The subcommittee markups were not held in party caucus but openly, in an ad hoc budget subcommittee, with all of the agricultural commodity groups there to bear witness.

Despite the variable conditions that committee members faced in reacting to presidential budget cuts, tables 5.4 and 5.5 provide consistent (if not always statistically significant) evidence that prosecuting the president's agenda is a category of interests that should not be assumed away. None of this is to say that members of a president's party are inclined to be lackeys for their chief legislator, dutifully carrying his water whether they prefer the taste of it or not. Members of Congress are independent sorts, with no qualms about increasing their distance from their president, publicly repudiating rather than actively prosecuting his agenda if they find it either ideologically unpalatable or politically unpopular. Rather, the interest I here label prosecuting the president's agenda is grounded in individual members' purposes. Leverage from the White House affects the strategic calculations of the member about the expected return of her investments in particular initiatives that are consistent with the members' own interests.

The Behavioral Importance of Institutional Position

The bill-specific interests that members bring to their subcommittee work affect their willingness to pay the time, information, and transaction costs associated with participation; they say nothing about members' variable ability to pay. Some members simply have greater resources in terms of access to policy-making networks and political actors that pay attention to particular subcommittees' domains; others have greater resources in terms of legislative staff; and some enjoy positions or procedural prerogatives that lead them to anticipate significant political and policy returns for relatively low-cost investments.

At this stage the variation in nonleaders' resources is least pronounced, however. A member on the subcommittee of jurisdiction has a seat at the center table, where information gets gathered. Virtually all legislative hearings in the House are held in subcommittee. Within interest groups, subcommittee members are viewed as key actors with whom communication is essential. Administration officials see subcommittee members as the principal overseers of their programs, with whom they must interact on any legislation affecting their agency.

But within subcommittee, the resource advantages listed above accrue most to subcommittee leaders. As predicted, the results presented in tables 5.4 and 5.5 reveal the dramatic effects on participation of holding the chair. In decision making behind the scenes, subcommittee chairs are invariably at the legislative center: chair status alone accounts for movement from two-thirds to three-quarters along the informal participation scale. Ranking minority subcommittee members, who have fewer agenda prerogatives and smaller staff and budget subsidies, show coefficients less than half those of subcommittee chairs for all three committee samples. Even so, the advantages of ranking minority status are substantial. We see large, positive, statistically significant effects on behind-the-scenes participation. Ranking minority members are likely to be central players, whether in negotiating with the subcommittee majority in the early stages of bill drafting or in working with interested minority colleagues in developing counterproposals or party strategy. As subcommittee bills move from off to on the public stage, in turn, the behavioral effects of leadership status remain clearly evident.

How can the leadership coefficients be interpreted specifically and concretely? As I emphasized in the last chapter, these simple dichotomous variables are associated with a range of factors likely to enhance a member's participation. For instance, subcommittee leaders are likely, for any of several reasons, to be more interested in issues that come before their panels than nonleaders. I control for at least three of these factors in the model, however. Subcommittee leaders are likely to be more experienced, perhaps more expert, in the issues that come before their panels, and to be able to participate at a lower marginal cost. I control for seniority as well, and find that even on the single set of subcommittees (Energy and Commerce) where seniority exerts a positive and appreciable effect, both subcommittee leadership coefficients remain large and statistically significant.

However, we cannot disentangle with a simple, dichotomous variable the importance of the several and different advantages that leadership status bestows. As I have noted, one of the most important of these is the size of jurisdiction-relevant staff, which is highly collinear with leadership position. Neither can we assess the relative importance of whatever agenda power or other procedural prerogatives leaders can strategically manipulate. The variable whose effects are estimated here, in short, serves simply as a surrogate for the package of institutionalized advantages that subcommittee leaders may enjoy.

Finally, tables 5.4 and 5.5 provide little or mixed support for the hypotheses about the direct effects of minority status. Given that the majority party largely controls agenda setting and other premarkup deliberations and that majority members have somewhat greater access to professional staff, I argued that minority members should face higher barriers to entry at this stage of the legislative game. Hence minority status should diminish informal participation for the typical backbencher. Table 5.4 suggests that, if anything, the opposite is true. The coefficients on minority status are positive, not negative, in the equations for all three committees. The magnitudes for two of the committees are slight, but the coefficient for House Agriculture is positive, large, and statistically significant.

I also hypothesized, though, that minority members, having had less influence on the markup vehicle than their majority counterparts, should be all the more active in public markup. Hence, the sign on the minority status coefficient should be positive for formal participation. On this score, the results exhibit a better fit with the prediction. The coefficients are correct in sign for the panels of all three committees, and substantively and statistically significant for two of the three.

SOCIOLOGICAL NORMS IN THE CONTEMPORARY CONGRESS? THE EARLY RETURNS

The principal emphasis in the results of the empirical analysis has thus far been properly placed on the interests that motivate members as they set their legislative priorities in House subcommittees. The results provide strong evidence for the expected utility framework elaborated in the preceding chapters.

This theory of participation stands in contrast to the sociological account of legislative participation. What evidence do we find in the subcommittee results to support the prescriptive or proscriptive norms that informed earlier scholarship? Does the sociological model still work well as an alternative (or supplementary) explanation?

We have already filled in part of the answer with respect to the norm of apprenticeship. A social norm is nothing if not recognized and shared by most members in the group — enough at least that a member who does not share the norm is readily recognizable as a maverick. As the interview evidence has already revealed, however, on all of the three committees studied here, the subservient status of freshmen is positively repudiated, by junior and senior members alike.

Contrary to any expectation one might derive from the contemporary literature on Congress, the results of tables 5.4 and 5.5 clearly bear out the prediction that some sort of apprenticeship is alive and well. Freshman status significantly reduces subcommittee participation on the panels of all three committees in both public and nonpublic forums.

But how can we be confident that the coefficients do not simply reflect the old apprenticeship that earlier sociologists of Congress described? Perhaps only the rhetoric of an imposed apprenticeship has given way — suppressed, say, out of respect for the still lowly newcomers' need to save political face in an electorally competitive world?

This question can be better answered in the next chapter, where we will have more and different data with which to address it. But for now, two patterns in the multivariate analyses of tables 5.4 and 5.5 suggest that this possibility is remote. First, the traditional apprenticeship norm held that newly elected members, individuals unknown to the powers that be and unaccustomed to the ways of their chamber, should be seen and not heard. The same could not be said, however, for individuals who could already boast at least two years of service, of learning, of developing colleagues and contacts, and who had at least one reelection victory under their belts. These were not of the lower caste, even if they had transferred to a new committee where they lacked expertise. Nonfreshman transfers should not bow to the apprenticeship norm presumed to hold in check their junior colleagues' participation.

Yet diminished participation on the part of transfers is precisely what we find. Moreover, the negative effects transfer status has on participation are somewhat larger than for freshman status, a difference that holds for all three committees. Such patterns are hardly consistent with apprenticeship as a proscriptive norm, at least insofar as that norm can be reconstructed from the sociological accounts of the 1940s and 1950s. Lower participation by transfers, however, *can* be explained by the higher information and transaction costs of participation that transfers (and freshmen) face by comparison with their colleagues who enjoy greater political and policy experience in the areas within the panel's jurisdiction.

The admonition that freshmen be seen and not heard reflected a more general seniority-based pecking order thought to structure interactions in small legislative groups. Indeed, vestiges of seniority as a participation norm still appear in subcommittee hearings, where members are recognized for the purpose of questioning witnesses in order of their seniority. In subcommittee markup, likewise, members who wish to give opening statements are called in order of seniority. If the seniority norm still has a structuring effect on the legislative roles that members play, we should see a positive effect of years of panel service on both informal and formal participation, ceteris paribus. In fact, the positive effect of seniority appears only in one set of subcommittees, those of Energy and Commerce, and even there the effects are significant only for participation in committee markups.

Finally, there is little support in the analysis presented thus far for the hypothesis that a norm of deference affects individual behavior within these legislative groups. Chairing another subcommittee, for example, ought to have a negative effect, yet no such effect appears in the multivariate analysis of informal participation on the panels of any of the three committees, and the coefficient is negative only for Energy and Commerce in markup. Data on subcommittee amendments only confirm that no norm of interchair deference is in operation. Chairs of other subcommittees are just as likely to offer amendments in someone else's subcommittees as are rank-and-file majority members. Such amending, in fact, was fairly common, occurring in the subcommittee markups of one-fifth of the bills sampled here.

Conclusion

Students of Congress have frequently commented on a division of labor within the House. In so doing, they invariably repair to the jurisdictional divisions and membership lists of House subcommittees. But the official lists mislead us. Even in the most narrowly focused, officially sanctioned panels of the chamber, participation is highly selective, with the legislative labor typically undertaken by small subsets of members, which change in size and composition from bill to bill. The division of labor is thus a behavioral rather than an institutional thing. How might we explain it?

First, it is indispensable to understand how individual members' several and variable interests affect their behavioral choices on specific bills. Constituency interests as they are perceived inside the enterprise directly affect members' resource-allocation decisions in the legislative labors of their subcommittees. In this respect we find robust evidence of dyadic representation at a stage of the legislative process and in a type of legislative behavior that students of representation have not systematically studied.

Second, participation is motivated by other interests as well. The evidence on this point is clear. Members may seek reelection, but they do so with a postelection purpose. In particular, they have their own policy agendas, which they actively pursue, independent of their district interests. We can also conclude that a partisan few invest resources of their own in prosecuting the president's agenda.

Finally, it bears repeating that the results regarding the effects of members' extra-constituency interests held for the panels of three different committees. Thus does the multidimensional conceptualization of member interest prove important across observations from three different jurisdictions, twenty subjurisdictions, and hence widely varied subsets of bills — of both high and low salience, conflictual and consensual, parochial and national in focus. At the same time, these relatively robust results hold true across subsets of members from different regions of the country, with diverse backgrounds, representing very different districts, acting at different times, in different contexts, under different chairs, and in different forums. In short, a rational-choice reductionism that imputes a single, reelection-minded component to members' expected utility calculations cannot be sustained.

Turning to a related set of results, members appear more inclined to pursue their own policy priorities as opposed to those of their constituency in behind-the-scenes action, a preference that supports the hypotheses underlying the Workhorse–Show Horse distinction. Similarly, constituency effects tend to be more pronounced than policy effects in public markups, which representatives of interested subconstituencies can monitor. Minority party membership diminished the behavioral effect of district interest, thereby supporting the logic underlying the Blame-Avoidance Hypothesis. Members do not make their legislative investments with a blind eye to the political consequences; they know that those vary according to whether their actions are public or non-public and according to whose party controls the agenda.

In addition, staff, budget, procedural prerogatives, and other resources exert a powerful effect on subcommittee participation. Subcommittee leaders may be strategic and purposive, like their rank-and-file counterparts, but their ability to pay the information and transaction costs of a significant legislative investment is far greater. One-person-one-vote may appear on the parchment of panel rules, but all members are not equal.

It is important also to point out two things that I do not directly address in this chapter. First, while subcommittee self-selection appears relatively unconstrained, one cannot infer from the analysis here that subcommittee members are preference outliers, only that they are interest-intensity outliers. Nor can we infer from the coefficients on the interest variables that preference outliers tend to be more active; again, the valid inference is that interest outliers tend to be more active. The intensity and valence of members' positions on particular issues may, under specifiable conditions, be related. But those conditions and the relevant empirical analysis are not the subjects here.

Second, I do not directly discuss whether and to what extent individual members or groups of members are influential in shaping the collective choices of their panels. Legislative influence is a notoriously slippery notion (see Hall 1992), and in any case, one understands it only by investigating the connection between member preferences and collective outcomes. My level of analysis is individual, not collective. Thus we can say which particular members participate and why, but it is a matter for further research to comprehend the extent to which and the conditions under which participation and influence are related.

6

Congressmen in (and Absent from) Committees

The standing committee [is] the eye, the ear, the hand and very often the brain of the House. — Thomas Brackett Reed, circa 1890

On a good day half of them know half of what's going on. Most of the time it's only five or six who actually mark a bill up. — House committee staffer, 1987

In the previous chapter I demonstrated that the subcommittee assignment process is built on the twin pillars of interest and self-accommodation, so that subcommittees are nonrandom samples of the committees from which they are drawn. For critics of the legislative system, in turn, such a process contributes to all manner of institutional ills, including runaway bureaucracies, uncontrollable spending, and enhanced influence by narrow interests. Some have even looked back longingly to the prereform days when a "full committee maintaining a broader representation of interests could mute the excessive enthusiasms of each of its subcommittees" (Hardin, Shepsle, and Weingast 1983).

But the subcommittee reforms of the mid-1970s did not abolish the right of full-committee review nor did they impoverish the formal powers of the full-committee chair nor did they limit the legislative capacity of the chair's enterprise. Neither did the reforms to the committee system of the mid-1990s — quite the contrary. While committee staffs suffered across-the-board cuts, the preexisting guarantee that subcommittee leaders would enjoy at least one full-time staffer was rescinded, and formal control of all staff was centralized in the offices of full-committee leaders. In any case, pre-1974, post-1974, and post-1994 committee majorities have had in principle the ability to retain legislation in full committee with a simple majority vote. If legislation is reported from subcommittee, a committee majority has had formal opportunity to control it in the same way. Then and now, the subcommittee bill comes before full-committee markup under the equivalent of a perfectly open rule, so that, procedurally speaking, a full committee containing a broader representation of interests could always mute — or, alternatively, amplify — the "enthusiasms" of its subcommittees whenever its members pleased. Whether individual committee members use the available opportunities to inject their own views, values, and interests into the deliberations on bills that originate in subcommittee, then, is an open question that requires behavioral analysis.

In this chapter I adapt to the full-committee context the model of participation specified in Chapter 5. Beyond testing the robustness of the model at a second, important stage of the legislative process, I have two aims in extending the analysis to full committee.

The first is to investigate the behavioral effects of subcommittee position once a subcommittee opens its gate and begins to move a bill. The account I have developed thus far suggests that the concerns of the critics have a strong basis in behavioral theory. In the main, full-committee members should be relatively uninterested and their enterprises less able to consistently match wits with their self-selected subcommittee colleagues, many of whom have already paid the information and transaction costs on the particular bill before the full committee.

An important extension of my first aim is to investigate the extent to which full-committee leaders remained main players in the postreform games. Specifically, how much do they invest themselves and their enterprises in agenda action, informal negotiation, and committee markup action on bills arising from subcommittees on which they do not officially sit? And to what extent do subcommittee leaders dominate the stage in full committee, leaving the full-committee leaders behavioral shadows of their prereform selves?

Second, the broader scope of the empirical analysis at the full-committee stage throws additional light on purposive versus sociological explanations. I reexamine the nature and importance of purpose, apprenticeship, specialization, and deference. Besides testing the competing hypotheses at a second, more data-rich stage in the context of the cross-sectional model, I also exploit data from the closed markups of one committee in the prereform 87th Congress (1961–62) to assess whether and to what extent the sociological norms so often voiced in the past did in fact have behavioral consequences or, alternatively, whether the revisionist account I offer here is generalizable to the prereform congresses of more than three decades ago.

Subcommittee Members Beyond the Subcommittee Stage

Recall from Chapter 2 that, on the whole, member participation in committee is highly selective. Across the samples of bills from the three committees, attendance at markups averaged less than 80 percent, voting participation less than 60 percent, participation in markup debate less than 40 percent, amending action less than 20 percent, and agenda action less than 10 percent. Also infrequent was behind-the-scenes participation: in fewer than 25 percent of the observations did a member play a discernible role at any point in the informal discussions or negotiations.

We are now in position to compare the behavior of subcommittee members and committee members on common ground. How does the participation of committee members and leaders compare with that of their subcommittee colleagues when all are eligible to enter the game? I begin by examining the aggregate patterns of subcommittee member and nonmember participation. I then turn to the analogous patterns for subcommittee and full-committee leaders.

SUBCOMMITTEE MEMBERS AND NONMEMBERS COMPARED

In line with both the concerns of congressional critics and the behavioral theory under examination, table 6.1 reveals that subcommittee members exhibit much greater involvement than subcommittee nonmembers in committee deliberations. On the whole, subcommittee members were three to four times as likely to be involved in behind-the-scenes action at any point up to the committee's report to the chamber. These dramatic differences are consistent with the earlier description of agenda setting and drafting. Most of this action occurs long before a bill appears on the full committee's radar. Except for reauthorizations, budget reconciliation, or bills that touch a committee chair's widely known priorities, subcommittee nonmembers are often unaware that a particular bill will be coming before them until the subcommittee of jurisdiction actually schedules a markup. A subcommittee nonmember thus would have to be especially attentive and resourceful in monitoring what other panels are doing behind the scenes in order to introduce his enterprise into the mix in a timely fashion. Of course, behind-the-scenes negotiations do not end with the first subcommittee markup. In many cases, they continue — sometimes in earnest — before and during committee markup, and interested subcommittee nonmembers can participate in informal forums, though there may be informal barriers to entry. Because those barriers limit their ability or because self-selection has generated a relative thinness of interest, however, subcommittee nonmembers participate infrequently in these negotiations.

Full-committee markups, however, provide full-committee members fully guaranteed opportunities to participate — to mute or amplify, as it were, what the subcommittee has done. Indeed, the patterns of committee markup participation should be more likely to reveal legislative involvement of subcommittee nonmembers, for several reasons. Official barriers to entry into the

Table 6.1   Who Gets into the Game? Subcommittee Members and Nonmembers

	Agriculture		Education and Labor		Energy and Commerce	
Players behind the scenes	27%	(181)	20%	(99)	17%	(111)
Subcommittee nonmembers	13	(56)	10	(32)	10	(44)
Subcommittee members	51	(125)	42	(67)	31	(67)
Players in committee markup	30	(247)	25	(124)	26	(171)
Subcommittee nonmembers	21	(88)	18	(61)	18	(81)
Subcommittee members	45	(112)	40	(63)	41	(90)

Source: Interviews with committee and subcommittee staff and minutes of committee and subcommittee markups. (See Appendixes B and C.)

Note: Entries are the percentages of members of the row category classified as active players, with the numbers of players in the row category shown in parentheses. The number of observations, by committee, was as follows: Agriculture, 672; Education and Labor, 493; Energy and Commerce, 660.

legislative game are proscribed at this stage. All committee members enjoy full, formal eligibility. Parliamentary rules are in force. There is no equivalent of a restrictive rule to delimit the ability of some committee members — however mischievous their intentions — to speak to the merits of the bill, speak to the merits of individual amendments, propose amendments of their own, exploit procedural options, or engage in dilatory tactics. At the same time, neither are there limitations on subcommittee members', subcommittee leaders', or others' right to respond with counterproposals that Weingast has aptly referred to in a different context as "fighting fire with fire" (1989). In sum, if subcommittee nonmembers have been excluded from prior deliberations or if the subcommittee bill that now comes before them has piqued their interest, they are free to enter the mix in full committee.

The second two rows of table 6.1 show that subcommittee nonmembers are far from invisible in full-committee markup. Roughly one in five are major speakers in the markup deliberation or take some form of procedural, amending, or agenda-setting action. In each committee, most of these actors are committee backbenchers, who have relatively few resources to draw on. At the same time, however, subcommittee members are more than twice as likely to meet the "active player" threshold in full committee, despite their having already had an official crack at the bills and privileged access to unofficial negotiations for all but a very few bills that bypassed subcommittee markup.

In sum, subcommittee members are more likely to participate in full-committee markup than their nonmember colleagues. But subcommittee nonmembers do not always sit idle when subcommittees bring bills before them. The importance of this point becomes more visible when one considers that far more subcommittee nonmembers than members are eligible to participate in full-committee markup; rarely does subcommittee size come close to half the full-committee membership. The actual numbers as opposed to the percentages of participants within each category reveal that almost as many players in full-committee markup are not subcommittee members as are.

One should not infer from the aggregate patterns of table 6.1 that committee members passively ratify the decisions of their subcommittees. This does not occur even on House Agriculture, where a long-standing logroll among the several commodity subcommittees is widely asserted to exist. On the other two committees, subcommittee nonmembers frequently enter the committee markup action.

That the glass of full-committee member participation is partly full is reinforced by amending patterns. It is important to bear in mind, of course, that amending data do *not* necessarily tell us anything about whether committee members are rolling the reporting subcommittees (Hall 1992; Hall and Evans 1990). Amending data tell us only who is amending, not who is influencing, the legislative provisions under consideration. Still, this form of markup participation does provide a window on whether the full committee passively ratifies its subcommittees' bills, however excessive the enthusiasms expressed in them. Though subcommittee members offer and pass more amendments in full-committee markup than their full-committee colleagues, the latter often offer and pass amendments as well. On average, subcommittee nonmembers offer approximately three and pass approximately two amendments for each bill that sees a committee markup, with a variation from zero to more than a dozen per bill.

Similar patterns materialize in comparisons of full- and subcommittee leaders. In both formal and informal forums, the behavioral advantage consistently goes to the latter. Subcommittee leaders were active players behind the scenes in approximately 90 percent of the sixty bills considered by three committees—roughly half again as often as their full-committee counterparts. Likewise, subcommittee leaders were consistently more active than their full-committee counterparts even as the action moves to full-committee markup. Indeed, the participation of subcommittee leaders at this stage appears barely selective: rare is the subcommittee chair or ranking member who did not play a leading role when one of her bills is on the full-committee stage.

I do not intend to suggest, however, that full-committee leaders were inattentive to or disengaged from the legislative business of their subcommittees during the period under study. Committee leaders were active in both behind-the-scenes deliberations and formal markup action in well over half of the cases for each of the three committees. Most revealing, however, are the comparisons of the participation patterns of subcommittee and full-committee chairs. The literature on the reforms of the early 1970s and the ensuing literature on the postreform Congress has made much of the decentralization of legislative authority away from reputed autocratic chairs toward subcommittee barons of narrow and newly institutionalized fiefdoms. The final rows of table 6.1 mask the fact that variance in participation by committee leaders occurred mostly among ranking minority leaders, not full-committee chairs.

In the statistics of table 6.1, of course, we have no historical baseline against which to judge whether the alleged shift was monumental or incremental. But whatever advantages the past procedural prerogatives of committee chairs may have wrought, the behavioral evidence leads one to infer that supposed diminution in the powers of postreform committee chairs was probably overblown. Full-committee chairs remained at center stage in the decision-making processes of their committees well after the procedural reforms had time to play out in practice. Hence the significance of recentralization in the mid-1990s may be overblown as well.

INSTITUTIONAL POSITION AND LEGISLATIVE ADVANTAGE: PRELIMINARY FINDINGS

In distilling the lessons of the previous sections, it is important to keep in mind the aggregate nature of the data. In the main, the patterns of subcommittee member and nonmember participation are consistent with the behavioral theory I have advanced. For reasons of both interest and ability, subcommittee members should be more active at every stage than their full-committee colleagues. This is what we find. But the finding is a matter of *central tendency,* and one transforms it into a stylized fact at risk of throwing away *significant* variation. Full-committee leaders and members can and often do inject their own views, values, and interests into the deliberations on a bill originating from a subcommittee on which they do not sit. Whether they thereby mute or perhaps even amplify the enthusiasms of their subcommittees we cannot tell from the data available. But we can tell that subcommittee autonomy is not a constant of legislative life. Understanding when and under what conditions full committees mute the enthusiasms of their subcommittees requires an analysis not simply of comparative institutional foundations but of variable behavioral incentives and constraints, regardless of the legislative period under study.

Explaining Participation in Committee

The aggregate patterns just described provide more description than explanation. They tell us what different categories of members do during committee deliberations, not why they do it. As I discussed in previous chapters, there are strong theoretical reasons to believe that institutional position is inherently related to member interests and seniority-related factors — factors that I also hypothesize to affect members' involvement in particular legislative games. Hence it is even more important in this chapter than the last that institutional variables be embedded in a larger multivariate model. In this section I do that, adapting the model of the last chapter to the different and more data-rich context of full committee.

The adaptations of the model are simply these: institutional variables that do not vary at the subcommittee level — that is, full-committee chair, full-committee ranking position, and membership on the reporting subcommittee — are included in the full-committee model. Table 6.2 presents the analysis of members' behind-the-scenes participation on three committees. Table 6.3 presents the comparable analysis of participation in full-committee markup.

The analyses here involve substantially larger samples of members, drawn from different populations, acting in different legislative forums. Such differences notwithstanding, the various components of the theory find strong support in the analysis of committee participation. Moreover, the signs, significance, and patterns of coefficients exhibit substantial similarity when compared to the subcommittee results, providing further assurance that the model is quite generalizable — across panels, across deliberative forums, and across stages in a sequential legislative process.

First I take up the results regarding the importance of the several institutional positions. When we move to forums where interested committee members without portfolio are eligible to participate, what behavioral difference does institutional position make?

PARTICIPATION AND SUBCOMMITTEE POSITION IN COMMITTEE DECISION MAKING

The effects worth noting first involve the importance of subcommittee position once the subcommittee has opened its gates. As the tables show, subcommittee membership exerts a statistically significant, independent effect on committee members' participation — despite subcommittee members' having by this point in the process enjoyed more and better opportunities to be counted and heard. This finding holds for all three committees and in both formal and informal settings. In part, at least, the preliminary inferences of earlier sections remain intact in the face of appropriate multivariate controls. Insofar as I am able to measure, the behavioral importance of subcommittee membership is not wholly reducible to self-selection driven differences in individuals' interests.

Table 6.2   Participation Behind the Committee Scenes: Multivariate Analyses

	Agriculture		Education and Labor		Energy and Commerce	
Intercept	−.04	(.05)	−.02	(.04)	−.08***	(.02)
Bill-specific interests						
District	.07***	(.03)	.06*	(.04)	.07**	(.02)
Minority-district interaction	−.12**	(.05)	−.05	(.06)	−.07**	(.03)
Electoral insecurity	.01	(.02)	.06*	(.04)	.00	(.02)
Policy	.12***	(.03)	.17***	(.03)	.08	(.05)
Prosecuting the president's agenda	−.01	(.04)	.10*	(.06)	.06**	(.03)
Institutional position						
Full-committee chair	.25***	(.06)	.25***	(.06)	.51***	(.04)
Ranking full-committee member	.03	(.05)	.25***	(.06)	.29***	(.03)
Subcommittee chair	.66***	(.06)	.64***	(.05)	.82***	(.06)
Ranking subcommittee member	.36***	(.05)	.28***	(.05)	.25***	(.06)
Subcommittee member	.17***	(.02	.12***	(.02)	.07***	(.01)
Minority party member	.05	(.04)	.00	(.03)	.02	(.02)
Seniority status						
Committee seniority	.02	(.06)	.09**	(.05)	−.09**	(.04)
Freshman status	−.08***	(.03)	−.12***	(.03)	−.04**	(.02)
New transfer	−.07**	(.04)	—		−.03	(.03)
Chair, other subcommittee	.01	(.04)	−.04*	(.03)	.03*	(.02)
Adjusted R²		.48		.55		.63

Source: Committee markup records and interviews with congressional staff.
Note: Parameter estimates are OLS coefficients. Standard errors appear in parentheses. Education and Labor had no new transfers in the congress under study here. Six Energy and Commerce observations contained missing values and were eliminated from the analysis. The number of observations, by committee, was as follows: Agriculture, 672; Education and Labor, 493; Energy and Commerce, 654.

*Statistically significant at .10, one-tailed test. **Statistically significant at .05, one-tailed test. ***Statistically significant at .01, one-tailed test.

Institutional Subsidies to Subcommittee Leaders

More dramatic are the effects associated with subcommittee leadership position. The resources and prerogatives associated with holding the reporting subcommittee chair push a member two-thirds to four-fifths along the informal participation scale and one-third to three-fifths along the committee markup scale. As predicted, subcommittee ranking minority status also has a positive and significant effect on participation, both formal and informal. But also as predicted, this less resource-rich position has a behavioral effect consistently lower than — typically half the size of — the effect associated with the

Table 6.3   Participation in Committee Markups: Multivariate Analyses

	Agriculture		Education and Labor		Energy and Commerce	
Intercept	.32***	(.06)	.02	(.05)	.06*	(.04)
Bill-specific interests						
District	.10***	(.04)	.11***	(.04)	.08**	(.05)
Minority-district interaction	−.04	(.06)	−.08	(.08)	−.03	(.06)
Electoral insecurity	.03	(.06)	.03	(.03)	.02	(.04)
Policy	.09***	(.03)	.22***	(.04)	.13***	(.03)
Prosecuting the president's agenda	.09**	(.05)	.27***	(.07)	−.08	(.06)
Institutional position						
Full-committee chair	.19***	(.07)	.33***	(.07)	.56***	(.07)
Ranking full-committee member	−.01	(.06)	.25***	(.08)	.24***	(.06)
Subcommittee chair	.33***	(.08)	.58***	(.06)	.59***	(.07)
Ranking subcommittee member	.20***	(.06)	.30***	(.07)	.24***	(.07)
Subcommittee member	.20***	(.02)	.30***	(.07)	.24***	(.07)
Minority party member	.07**	(.04)	.09**	(.04)	.13***	(.03)
Seniority status						
Committee seniority	.02	(.07)	−.07	(.07)	−.26***	(.07)
Freshman status	−.10***	(.04)	−.16***	(.04)	−.10**	(.05)
New transfer	−.10**	(.05)	—		−.08*	(.06)
Chair, other subcommittee	−.15***	(.05)	.01	(.04)	.04	(.04)
Adjusted R²		.28		.44		.31

Source: Committee markup records and interviews with congressional staff.
Note: Entries are OLS coefficients. Standard errors appear in parentheses. Education and Labor had no new transfers in the 97th Congress. Six Energy and Commerce observations contained missing data and were excluded from the analysis. The number of observations, by committee, was as follows: Agriculture, 672; Education and Labor, 493; Energy and Commerce, 654.
*Statistically significant at .10, one-tailed test. **Statistically significant at .05, one-tailed test. ***Statistically significant at .01, one-tailed test.

position of subcommittee chair. Subcommittee minority leaders do tend to have (or quickly acquire) greater experience and policy expertise as well as better lines of communication. They also usually benefit from some additional staff support, which enables them to pay the marginal information and transaction costs more easily than most backbenchers can. However, staffers from all three committees and most subcommittees emphasized the legislative importance of the differential staff subsidies allocated to majority and minority leaders. For instance, the minority Commerce staffer assigned to handle a bill governing implementation of the Strategic Petroleum Reserve catalogued the obstacles confronting the minority by comparison with the majority leaders: "We really only had two guys who cared about this bill in the early going, [A] and [B], and they delegated it to the staff, which was me. [Subcommittee Chair] Sharp has a fairly large staff. He probably had five people working on this at different times. He himself was involved. [Subcommittee member] Mike Synar had access to three or four staffers. They were bouncing their proposal around to all kinds of people."

The same staffer also emphasized the barriers that his boss faced because of the agenda power of the subcommittee chair. "The Administration gets involved with Sharp and Synar because [Secretary] Hodel wants to work with them — he knows he can't get a consensus bill [otherwise]. . . . We had wanted to involve ourselves in the negotiations between Synar and Sharp's staff and the Administration's staff. However, that did not work out . . . [which] pushed us onto the margin."

A member of the minority Agriculture staff noted that although Agriculture had among the smallest staff contingents in the House, the majority still outnumbered the minority staff three to one. As an organizational matter, he pointed out, minority ranking members received no official staff allocation. Referring to one of the majority staffers with whom he worked on the wheat and feed grains title of the Omnibus Farm Bill, another minority staffer observed: "[D] handles wheat. That's it, wheat — which also took him into the embargo protection issue in a big way. But he's got someone else to handle all of the other [subcommittee] issues. I've got to handle all of those, plus help out on farm credit."

My interviews with the subcommittee's majority staff confirmed that these were not merely the self-indulgent moanings of a resentful minority staffer. Without my having prompted any comparison with the minority, in fact, two majority subcommittee staffers (including the one referred to in the quotation above) separately mentioned that they didn't know how their minority counterparts kept up.

The procedural prerogatives of the Democratic majority visibly affected what ranking subcommittee members found themselves able to do. For several decades leading up to their takeover of the House in 1995, Republicans had called for the abolition of proxy voting in committees and subcommittees, arguing that it allowed an indolent Democratic majority to move legislation through committee with antimajoritarian procedures.[1] Several staffers whom

---

1. The new Republican majority abolished proxy voting in committee in the 104th House, despite the advantage it gives to the majority — especially a slender majority — in committee. See Chapter 8 for a fuller discussion.

I interviewed complained about the majority party's abuse of proxy voting in committee, noting that bills the minority opposed in subcommittee would often be marked up with as few as two or three majority members present, with the subcommittee chair or other majority player casting their absent colleagues' proxies. "They ramrod things through subcommittee even when we have them outnumbered. We know that [subcommittee chair] doesn't actually have the proxies half the time. Neither do we. It's just a joke. Except when it comes time to report a bill, when everything is pretty much a done deal, the majority almost never has an actual majority."

The staff, agenda control, and other procedural advantages of subcommittee chairs, then, are widely acknowledged by both majority and minority members and are clearly consistent with the statistical results regarding their full-committee participation.

The "Role" of the Subcommittee Chair

At the same time, however, numerous subcommittee staffers pointed to a different kind of behavioral process at work in the actions taken by subcommittee chairs, a process that an issue-specific optimization theory of participation does not easily encompass. The language that majority respondents frequently invoked pointed to what one might well interpret as the role obligations of the chair:

> Everything is up for grabs in a farm bill. Every program gets reauthorized, tinkered with. We had to rewrite the wool and mohair section. A friend of mine was handling honeybees. [Neither of our bosses] could care less, but it was their subcommittee. [Agriculture]

> We knew that we had to move a bill, so there wasn't a whole lot of choice. He [the subcommittee chair] told us to put together a bill. [Agriculture]

> Why do members get involved? A lot of it is simply like the situation with JTPA or the 1978 amendments to CETA.[2] Legislation is expiring; the chairman of the subcommittee has responsibility for reauthorizing it, and it's as simple as that. [Education and Labor]

> In terms of developing interests on individual bills, [members] usually do so for one of two reasons: because they want to or because they have to. As a [chairman] of a subcommittee, you have an obligation to attend to all bills at

2. JTPA refers to the the Job Training Partnership Act of 1982. Excepting the conglomerate of statutory changes packaged in the 1981 Budget Reconciliation bill, JTPA was perhaps the most important domestic policy initiative during Reagan's first congress. CETA refers to the Comprehensive Employment and Training Act, a program long reviled by conservative Republicans and replaced in 1982 by JTPA.

the subcommittee level. You owe it to the full committee to sort out what the impact will be and try to deal with it before it gets to full committee. If you want to protect your professional reputation, you have to get involved. [Education and Labor]

We had a joint referral with Banking on that one. We hadn't even held hearings. But word came down that we get our own bill in. To Dingell, jurisdiction is everything. The subcommittee chairs are expected to watch out for their part of it. [Energy and Commerce]

The initiative on that bill came from the Republicans, who were carrying water for the administration. To tell you the honest-to-God truth, [L] didn't know much about this issue when we started and probably didn't want to. But we couldn't just sit on the thing. It was too visible at that point. [Energy and Commerce]

Such quotations suggest, then, that subcommittee chairs cannot be as selective in their participation as their colleagues. This appears true even by comparison with full-committee chairs; when it suits their purposes (or lack thereof), committee chairs can elect simply to leave the bucket in the subcommittee chair's hands. On bills that fit within what Walker (1977) has labeled the "non-discretionary side of the legislative agenda," the subcommittee chair may find himself carrying water he cares little about. Among subcommittee chairs, one thus finds bill-specific participation without bill-specific purpose: subcommittee chairs were ten times as likely as committee backbenchers to be active on bills in which they had little interest along any of three dimensions.[3]

In sum, considerable interview and behavioral evidence suggests that in my attempt to clarify the psychology of participation among this central set of actors, I encounter at least one real limitation to my optimization theory. Rather, that framework provides a backdrop against which certain behavioral patterns evident among subcommittee chairs appear not to fit, patterns that suggest at least two alternative explanations. One is sociological, namely, that members who become chairs walk into a legislative role, the behavioral requirements of which precede and imperfectly mesh with their issue-specific purposes. Viewed in this theoretical light, the position exhibits something like a bona fide job description: a set of role obligations, a widely recognized set of peer expectations.[4]

3. I attempted to better quantify such effects in the pilot study for this project (Hall 1987) by including interactions of reporting subcommittee chairs and the several interest variables. While all coefficients were negative, as predicted, none were statistically significant at generous levels.

4. Note that although such evidence is consistent with traditional sociological theory, the role orientations of subcommittee or committee chairs were not prominent themes in

But there is a second explanation. The evidence can be read to suggest a more fully elaborated theory of purpose, one that takes into account the long-term reputational interests of ambitious subcommittee chairs in addition to their more immediate, issue-specific interests. According to this view, subcommittee chairs will invest their enterprises in bills they are otherwise inclined to neglect, to promote a favorable reputation, which in turn renders more secure their current position and enhances any ambitions they may have for upward mobility within committee or House. While I cannot here systematically assess the relative evidentiary weight one might attach to either line of argument, the implication is that a full understanding of the behavior of formally designated leaders requires research designed to disentangle the theoretical alternatives.[5] For my part, I simply cannot unpack the full meaning of this simple but important variable.

FULL-COMMITTEE LEADERS AND THE
IMPORTANCE OF LEADERSHIP "STYLE"

The identities, personalities, and legislative styles of House legislators who have held the chairs of standing committees in this century infuse House legend and lore. Chairs' importance in legislative decision making has been emphasized less since the mid-1970s, however, to the point that a committee chair reputed to dominate his panel was generally characterized as a throwback to an earlier era.

Participants' observations about the diminution in these offices notwithstanding, I have argued that full-committee chairs still retain substantial staff and procedural advantages that render negligible the barriers to entry that they face on the range of bills before their panels. To a lesser extent, such

---

the literature on participation patterns in the prereform Congress. More prominent were sociological versions on apprenticeship, hard work, specialization, and deference — the nature and importance of which I am better able to disentangle.

5. While the second interpretation appears to be a natural extension of the theoretical framework I employ, I would simply confess my concern that the rational-choice concept of reputation in this context does little more than smuggle in some sociological theory. Simply put, reputation is a pattern of continually updated peer evaluations. Though a chair might care about such evaluations, it is not clear what sort of self-interested calculations by individual peers would collectively incline them to penalize a chair for not acting in a selfless manner. If a chair is not interested in some nondiscretionary agenda item, nothing prevents him from abdicating leadership responsibility to some other interested, credit-seeking member. Indeed, he might gain favor in doing so. Alternatively, if no one cares, why would the uncaring hold accountable a chair for not doing his duty? In short, there are logically prior conceptual issues to resolve before meaningful research on alternative theoretical accounts of reputation can proceed.

advantages accrue to their minority counterparts as well. These arguments find strong support in the multivariate results. In participation both behind the scenes and in full-committee markup, the effect of holding committee chairmanship was substantial for all three committees, whereas the effect for committee ranking minority member was substantial for two of three. At the very least, we can safely conclude that full-committee leaders do not sit passively by as subcommittee leaders and members bring their bills to committee for ratification.

There are variations, however, in the relative size of the respective coefficients within each model. For instance, although it is substantively large and statistically significant, the coefficient that captures the effect of Agriculture chairmanship is underwhelming when compared to the other institutional effects — less than that for ranking subcommittee minority status and half the size of that for the reporting subcommittee chair. Nor has the Agriculture chair simply exploited his resources and involved himself behind the scenes to ensure that his bidding is done prior to markup; the comparisons favor him even less in the model of informal participation. At the other end of the spectrum, the analogous effects of the Commerce chair are much larger. In full-committee markup, for instance, the coefficient for the full-committee chair is responsible for movement halfway along the participation scale — a coefficient more than twice the size of the ranking subcommittee minority member and nearly identical to that of the subcommittee chair, whose status and advantages are concentrated in a much more narrowly defined legislative venue.

It is tempting to interpret such central tendencies in leaders' behavior as functions of their personal leadership "styles." Indeed, most Congress-watchers and many Congress scholars have been inclined to do just that, cataloguing how the unique personalities of chairs emerge in the committee politics of Congress. For instance, numerous accounts testify to the aggressive and heavy-handed approach to committee lawmaking by Representative John Dingell (Democrat of Michigan), who chaired Energy and Commerce continuously from 1981 to 1994. Dingell was variously referred to as Big John, "the Chairman," and "the most powerful chairman in the House," as if he were a throwback to a prereform era of autocratic chairs. By contrast, Agriculture Chair Kika de la Garza (Democrat of Texas) was widely perceived as "clerk-like," inclined more to allow his various subcommittee leaders to negotiate within their respective jurisdictions. In reflecting on de la Garza's leadership in the congress under study here, for instance, a writer for the *Almanac of American Politics* commented that " 'no one expected de la Garza to be an overbearing chairman, and he apparently hasn't been' " (Barone and Ujifusa 1983, 1156). Between these apparent polar opposites in reputed style, Dingell and de la Garza, was Carl Perkins, Chair of Education and Labor. The same insider source characterizes Perkins thus: " 'He is one of the few really strong committee chairmen left. One reason is that he—and organized labor—have made sure that only Democrats sympathetic to the committee's programs get on Education and Labor. Another is Perkins's own strength of character. Far from fashionable, he is one of those old-fashioned liberals . . . who know their legislation cold, negotiate like master poker players, and refuse to compromise their principles' " (Barone and Ujifusa 1983, 469).

The danger in such commonsense explanations, however, is that the ill-defined and unobserved categories *character* or *style* do little more than generalize and label what they purport to explain. Alternatively, the constrained optimization account I have elaborated suggests that there are theoretically plausible but qualitatively different factors that may account for the behavioral tendencies we observe in particular leaders. For instance, the committee chair coefficients map remarkably well onto the differences in staff allocations for different committee chairs and onto the differences between chairs and their minority counterparts. Recall from Chapter 4 (table 4.1) that the full-committee legislative staffers available to Chairs Dingell, Perkins, and de la Garza were twenty-five, fifteen, and five, respectively. Dingell had a staff salary budget of $1.3 million, Perkins a budget of $.5 million, and de la Garza a budget of $.2 million, figures I assume to have some bearing on staff quality as well as numbers. Similarly, differences in staff allocations between chair and minority leader within committees fit the multivariate results: estimates of participation by the chair are consistently higher than they are for the minority leader. Energy and Commerce Chair Dingell had nineteen more legislative staffers than the ranking committee minority member; Perkins had eight more than his minority counterpart; and de la Garza had two more (five versus three) than the Agriculture minority leader.[6]

Unfortunately, it is hard to ascertain which factors may be responsible for the substantial but variable effects of the committee leaders' positions. For instance, the strategic considerations of coalition politics might fit the pattern of coefficients. Staff size and leadership position, in turn, are so highly collinear that one cannot disentangle statistically the behavioral advantage attributable to size of staff from other factors.

6. Neither should we assume that such resource levels are endogenous with respect to leadership style, that is, that a chair with, say, an aggressive "style" aggressively seeks and receives a larger staff to help prosecute his agenda. To take our two cases of reputedly opposite styles, Dingell and de la Garza were both new to their jobs during the period analyzed here and had largely inherited the staff size and within-committee staff allocations from their predecessors.

However, we can conclude that the observed behavioral differences across committee leaders are consistent with an explanation that need not repair to the categories of personality or style. Were one inclined to do better, in any case, it is difficult to imagine what a systematic investigation of leadership style would look like. This concept is notorious for being vaguely conceptualized. Indeed, one plausible interpretation is that style simply labels the breadth and intensity of the leader's interest in his jurisdiction, two general factors controlled for in the analysis. For instance, Dingell's level of interest in bills within his jurisdiction was higher across the board than was the interest of the other two chairs in bills reported from their committees. And even could we sort out the independent effects of staff, other residual factors associated with leadership status should enhance a leader's participation, not least of which are the procedural prerogatives likely to inflate the expected efficacy of the leader's legislative investments.

None of this is to imply that the personalities or idiosyncratic tendencies of individual leaders are entirely epiphenomenal — that participant-observers mistakenly assume the personal factors to matter when in fact other ill-considered and more generalizable factors do. In the legislative action on particular issues, leaders' personal attributes may have a prominent and important effect on the deliberations. At the same time, however, the theory and evidence here caution strongly against the participant-observer's inclination to personalize the explanation of patterns that emerge over time and across contexts. Whatever the other advantages of this mode of inquiry, participant-observation does not provide the range of vision that is needed to render even casual comparative analysis across differently situated leaders, much less the analytical leverage needed to disentangle the substantial structural factors that variously enable or constrain what individual leaders do.

Participation and Purpose in Full Committee

In several respects, the full committee provides a rich testing ground for the different hypotheses I have advanced about the nature and importance of members' interests. The preliminary analysis presented thus far suggests that institutional positions matter, sometimes a great deal, in full-committee participation. Is participation at this stage thus mostly "structured"? Or are the principal findings of the last chapter regarding the connections between selective participation and variable purpose confirmed in the full-committee setting? More specifically, do legislators pursue their interests, independent of the institutional position they hold, by entering legislative games in full committee?

Several features of full-committee deliberations should govern our expectations here. First, the behind-the-scenes deliberations begin long before a bill comes onto the committee's radar. To say that full-committee members are eligible to pursue their interests through informal participation is thus technically true, but the statement must be qualified by recognition of the relative disadvantages full-committee members face in acquiring the necessary political intelligence and bill-specific policy knowledge.

The rules of the standing committees do guarantee members advance notice when a bill is slated for formal markup and, save in extraordinary cases, require that the text of the bill and a section-by-section analysis of its provisions be available to all members. Like the subcommittee markup, the committee markup itself operates under the equivalent of an open rule: any panel member can speak to or offer amendments or procedural objections to proposed committee actions. Finally, the full-committee markup, like that of the originating subcommittee, is almost always held in open session. Indeed, the full-committee markup is far more likely to draw the attention of the press, the administration, organized interests, and other important outsiders, so that in practice full-committee markups tend to be more public than subcommittee markups.

Tables 6.2 and 6.3 exhibit the implications of such differences. Given the barriers to entry faced by purposive full-committee members, members' interests assume consistently greater importance in formal committee markup than in behind-the-scenes deliberations (once subcommittee positions have been controlled for). Several more specific findings bear emphasis, however.

CONSTITUENCY-MINDED COMMITTEE MEMBERS

Relatively inaccessible and publicly invisible though behind-the-scenes business is, responsiveness to constituency interests is nonetheless evident in the informal participation of members of all three committees. Indeed, the coefficients are remarkably similar across committees. Comparing constituency-oriented Agriculture with the reputedly policy-oriented Education and Labor Committee as well as with Energy and Commerce, for instance, we find that for all three, district effects are statistically significant and, more surprisingly, nearly identical in size (see table 6.2). As the strategic incentives implied by the Workhorse Hypothesis would predict, however, none of the direct constituency effects appears substantively all that large. This pattern of coefficients on informal participation, I would note, is similar to that at the subcommittee level (see table 5.4).

Table 6.3 provides somewhat stronger evidence that district considerations affect members' participation in open committee markup, thus adding support to the results of the last chapter regarding the importance of public opportunities to engage in the activities of position-taking and credit-claiming. All three coefficients are greater than or equal to the coefficient of the most often mentioned institutional variable thought to structure the chamber's reputed division of labor, namely, membership on the reporting subcommittee. All three district coefficients are statistically significant at conservative levels, and again, the similarity in the district coefficients across committee equations is more than a little remarkable. As we found in the analysis of informal participation, moreover, the estimates for Agriculture on the one hand and Education and Labor on the other are nearly identical.

Again, it is important to emphasize what such a similarity does not imply. It does not imply the counterintuitive conclusion that the issues falling within the jurisdictions of these two committees are similar in nature. Agriculture certainly allows individual members to better service district concerns. If my results implied the reverse, I would encourage the reader to doubt my results. Rather, the point is that the jurisdictionally grounded differences appear in the varying perceptions of district interest that members attach to committee bills, and hence in the different distributions on this particular independent variable. High levels of district interest (see table 3.1) are more likely to be evoked by Agriculture than by Education and Labor bills. But when district interests are evoked, even on Education and Labor, members' participation decisions are similarly affected.

The nature of members' optimizing calculations does not change with the committee room in which they happen to be sitting. For instance, the two members in my sample who sat both on Education and Labor and on Agriculture did not, so far as I could tell, change from policy-minded Jekylls into pork-minded Hydes when they moved between the former and the latter committee rooms. But given the very different sorts of issues they confront in these two locations, the particular bills to which they react are quite different in that they typically evoke different interests and provide different legislative opportunities to pursue them.

RESPONDING TO DISTRICT INTERESTS:
THE DISADVANTAGES OF MINORITY STATUS

Evidence in the analysis of strategic behavior with regard to committee agendas also differentiates between the incentives of majority and minority members to engage in setting priorities with the constituency in mind. To briefly recall the general argument, majority members are more likely to see legislation come before them that is conducive to district-endearing credit-claiming, while minority members, lacking agenda control, are more likely to see the advantages of a blame-avoidance strategy. Thus did I hypothesize that minority status should at least partly offset the otherwise clear incentive to participate when constituency interests are evoked. The coefficients on the interaction between minority and district, tables 6.2 and 6.3 show, are relatively stable across the committee equations, both in the informal and formal participation models. All are negative in sign, suggesting that agenda control by the majority party does, in committee as in subcommittee, provide greater opportunities for majority members to pursue constituents' interests without simultaneously suffering ideological or other cross-pressures from the constituency.

These results are not consistently strong, however, and even display some apparent anomalies. For instance, the strongest blame avoidance effect in the model of informal participation appears on Agriculture, a result that mirrors the finding for informal participation in subcommittee. In general, this is not the committee for which one would expect the strongest result — quite the contrary. A committee historically composed of homogeneous high-demanders for federally financed agricultural programs, House Agriculture has tended to be much less partisan that most House committees. One should thus see less strategic and potentially punitive agenda manipulation on the part of agenda setters from the majority.

Second, the Blame Avoidance Hypothesis finds greater support in the model of informal than in that of formal participation. While correct in sign, the minority-district coefficients are relatively small in the model of markup behavior, and we cannot be confident that any are nonzero. This apparent asymmetry between the informal and formal forums is just the opposite of what I predicted. Cross-pressured Republicans should find it especially risky in a public forum to promote or actively support program changes that redound to the greater good of Democratic constituencies or the greater ill of Republican ones. Absent a fuller specification and better measurement of the issue-specific conditions under which the committee majority leaders will engage in strategic agenda manipulation, however, one cannot say much more than that these preliminary results appear interesting but anomalous. In particular, I cannot here sort out the extent to which a plausible but countervailing incentive may be at work, namely, that a majority agenda may be designed to do tangible harm to the minority party's constituencies, in which case the committee markup sometimes becomes the best and perhaps only forum for minority expressions of protest or constituency-minded counterproposals.

PARTICIPATION AND EXTRAELECTORAL PURPOSES
IN HOUSE COMMITTEES

The more striking findings regarding participation in committee relate to the importance of members' policy interests. In the pilot study for this project, I reported that this variable exhibited a strong behavioral effect on decision making within the House Education and Labor Committee (1987).[7] Then as now, this finding is interesting or unsurprising, depending on one's point of view. It is unsurprising insofar as it follows Fenno's well-known conclusion in *Congressmen in Committees* that members seek assignment to Education and Labor, more than to most committees, with an eye to making good public policy (1973a). In this respect, my analysis extends Fenno's inductive study and tests its implications for members' post-assignment behavior. But the Education and Labor analysis remains noteworthy because theories of legislative behavior and systematic analysis have done little with Fenno's original insight that the motivational psychology of House members cannot be reduced to simple seeking of a single goal.[8]

Even if one assumes, following Fenno, that Education and Labor is an easy case for testing the importance of members' policy interests, one cannot assume the same for the other two committees — certainly not for House Agriculture. As House committees go, it is the limiting case insofar as constituency-driven assignment seeking is concerned (Jones 1961; Ferejohn 1975; Shepsle 1978; Smith and Deering 1984). Yet in Agriculture Committee decision making we find that members' policy interests figure prominently in the behavioral play. In participation behind the scenes, in fact, the effect of Agriculture members' policy interests is larger than that of their district interests. And in participation during committee markup, the the effect of policy interests is only slightly smaller than that of district interests.

In addition, one staffer implied that there might be something like an additive effect when a single issue evokes both district and policy interests for a member. When I asked him why his boss had gotten so involved in three bills, only one of which had emerged from a subcommittee on which the member sat, he observed: "The wheat and dairy subsidies are important to the district,

---

7. The results for that committee shown in tables 6.2 and 6.3, once the variables are transformed to the comparable scales (see Hall 1987, appendix, 123–24), are nearly identical to those first reported, despite subsequent modifications that gave rise to the somewhat more general model I estimate here.

8. Exceptions include Perkins 1980, Smith and Deering 1984, and Strahan 1989, though none of these develop a behavioral model on the basis of which one can confidently infer causal connections between extraelectoral interests and individual members' decisions. Except for Kingdon 1989, little analogous analysis in the literature on roll call voting offers more. For instance, Jackson and Kingdon (1992) demonstrate the inherent methodological and hence inferential flaws of virtually all roll call studies purporting to establish that ideology has an importance in members' voting decisions independent of constituency.

no doubt about it. And the producer groups make themselves heard. But the Congressman grew up there. It's an area of scattered farms and small towns. He really does see it as 'a way of life' — something he doesn't want to see die away. So the costs of the programs can be justified in those terms as well."

So too do we find important effects of members' policy interests on their participation in Commerce Committee deliberations. This is especially evident in full-committee markup, where — more than for most committees — major legislative battles are frequently fought. As one staffer put it and other majority and minority staff echoed, often there is "blood all over the committee room floor." Another added: "It's always a battle of wits; that's true whenever you're dealing with John Dingell, but it's also a battle of ideas. That's the fun part. You don't come [into a Commerce Committee markup] unless you can make your case, make it well. . . . You won't stand a chance otherwise."

In summary, in five of the six sets of estimates in tables 6.2 and 6.3, the behavioral effect of members' personal policy interests is greater than the effect of district interests, as those interests are perceived within the member's enterprise. Across very different committees and decision-making contexts, in short, this is a robust result.

Though less consistent across committees, there is additional evidence that members' interest in prosecuting the president's agenda matters as well. This interest appears most clearly on House Education and Labor, a committee with jurisdiction over a wide range of Great Society programs loathed by committee Republicans and targeted for the deepest cuts of any budget function by OMB director David Stockman. Yet prosecution of the president's agenda on Education and Labor was not limited to the now famous battles over the 1981 Budget Reconciliation. Perhaps the most important domestic program to emerge from Reagan's first term was the Job Training Partnership Act of 1982 (JTPA), the replacement for the expiring and much maligned Comprehensive Employment and Training Act (CETA). The strong preference of Employment and Opportunities Subcommittee Chair Augustus Hawkins (Democrat of California) was to include in the bill some significant provision for publicly funded jobs, to mitigate the burgeoning unemployment apparent in 1982. The Reagan White House was adamantly opposed to provisions for public jobs, and Reagan loyalists forced Hawkins to withdraw that title of the bill. Similar accounts characterize other Education and Labor bills. For instance, the scheduled reauthorizations of the Older Americans Act, the Head Start Act, and others were modest in scope, and the terms of their reauthorizations limited to two years, in the face of Republican opposition backed by the Reagan White House. "We were doing everything we could just to preserve as much of what we had already accomplished in the past," one majority staffer put it. "Expanding programs or doing anything positive was just out of the question."

Additional if somewhat weaker evidence appears in the results of the Commerce Committee analysis, where a number of programs opposed by the administration (Superfund, Low-Income Energy Assistance, health care programs for the unemployed) were also opposed by minority partisans. Staffers on both sides of the aisle observed that committee ranking minority member James Broyhill (Republican of North Carolina) and several other conservative members were, as one staffer put it, "more than happy to carry water for the administration." "[Reagan's] agenda wasn't exactly the same as our agenda," another minority committee staffer observed, "but there was plenty of overlap, and many of our members saw an opportunity to succeed."

Given the constituency-based homogeneity on House Agriculture, finally, otherwise conservative Republicans not only did not support but actively opposed administration proposals to cut deeply into agricultural subsidies, subsidies dear to districts represented by both parties. It is therefore not terribly surprising that the estimation of the presidential effect for that committee should be slight, if not negative. At the same time, however, this estimate reveals the limitations of the data in capturing the conditional nature of the relationship and, more generally, disentangling the effects when different interests conflict.

PARTICIPATION AND PURPOSE IN COMMITTEE: IMPLICATIONS

In sum, we can conclude with considerable confidence that it is the exception, not the rule, for district interests to dominate — much less exclusively govern — members' behavioral choices regarding the time and effort their enterprise will invest in advancing their views on particular legislative issues. Coupled with similar findings at the subcommittee level, this stands out as an important finding for future theorists of legislative behavior and institutions. Fenno's oft-cited study (1973a) to the contrary, the reductionist assumption that members act — or act "as if" — to pursue reelection-related interests has become a staple of our theoretical trade. It is the central theme in most studies of roll call voting (Fiorina 1974; Jackson 1974), casework and constituency service (Cain, Ferejohn, and Fiorina 1987; Fiorina 1989), committee assignment seeking (Shepsle 1978), legislative delegation to executive agencies (Arnold 1979; Fiorina 1989), and legislative organization (Cox and McCubbins 1993; Shepsle and Weingast 1987a; Weingast and Marshall 1988). It may be that this particular "as if" assumption works reasonably well for explaining members' public positions or extralegislative behavior. But the evidence accumulating in the several analyses of members' participation decisions strongly supports the view that that the investment of members' scarce legislative resources — their revealed intensities in specific legislative games — cannot be reduced to district considerations.

Did the Sociology of Congress Ever Hold?

In previous chapters I reviewed the once prevailing but now allegedly dated theory of legislative participation, a sociological approach that attached explanatory importance to the prescriptive and proscriptive norms of group life into which all but the occasional maverick became quickly socialized. But by the late 1980s, the institution had changed enough that scholars of both House and Senate described a Congress where legislators were unleashed to adopt new, more active "styles" (Sinclair 1989; Smith 1989). The apparent demise of the older participation norms, however, prompted few attempts to provide alternative explanations regarding when and why members participate. In this section, I extend the revisionist arguments of the previous chapter, both to participation at different legislative stages and to different legislative eras.

APPRENTICESHIP, SPECIALIZATION, AND DEFERENCE, REDUX

Evidence in support of the revisionist view of apprenticeship was clear and consistent in the subcommittee analysis. The sociological rhetoric may no longer be on the lips of participant-observers, but newcomers' legislative priorities and participation decisions are subject to greater constraints than those of the typical senior member. Freshmen participate in subcommittee significantly less, other things being equal.

The results of the committee-level analysis add a second, thicker layer in support of a rational-choice theory of apprenticeship. Tables 6.2 and 6.3 show that in participation both behind the committee scenes and publicly on the committee stage, freshman status exerts a consistently strong, negative effect on member participation. This finding holds across the three committees, despite controls for the interval-level variable of committee seniority, the several levels of member interest, and subcommittee assignments — all variables related to freshman status that might cause newcomers to participate less than they otherwise would.

So, too, we find evidence of specialization, though precisely what this norm described in the heyday of the prereform Congress is not altogether clear. As I discuss in Chapter 4, ordinary usage implies that specialization is two-dimensional, consisting of a behavioral means to legislatively practical ends. The means is to concentrate on a relatively small number and narrow range of issues; the specialist is thus the opposite of generalist. The end is to develop expertise in a specialty, which over time presumably leads to accomplishing the second-order ends of peer respect and hence greater legislative effectiveness (Matthews 1960).

Whether members develop expertise, peer respect, and indirectly greater effectiveness cannot be ascertained from the analysis here (nor, for that matter, from any evidence in the older literature). But we can tell that members invariably concentrate on a narrow range of issues. With the possible exceptions of the chairs and ranking minority members, generalists are nowhere to be found on any of the committees. Rather, as Chapter 3 revealed, the typical member was reasonably active on less than a fifth of the issues before his committee.

Such statistics say nothing about whether the sets of issues in which each member participates cohere as a definable policy area in which the member might earn a reputation for expertise. The results of the multivariate analyses of this chapter (tables 6.2 and 6.3) suggest, however, at least some coherence in the choices, at least insofar as subcommittee jurisdictional boundaries define loosely connected policy domains. Subcommittee leaders and members consistently participate more in issues arising within the jurisdiction of their committees, both in deliberations behind the scenes and in committee markups.

But does this mean that the older work-related norms are still at work despite their reputed demise? Decidedly not. Such patterns appear, but no interview or participant-observer report anywhere alludes to a hard work or specialization norm alive in the group life of contemporary committees. Rather, the patterns exhibit selective and purposive participation, the consequence of decisions made by rational legislators with differing institutional resources. If specialization exists, it is a rational specialization, distinguishable from the older sociological conceptualization. Moreover, the patterns revealed here imply only selective and hence relatively narrow patterns of individual-level participation, not substantive expertise in bill-specific policy issues. Previous participation is undoubtedly a necessary condition for expertise, but it is far from being a sufficient condition. Committee and subcommittee backbenchers frequently participate in the deliberations on specific bills, yet rare was the case when a staffer characterized his boss as an expert on a particular committee subject, except in the enterprises of committee leaders or relevant subcommittee leaders.[9]

9. In a pathbreaking book on legislative organization, Krehbiel (1991) emphasizes the informational basis upon which a rational, majoritarian legislature should induce subsets of its members to specialize, gain expertise, and then reveal their expertise to their col-

Finally, the committee-level evidence strongly suggests that rational abdication rather than social deference operates at this stage of decision making. Specifically, the disinclination of a subcommittee chair to involve himself in the jurisdiction of some other subcommittee fails to appear in the multivariate results. Rather, the sign on this coefficient is incorrect (positive) in four of the six equations, correct and substantively large only on House Agriculture and then only at the formal markup stage. Neither does increasing seniority generate any greater opportunities to participate, except in freedom from the legislative start-up costs that the typical freshman must pay.

HISTORICAL REVISIONISM AND BEHAVIORAL EXPLANATION

In sum, behavioral norms of a sociological sort are in fact dead. Properly reconceptualized in terms of optimization theory, however, the two behavioral phenomena most widely noted in the older, sociological scholarship — apprenticeship and specialization — appear very much alive.

But I wish to push my case a good bit further — further back in time — to a second nonintuitive assertion. To state the assertion baldly: it is not the case that the older, sociological norms were once alive but later gave way to the individualism of the contemporary congress, as various scholars have argued (Asher 1975; Sinclair 1989; Smith 1989). Rather, most norms of a sociological sort never were alive, behaviorally speaking. The complement of this claim, stated equally baldly, is that the optimization theory of participation developed here is quite general, as applicable in the heyday of the prereform Congress as it is now. One need not, in other words, change theories as one moves from explaining members' behavior in one era to explaining it another.

The contemporary behavioral analysis at both the subcommittee and the committee level has already rendered the older sociological explanation suspect. In congresses where not even lip service is paid to an apprenticeship norm, clear behavioral tendencies consistent with that norm flourish. They reflect a practical apprenticeship, in which newcomers face greater information and transaction costs than their more senior colleagues, and thus greater barriers to entry for the wide range of legislative issues that come before their panels.

There is every reason to believe that such costs were at least as important in

---

leagues. I focus here on the rational calculations of individuals to concentrate on a select set of issues, a different theoretical question from the one posed by Krehbiel. Still, the explanation of selective participation that I provide can be read as an individual-level account that buttresses several important features of Krehbiel's theory of legislative organization. I return to such issues in the concluding chapter.

the behavioral calculations of House freshmen in earlier times. Freshman members may well have participated less, but not because of the rhetoric of admonition that may have floated through freshmen's supposedly socializing conversations with committee elders. Rather, the argument here is that such rhetoric and its alleged effects were mostly epiphenomenal; the patterns of freshman behavior that coincided with the apprenticeship norm were due to nontrivial, nonsociological constraints.

Recall that the evidence that supported the sociological account prevalent in the 1950s and 1960s necessarily came from interviews with participant-observers, who characterized the norms as part of what newcomers learned and senior members helped to sustain. Group expectations and peer pressure, these informants reported, structured the extent to which and the domains in which members felt free to participate. What the actual behavioral patterns were at that time, however, we do not know and have never been able to determine. Committee markups prior to 1970 were invariably held in executive session and the records are hence inaccessible.[10] Even the most conscientious scholar of the pre-1970 period was forced to rely on expert informants for both a (general) description of the behavior of interest and necessarily speculative explanations for it. While committees were then as they are now the locations of most of the chamber's legislative work, one simply had no access to behavioral data with which to test alternative explanations.[11]

THE HISTORICAL DATA:
EDUCATION AND LABOR IN THE 87TH CONGRESS

By virtue of access I happily obtained to prereform markup records for one committee, I am able to test the alternatives here. The committee is House Education and Labor, for which I gathered participation data for all bills and all members in one congress (the 87th) two decades before the one I have focused on thus far.

The records from which the data are drawn are especially good for my

10. Because of recent congressional actions that diminish the barriers to access, however, such records have recently become more available to the historically minded student of legislative behavior and institutions. See Schamel et al. 1989.

11. Scholars interested in such issues have thus been forced to look where the light is, namely, the public floor behavior reported in the *Congressional Record* (see Matthews 1960; Sinclair 1989; Smith 1989). Of course, floor action is often quite important; thus do I adapt my model to analyze floor participation in the next chapter. But at the same time, it is almost certainly true that during most of this century, most of the most important participation in legislative deliberations has occurred in committee, and it is primarily there that the principal norms were reported to be important.

purposes because they were kept in identical form by the same person across the two decades that I will compare. The minutes for each markup contain almost all the information on which I have relied thus far — attendance, voting, amending, procedural action, agenda action — as well as short summaries of central parts of the markup debate in which the key discussants are identified. I thus was able to assign a markup index score in the same way as I did for Education and Labor in the 97th Congress, except that classification of members into minor or major speakers was somewhat less precise. To make the cross-congress comparisons as valid as possible, however, I reconstructed the index scores for the 97th Congress, using only the identically kept markup minutes, excluding the information on speaking culled from the verbatim transcripts that were available only for the later congress.[12]

Available for comparative analysis, then, are participation data for the same committee for one congress (1961–62) approximately one decade before and one congress (1981–82) a decade after the democratizing changes attributed to the reforms of the 1970s. The descriptive profiles of the two committees are shown in table 6.4 and exhibit remarkable similarity along the usual dimensions. Note that the committees are closely comparable in size, party ratios, and number of subcommittees. The seniority profiles are also very similar, with the Class of 1960 bringing six new freshmen to the committee, the Class of 1980 bringing five. The freshmen contingent was no more substantial (and thus no more threatening as a cohort) in one congress than in the other. Neither did the seniority of the nonfreshmen differ appreciably in the two periods.

SEEN BUT NOT HEARD?
THE PREREFORM NORM OF APPRENTICESHIP RECONSIDERED

The clearest statement of the older apprenticeship norm was that the newcomer should be seen and not heard. He should await the time when he has both experience and familiarity with the issues and the procedures, personalities, and politics of committee decision making. Table 6.5 enables us to look back and see if those patterns did in fact hold and compare them with a contemporary congress in which the norm was no longer acknowledged. Specifically, the table presents identical data from the two congresses on how

12. An ancillary benefit of this reconstruction is that it allowed a reliability check on the exclusively minute-based measure of markup participation. The latter measure correlated with the original, transcript-enhanced measure at .96. I thus can confidently assume that the participation measure adapted to the data available in the older committee minutes does not miss much. (It also implies that future students of legislative participation can do less labor-intensive data collection and not miss much.)

Table 6.4 Profile of House Education and Labor Committee, Two Decades Divided

Committee Statistic	87th Congress (1961–62)	97th Congress (1981–82)
Number of members	31	29
Party ratio (% minority)	.39	.38
Number of freshmen	6	5
Number of new transfers	2	0
Median years in house — nonfreshmen	8	7
Number of subcommittees	6	7
Median subcommittee size	7	8

Note: Statistics from the 87th Congress are based on full population of committee members who served for the entire congress. Statistics from the 97th Congress are based on a dense, stratified sample of members — 29 of 33 — who served for the entire congress.

frequently juniors and seniors appeared at committee business meetings and proportionately how much they spoke.

Depending on how one translates the older accounts of apprenticeship into behavioral hypotheses, the first row of table 6.5 is consistent with the sociological thesis regarding the prereform Congress. Freshmen attended committee markups just as often as their senior colleagues. But if one takes the admonition to mean that increasing seniority gives members greater latitude in choosing not to attend, then one ought to expect freshmen to attend more often than their senior colleagues in 87th Congress. This is not the case.

When one compares the attendance patterns of the two groups for the two congresses, however, evidence of the reputed decline in the prescriptive apprenticeship norm does appear. If freshmen during the prereform Congress were seen as often as their senior colleagues in 1961–62, they were far more likely to be truant at committee markups two decades later. Insofar as "being seen" goes, in sum, the comparative bivariate analysis suggests that the group apprenticeship norm of yesteryear may have existed and may well have had some behavioral effect.

However, no stronger behavioral evidence appears for the complementary admonition — that of not being heard — in the earlier than in the later congress. Indeed, junior and senior members' average share of markup speaking references appears almost identical. In both congresses freshmen participated in the markup debate far less than nonfreshmen, but freshmen were heard just as much in the 87th Congress, when the admonition to be silent was reputedly alive, as in the 97th, when it was indisputably dead.

In sum, a cross-congress comparison of attendance and speaking behavior

Table 6.5   *Freshmen Seen and Not Heard? The Education and Labor Committee a Decade Before and a Decade After Democratic Reforms*

	87th Congress (1961–62)		97th Congress (1981–82)	
	Freshmen (19%) %	Nonfreshmen (81%) %	Freshmen (17%) %	Nonfreshmen (83%) %
Average markup attendance	75	76	57	73
Average share of markup speeches per member	.7	3.8	.7	4.0
Number of observations	150	623	85	408

Source: Minutes of House Education and Labor Committee markups, 87th Congress (25 bills, 31 members); minutes of House Education and Labor Committee markups, 97th Congress (17 bills, 29 members).

provides at best mixed support for the view that much has changed with respect to apprenticeship. For good reasons already elaborated, however, the bivariate comparisons are limited in what they can tell us. Such comparisons are what the participant-observer may be able to make, but I have identified numerous other factors that confound the inferences one can make from bivariate analysis. In adapting the model of committee participation to the historical data, I apply the appropriate multivariate controls. Table 6.6 presents the results of the model for member attendance in the two congresses.

The multivariate analysis saves us from an incorrect inference suggested by table 6.5. Other things being equal, freshman status actually diminished committee attendance in the 87th Congress, even controlling for committee seniority, the coefficient on which is, predictably, negative. In fact, freshman status diminished markup attendance about as much as full-committee chair, subcommittee chair, and subcommittee membership increased it. Properly embedded in a more fully specified model of participation, then, the otherwise noteworthy bivariate evidence that freshmen were frequently "seen" cannot be interpreted to suggest that anything having to do with freshman status was responsible.

The second column of table 6.6 reports the estimates of the identical model of committee markup attendance for the 97th Congress. The patterns of behavioral effects are surprisingly similar. Freshman status per se causes a member to be seen less, even as increasing committee seniority does the same. As I have noted before, a negative coefficient on freshman status is not what one should expect, given the widely acknowledged demise of the apprenticeship norm well before the early 1980s.

Table 6.6 Being Seen: Multivariate Analyses of Education and Labor Markup Attendance, Pre- and Postreform

	87th Congress (1961–62)	97th Congress (1981–82)
Intercept	.73*** (.02)	.26*** (.08)
Marginality	.19*** (.04)	−.04 (.05)
Institutional position		
Full-committee chair	.11* (.07)	.65*** (.12)
Ranking full-committee member	−.14** (.08)	.29*** (.13)
Subcommittee chair	.15** (.08)	.40*** (.11)
Ranking subcommittee member	.04 (.08)	.12 (.11)
Subcommittee member	.09*** (.04)	.05* (.04)
Minority party member	−.15*** (.03)	.31*** (.07)
Seniority/status		
Committee seniority	−.32*** (.12)	−.46*** (.12)
Freshman status	−.11** (.05)	−.26*** (.07)
New transfer	−.06* (.04)	—
Chair, other subcommittee	.24*** (.08)	.11** (.06)
Adjusted R^2	.13	.12

Source: Minutes of House Education and Labor Committee markups, 87th Congress (25 bills, 31 members); minutes of House Education and Labor Committee markups, 97th Congress (17 bills, 29 members).

Note: Entries are OLS coefficients. Standard errors appear in parentheses. The number of observations, by Congress, was as follows: 87th Congress, 773; 97th Congress, 493.

*Statistically significant at .10, one-tailed test. **Statistically significant at .05, one-tailed test. ***Statistically significant at .01, one-tailed test.

Similarly revealing are the comparisons available in table 6.7, which estimates the same model using percentage of speaking references as the dependent variable. Freshman status caused members of the 87th Congress to be seen relatively less, not more, but the evidence does *not* suggest that their status made them less likely to be heard in markup debate, as the prescriptive apprenticeship norm would predict. Again, the result is similar to that of the postapprenticeship congress. In sum, freshmen were seen less but heard as much as nonfreshmen in both eras, patterns that perfectly contradict the predictions of the literature on institutional change.

THE DETERMINANTS OF COMMITTEE PARTICIPATION
TWO DECADES APART

To this point in the cross-congress analysis, I have analyzed only two specific types of markup activity — attendance and speaking. Such analysis

Table 6.7   *Being Heard: Multivariate Analyses of Speaking in Education and Labor Markup Debates, Pre- and Postreform*

	87th Congress (1961–62)		97th Congress (1981–82)	
Intercept	.21***	(.00)	.03***	(.01)
Marginality	−.01	(.01)	.00	(.01)
Institutional position				
Full-committee chair	.06***	(.01)	.11***	(.02)
Ranking full-committee member	.01	(.02)	.16***	(.02)
Subcommittee chair	.25***	(.02)	.26***	(.01)
Ranking subcommittee member	−.01	(.01)	.07***	(.02)
Subcommittee member	.02***	(.01)	.03***	(.01)
Minority party member	.00	(.00)	−.00	(.01)
Seniority/status				
Committee seniority	−.01	(.02)	.02*	(.02)
Freshman status	−.01	(.01)	−.01	(.01)
New transfer	−.00	(.01)		—
Chair, other subcommittee	−.00	(.01)	−.01	(.01)
Adjusted R²		.39		.58

Source: Minutes of House Education and Labor Committee markups, 87th Congress (25 bills, 31 members); minutes of House Education and Labor Committee markups, 97th Congress (17 bills, 29 members).

Note: Entries are OLS coefficients. Standard errors appear in parentheses. The number of observations, by congress, was as follows: 87th Congress, 773; 97th Congress, 493.

*Statistically significant at 1.0, one-tailed test. **Statistically significant at .05, one-tailed test. ***Statistically significant at .01, one-tailed test.

was appropriate and revealing in light of the prescription that apprentices should be seen but not heard, but it limited our view of the full range of activities in which committee members may engage. It was also less appropriate for examining sociological hypotheses other than those related to apprenticeship. In this section I reestimate the model using a broader scale participation in markup.

Rational Apprenticeship in Different Eras

The results of this analysis are reported in table 6.8, where I present estimates of two slightly different models. The estimates of Model 1 appear far more similar across the two congresses than one could reasonably expect. On a scale that captures the full range of possible markup activities, freshman status has a negative and highly significant effect in both the prereform and postreform periods. If apprenticeship once had a prescriptive as well as a rational dimension to it, moreover, one should expect to see a discernibly

Table 6.8   Were Presciptive Norms Ever Potent? Multivariate Analyses of Education and Labor Markup Participation, Pre- and Postreform

	87th Congress (1961–62)		97th Congress (1981–82)	
	Model 1	Model 2	Model 1	Model 2
Intercept	.35*** (.02)	.35*** (.02)	.27*** (.07)	.27*** (.07)
Marginality	.04* (.03)	—	.01 (.04)	—
Marginality, year 1	—	.10*** (.04)	—	.11** (.06)
Marginality, year 2	—	−.02 (.04)	—	−.07* (.05)
Institutional position				
Full-committee chair	.24*** (.05)	.24*** (.05)	.43*** (.10)	.43*** (.10)
Ranking full-committee member	−.03 (.06)	−.03 (.06)	.27*** (.10)	.27*** (.01)
Subcommittee chair	.51*** (.06)	.52*** (.06)	.54*** (.08)	.53*** (.08)
Ranking subcommittee member	.02 (.06)	.03 (.06)	.30*** (.08)	.30*** (.09)
Subcommittee member	.11*** (.03)	.10*** (.03)	.12*** (.02)	.13*** (.05)
Minority party	.01 (.02)	.00 (.02)	.02 (.05)	.02 (.05)
Seniority/status				
Committee seniority	.04 (.09)	.09 (.09)	.07 (.09)	.07 (.09)
Freshman status	−.15*** (.04)	—	−.13*** (.05)	—
Freshman status, year 1	—	−.15*** (.05)	—	−.12** (.08)
Freshman status, year 2	—	−.14*** (.05)	—	−.07** (.03)
New transfer	−.15*** (.05)	−.12** (.08)	—	—
Chair, other subcommittee	.09* (.06)	.09* (.06)	−.04 (.05)	−.04 (.05)
Number of Observations	773	773	493	493
Adjusted R²	.21	.21	.25	.25

Source: Minutes of House Education and Labor Committee markups, 87th Congress (25 bills, 31 members); minutes of House Education and Labor Committee markups, 97th Congress (17 bills, 29 members).

Note: Entries are OLS coefficients. Standard errors appear in parentheses.

*Statistically significant at .10, one-tailed test. **Statistically significant at .05, one-tailed test. ***Statistically significant at .01, one-tailed test.

larger negative effect in the earlier relative to the later period. But that is not what we find. In both congresses, freshman status pushes a member downward approximately one-seventh along the formal participation scale.

Model 2 is identical to Model 1 except that I separate the effects of freshman status and electoral marginality into their first- and second-year effects. The purpose here is to test a corollary hypothesis associated with the sociological account of apprenticeship. According to this account, norms exist as part of the multifaceted nature of a group's unwritten social order, which the newcomer comes to understand during his early experiences in the group. Socialization or learning must take place with respect to the relevant group expectations (see Asher 1975), and this learning occurs over time. It is not as though a single admonition from a senior member on the first day of the congress magically causes a freshman to know his place and keep it. To the contrary, the newly elected member may be unusually eager to enter the mix, but during his first months on the job, the sociological story goes, he learns from his experience — perhaps from repetition of the norm; perhaps from scowls, frowns, or raised eyebrows; perhaps from various sorts of sanctions, such as finding himself either ignored or explicitly repudiated on some legislative matter or request. If the sociological account of apprenticeship is correct, then, the negative effect of freshman status ought to be stronger in the member's second year, after the appropriate socialization would have taken place. The newcomer may be overly eager (from his elders' point of view) in early committee deliberations, but by the second year he certainly should have learned his place in the social order.

Once again, the analysis suggests that this is not the case. In the prereform congress, the negative effect of freshman status in the second year is almost identical to that in the first. Indeed, the coefficient estimate for year two is slightly smaller, not larger, than for year one. So too in the analysis of the 97th Congress. Freshman status is negative and statistically significant for both the first and second year of the congress, but the coefficient's size is smaller in the second year. Hence, for neither the postreform nor the prereform congress do we find evidence of a socialization period during which the apprenticeship norm is learned.

At the same time, the results from both congresses suggest that a different type of learning does take place. It is not learning about the "group life," as Matthews (1960) or Fenno in his early work (1962, 1966) put it. Rather, as members spend time on the committee, they develop political networks and gain greater policy-related knowledge, and their transaction and information costs come to approximate those of their more experienced colleagues. According to this account, the negative effect of freshman status should gradually decline over time, in line with what we see in table 6.8.

Rational Specialization in Different Eras

The evidence for a prescriptive dimension to specialization, even in the prereform congress, is likewise thin. In both congresses, members do concentrate on a fairly narrow range of issues, but there is no evidence that members concentrate more narrowly in the earlier period and branch out more in the latter. In the 97th Congress, the typical member could be counted an active player on approximately one-fourth of the bills in the sample, a ratio that closely approximates that of the 87th Congress. More noteworthy, table 6.8 exhibits an uncanny consistency regarding the participation of subcommittee members in the two different periods. Members of the reporting subcommittees in both congresses tended to participate more in the full-committee deliberations. So far as these data reveal, committee members of the earlier period concentrated their energies no more in domains of their comparative advantage than did their postreform colleagues. So too do we find that the subcommittee chair position pushes a member approximately halfway along the formal participation scale in both congresses, and in both congresses, the behavioral effect of a subcommittee chair position is noticeably greater than that of full-committee chair.

The only significant, subcommittee-relevant difference evident in table 6.8 involves the participation of ranking subcommittee minority members. Once minority status itself was controlled for, these were relatively resource-rich positions in committee decision making, in both the 87th and 97th Congresses. But evidence of such advantage appears only in the latter period, a pattern that is mirrored by the contrasting coefficients of the full-committee ranking member across the two congresses. Does this suggest that something like a specialization norm is actually stronger, not weaker, in the later congress? Probably not. Again, norm-speak about hard work and specialization is no more on the lips of the contemporary House member than it is with apprenticeship. (If anything, the newcomer is more likely to consider committee elders presumptuous should they tell him to concentrate on only a few issues and to work hard.) And majority grants of staff and budget to the minority only increased over the period spanning these two congresses.

Still, there is certainly no greater and maybe somewhat less evidence that classic specialization operates in the prereform period. A more definitive test would require not simply more and better data (to allow us to disentangle the narrowness of participation from expertise) but also a clearer definition of specialization implied by the older sociological theory.

DEFERENCE AND RATIONAL ABDICATION IN DIFFERENT ERAS

Perhaps the best operational definition of deference one can distill is noninterference in the niche that has been rightfully claimed by another. Members of the group have been socialized over time to accept this definition. In the committee context, the clearest hypothesis one can derive is that a subcommittee chair will go out of his way to forgo activism on bills reported from subcommittees on which he does not sit and will expect that other subcommittee chairs do the same.

If anything, the results of table 6.8 suggest that deference appears greater in the normless 97th than the socially structured 87th. Chairs of subcommittees other than the one reporting a bill tended to participate slightly more at the full-committee stage during the Education and Labor markups of 1961–62, ceteris paribus. In contrast, such chairs were slightly less likely to participate in the committee markups held during 1981–82. But on the whole, there is little difference in the results when we compare the two congresses. If a traditional norm of deference operated among fellow chairs in the earlier congress, it operated too in the later congress, at a time when no such norm was recognized by the participants themselves.[13] But the best inference is that it operated in neither.

Of course, it remains possible that group prescriptions did — at some point in time on some committees — make a behavioral difference. But at the very least, this section has accomplished two things. First, it provides conceptual distinctions and a behavioral model with which to empirically assess (rather than passively accept) the received wisdom that a different sort of theory is needed to understand members' behavior in pre- versus postreform eras. Second, it provides systematic evidence that the sociological explanations in vogue three decades ago are theoretically misguided, not simply dated. Reports of the life of prescriptive norms now appear premature, to invert and paraphrase Mark Twain's remark. In contrast, the cumulative weight of what Twain would refer to as "facts and figures" suggests that the optimization theory elaborated here does the better explanatory work, in diverse policy domains and legislative eras.

Conclusion

The data of this chapter have provided a rich basis for investigating the several hypotheses implied by the optimization theory of participation: some eighteen hundred observations of member participation, measured in both formal and informal forums, drawn from some sixty bills considered by three committees in the postreform period. To this I added comparable historical data from one committee, consisting of some eight hundred observations

---

13. To clarify, I do not suggest that mutually beneficial noninterference pacts are not worked out between subcommittee chairs. Rather, I want to point out that such agreements are more likely to be the product of ad hoc negotiation than of some collective understanding that a member should not violate territorial imperatives recognized by the group. More probable still is that noninterference among fellow chairs reveals rational abdication, where subcommittee chairs concentrate on their own business because they have scarce resources to extend their efforts into other panels' domains. See Chapter 9.

drawn from a sample of twenty-five bills that were marked up in the early 1960s. The combination provides analytical leverage of several sorts and suggests several important conclusions.

First, members and leaders of reporting subcommittees are far more likely to voice their views and take action on them than are other committee members. However, these behavioral patterns do not imply that something like a formal division of labor operates in the U.S. House. Subcommittee members are largely self-selected, not assigned. And even among subcommittee members, participation is highly selective at every stage of play. For those who do participate, in turn, much of their effort is driven by their own calculations of interest, not an institutionally sanctioned allocation of tasks. If collective burdens fall anywhere, they are concentrated on members who chair the reporting subcommittees. Other formal leaders tend to be far more active as well, but the most plausible inference is that such tendencies follow from the staff subsidies and procedural prerogatives that defray information and transaction costs and enhance expectations of efficacy. While such benefits are in some sense institutionally provided, it is also true that they can be selectively deployed by the beneficiary.

Second, the results of the committee-level analysis confirm the earlier conclusion regarding subcommittees that legislative participation is not only purposive but that an array of individual purposes are at work. At the stage of full-committee action, differently positioned individuals tend to participate because they want to, and what they variously want is to serve district interests (service that presumably enhances their reelection chances), pursue personal policy interests or ideological agendas, or promote the agenda of a president from their own party.

Third, the comparative analysis of participation on House Education and Labor pre- and postreform provides clear and consistent evidence that the older sociological take on member participation is not simply dated. In the glare of systematic analysis, we find that it did not work well even at the time it was first applied. Theorists of legislative behavior should retain the concepts of apprenticeship and specialization, but as vessels into which we must pour new theoretical meaning. Apprenticeship and specialization both represent sets of identifiable constraints, unrelated to the expectations of the group, that affect the rational calculations of autonomous legislators about how to invest their time and legislative resources. Ideas about the deference reputedly paid those who rank high in the group social order should probably be dropped from theory on legislative behavior, regardless of the era under study.

7

Going to the Floor

In both chambers members now look to the floor as an avenue for pursuing their legislative interests far more frequently than they did in the 1950s. — Steven S. Smith, "Why Don't We Do It on the Floor?"

With good warrant, I have focused in the foregoing chapters on legislators' participation in the committees and subcommittees of jurisdiction. As scholars at least since Woodrow Wilson have noted, the United States Congress is distinctly different from most parliamentary assemblies in the policy-making importance of its committees. At the same time, however, action on the House floor is much more than symbolic action or mere ratification, much more than Congress on exhibition, as Wilson put it. Historically, some of the most important and most hotly contested issues have been decided there. If anything, the importance of the floor as an arena of substantive policy making has only increased over the past three decades, a trend documented in Steven Smith's well-known essay "Why Don't We Do It on the Floor?" (Smith 1989), and that continued into the mid-1990s. This is an important trend, to be sure. If a wide range of views, values, and interests is to find full expression in the legislative deliberations of the chamber, the floor is the ideal place for that to occur.

In this chapter I thus focus on members' involvement in decision making on the floor. As legislation moves from committee to the floor, who participates and why? What determines the character of the legislative deliberations there? To what extent, for instance, is floor action committee-centered, as Wilson suggested a century ago, or even subcommittee-centered, as postreform scholars have asserted? In an effort to address these questions, I adopt the theoretical perspective to understanding participation in committee and subcommittee that I have applied in the previous chapters. I begin by exploring the practical limits that a House member faces as she contemplates floor action on bills beyond the scope of her own committees. Focusing on six bills from three committees, I then explore the behavioral consequences of those limits. Participation on the floor, not surprisingly, is far more selective than in House committees, and I briefly explore the extent to which members of the originating panels dominate deliberations at this stage. In the fourth and fifth sections, I adapt the model of participation to floor decision making under an open rule and hence to a larger and more diverse population of actors who are formally eligible to participate.

Why Don't *Members Do It on the Floor?*

In one sense, the House floor fulfills the politician's fondest dream. Issues of every sort are taken up there, issues great and small, issues that affect the public welfare or private interests in important ways, that affect different countries and economies, different states and communities, different industries and employees, and different categories of people about which the member might especially care. Issues of rights, justice, fairness, freedom, equality, efficiency, and morality are variously evident, if sometimes under the surface, in the legislative measures that are considered there. And the floor provides the member with a highly visible (often televised) location in which to take up such issues, perhaps even to affect the final shape of legislation written to address them.

At the same time, given the range and number of measures that Congress takes up each year, the sweep of legislative action appears to most members as a blur, sounds to them something like a Doppler-effect din. "What did we do [in the last session]?" one member commented to me. "Give me a day or two and I might remember something we did last week." One staffer's remarks about her boss echoed the same theme: "Ask him what's on the floor today, he'll pull out his 3 by 5 [card with his daily schedule]. . . . Ask him what was on the floor yesterday or last week and he wouldn't be able to tell you. . . . That's really not fair — he could tell you the three or four major bills that have come up, but I doubt that he could remember half of the bills he's voted on, what they were about. . . ." More telling is John Kingdon's summary (1989, 231) of his in-depth interviews with House members regarding action on the House floor, interviews that were generally conducted within a week of the floor action in question:

> When asked if he was satisfied with the tax reform package, for instance, one congressman replied, "I told you, I don't know what's in the bill." Another, when asked about the supplemental appropriations bill, replied, "I voted for it, didn't I? Frankly, I don't remember much about it." Another admitted with

regard to as high-visibility a vote as the surtax extension bill, "I didn't know what was in the bill. It was as simple as that." I encountered another congress-man, a member of the committee that reported the bill, who had not the foggiest notion of what he had voted on the day before, and was reading the previous day's *Congressional Record* to find out what had happened. He even confused William Scherle (Republican from Iowa) with Shirley Chisholm (Democrat from New York) when asked about the "Scherle amendment," because their names are pronounced similarly.

However disquieting such reports might be to the idealist of informed delib-eration, the causes of such patterns have little to do with member indolence, incompetence, or irresponsibility. They reflect the simple, unsatisfying fact that members are continually confronted with too many issues on which there is too much to know, too much to do, and too little time to learn to do it.[1] We have already noted the substantial limits on a member's capacity to participate in the much smaller and more specialized set of issues that fall within the jurisdiction of the one or two major committees to which she holds assign-ment. Such limits are even greater when the member's participation choices involve the plethora of issues that come up for action on the House floor.

Indeed, the above quotations focus on the difficulty for a member to do well in what is perhaps the simplest, least time-consuming form of participation — casting a yea or nay in a formal roll call. Any participation beyond the simple act of voting requires considerably more effort. To become a serious and significant player in the floor action on a bill requires a substantial mobiliza-tion of staff and a serious commitment of time and energy. Observed one member three decades ago: "I don't believe there is any man in the House who can do a really effective legislative job on more than two bills in a year. If you do that you have a full-time job. This implies that you know reasonably well the position of each of the other members on the bill and the important amendments that may be proposed, and that is an incredibly time-consuming job. I am frustrated because I can only work on a couple of bills a year. The legislative process could absorb all our time and still cause frustration" (quoted in Clapp 1963, 120).

Speaking three decades later, a former House member described the con-straints he faced in taking action on the Senate floor: "It takes a lot to partici-pate on the floor. I noticed today that [P] offered a couple of very good amend-ments to the Hunger Relief Bill today. I would have liked to have been in there too. But that takes a lot of work, a lot of man hours, a lot of my time. I just can't do it most of the time. Most of the bills that go through down there, I

---

1. See Kingdon's discussion of such constraints as they relate to the information searches that typically accompany members' roll call voting decisions (1989, chap. 9.)

hate to admit it, I don't even know what they're about. God help me if anybody asks me and expects an intelligent answer."

In sum, members must make hard choices about going to the floor, choices constrained by the limits on the member's time and made with an eye to the almost infinite range of alternative opportunities for legislative and extralegislative action. The first and least surprising generalization one might make about participation on the House floor is that it is highly selective, if not very infrequent. For those legislative issues that come up for floor consideration, the group of representatives that can be counted as significant players is typically small in number and variable in composition — patterns readily apparent to the occasional visitor to the House gallery but altogether unexplained by students of legislative behavior.

Who Goes to the Floor? Six Bills from Three Committees

The investigation of floor participation in this chapter focuses on six bills from the sample of sixty analyzed in the preceding pages. The bills are briefly summarized in table 7.1. To be sure, this is a limited empirical focus — one forced upon me by the practical problems associated with data collection for 435 observations per case — and I make no claim that the cases are representative along all of the relevant dimensions. But the bills do capture variation relevant to several themes that have proven important thus far in the investigation. Two each were taken from the samples of the three committees, and each from a different subcommittee. For each committee, one bill counted as one of the most important that it reported in that congress, the other bill one of the least. Within Agriculture's jurisdiction, the dairy provisions constituted one of the two most important titles of the 1981 Farm Bill; once in place, they cost the federal government $2.6 billion in the first full marketing year, approximately $13,000 per dairy farmer, making it one of the three most expensive programs administered by the Department of Agriculture (U.S. Department of Agriculture 1984a, 22–23). In Education and Labor, the Job Training Partnership Act was to be a $5 billion initiative, replacing the most important public employment training program of the 1970s at a time when structural unemployment was reaching postwar highs. And the Commerce Committee's Universal Telephone Preservation Act involved a major effort on the part of Congress to regulate the continuing effects of the divestiture of AT&T. At stake were important protections for communications industry employees, the distribution of perhaps $25 billion in long distance costs across different categories of users, and the availability of basic telephone service for low-income households (House Committee on Energy and Commerce 1983b).

Table 7.1   Six Bills from Three Committees

Committee	Bill and Major Provisions
Agriculture	**HR3286: Peanuts Title, 1981 Omnibus Farm Bill** Major provisions: Extend the existing pricing and production system for peanuts; increase the minimum price support level from $420 to $600 per ton; decrease the poundage quotas from 1.44 million to 1.3 million tons; permit growers to carry forward their marketing quotas for succeeding years. *Subcommittee: Tobacco and Peanuts.* **HR2401: Dairy Title, 1981 Omnibus Farm Bill** Major provisions: Reauthorize system of federal milk marketing orders and the existing dairy price program; restrict budget-driven reductions in the support price to 75 percent of parity. *Subcommittee: Livestock, Dairy, and Poultry*
Education and Labor	**HR3046: Older Americans Amendments of 1981** Major provisions: Reauthorize the Older Americans Act for two years at successively higher levels; add education and training to the objectives of the act; establish level of commodity assistance at thirty cents per meal, adjusted for changes in the Consumer Price Index. *Subcommittee: Human Resources* **HR5320: Job Training Partnership Act of 1982** Major provisions: Replace the expiring Comprehensive Employment and Training Act (CETA) with a public-private system for training structurally unemployed workers; reauthorize the Job Corps; reauthorize employment programs for Native Americans, youth, veterans, and migrant farmworkers. *Subcommittee: Employment Opportunities*
Energy and Commerce	**HR2615: Weatherization and Employment Act of 1983** Major provisions: Authorize $500 million per year for the low-income weatherization program; create employment and training opportunities in weatherization; require Department of Energy to devise a ten-year implementation plan for weatherizing thirteen million homes. *Subcommittee: Energy Conservation and Power* **HR4102: Universal Telephone Service Preservation Act of 1983** Major provisions: Require all long-distance companies and customers to contribute to local system maintenance; reverse FCC access charge decision; create lifeline rates for low-income customers; establish Universal Service Fund to ensure telephone access in high-cost rural areas. *Subcommittee: Telecommunications, Consumer Protection, and Finance*

Source: Reports of the House Committees on Agriculture, Education and Labor, and Energy and Commerce, and interviews with committee staff. (See Appendix F.)

While the other three bills were hardly trivial, by comparison they were significantly more modest in scope and impact. The peanuts title of the 1981 Farm Bill dealt with federal programs concerning a single crop, one that is produced in only eleven states at that, for which federal outlays averaged approximately $40 million per year (U.S. Department of Agriculture 1984b, 16). The Older Americans amendments dealt with programs affecting a large number of low- to middle-income elderly in almost every congressional district, but the 1981 act consisted mostly of a straight reauthorization of existing law, with little in the way of program expansions or modifications. Finally, the principal purpose of the Commerce Committee's weatherization bill was to reauthorize a preexisting program, the Low-Income Weatherization Program, while increasing the authorization levels by approximately $500 million.

The data collected on floor participation for these six bills are analogous to the formal participation data collected for the committee and subcommittee level (see Appendix F). From the transcripts of the floor action published in the *Congressional Record,* I collected for each bill data on (1) whether each member participated in one or more roll call votes (either in person or in parliamentary pairs); (2) whether and to what extent each member participated in the floor debate, with participation ranging from simple insertions into the *Record* to major dialogues with other floor actors; (3) whether a member engaged in any parliamentary maneuvers on the floor or offered any technical amendments to the floor vehicle; (4) whether the member offered or coauthored any substantive first or second degree amendments; and (5) whether the member engaged in any significant agenda action, by participating in the debate over the special rule governing floor consideration, by (co)authoring the floor vehicle, or by (co)authoring an amendment in the nature of a substitute to it.

On the basis of the data from these six bills, how extensive is member involvement in floor decision making? On the floor, as in committee, the answer to this question depends in part on the specific activity one has in mind. Participation on roll call votes for these six bills was uniformly high. Between 88 and 95 percent of House members participated in person in every recorded vote that was held on the respective bills — rates that are consistent with the overall voting participation statistics for the past two decades. But once one examines other, more demanding forms of participation, the number of members involved drops off quickly. On average, approximately 15 percent of House members did something more than insert their cards at an electronic voting station.

Participation rates were especially low for amending activity, despite the fact that all six bills were considered under an open rule.[2] The percentage of members who engaged in this important activity was tallied for each bill, credit being given to any member who (1) authored any kind of amendment or procedural motion; (2) coauthored any amendment or motion; or (3) was mentioned in any speech in the *Congressional Record* or committee records as having helped develop the amendment. Amending is thus based on a generous coding scheme, yet less than 5 percent of the members counted as authors or coauthors of a floor amendment. And on the basis of similarly generous coding rules, in no case did as many as six members, alone or in concert, make significant attempts to cast or recast the agenda defined by the legislative vehicle before the chamber (see Appendixes B and F).

In sum, while it may be true that floor activity increased during the 1970s and 1980s, participation is anything but broad, and decision making is anything but "collegial."[3] Indeed, to make much of such trends is to emphasize modest changes in the time series that have not significantly altered a robust regularity of the cross-section. Even when highly salient and controversial issues are taken up under an open rule, a relatively small (but changing) contingent is largely responsible for the legislative action that occurs on the House floor. The vast majority of members react to the agenda set by these few and the signals that they provide. It thus becomes a matter of some importance to understand who participates at this stage, to what extent, and why.

The Committee on the Floor

Both casual observation and systematic evidence suggest that once bills leave the exclusive confines of the committee room, committee membership provides an important point of departure for any attempt to understand subsequent participation. Committee and subcommittee members constitute a disproportionate share of those who express their views, give cues, offer amendments, and maneuver on the floor. The floor managers of legislation, for instance, are almost always the ranking members of the committee or subcommittee of jurisdiction (Deering 1982; Shepsle and Weingast 1987a). In

2. On the substantive and strategic importance of amending action on the floor, see especially Krehbiel 1991; Smith 1989; Weingast 1989.

3. The term is Smith's and refers to an ideal type of decision making characterized by egalitarian norms and widespread participation by the House membership on the floor. Smith may be right that the glass of participation has become fuller over time, but it is still about 90 percent empty. See Smith 1989, chap. 1.

addition, Smith (1989) finds that committee members are disproportionately responsible for the amendments offered on the floor, even in the latter days of the postreform period. The average committee comprises approximately 9 percent of the House membership, yet the percentage of House floor amendments sponsored by members sitting on the committee of jurisdiction has consistently averaged about 50 percent over several decades. Such findings led Smith to emphasize the "structuring effects" of committee and subcommittee position (1989, chapters 5 and 6).

Such patterns correspond to the parts played by subcommittee members, committee members, members of related panels, and committee nonmembers in the six bills described above. Voting tends to be very nearly universal regardless of institutional position, but in every legislative activity that requires something more than a momentary visit to an electronic voting station, committee members are far more likely to participate. Among committee members, in turn, members of the reporting subcommittee are even more likely to play the lead in debate on the floor and in procedural maneuvers, amending activity, and agenda action. For the six bills analyzed here, at least one in two subcommittee members occupied center stage at some point in the floor deliberations, while at most one in twelve subcommittee nonmembers so much as achieved recognition from the chair.

Such results, of course, are consistent with the general account of legislative participation articulated in Chapter 3 and applied to the study of committee participation in the last two chapters. The procedural prerogatives and resource advantages that derive from institutional position have been prominent themes up to this point, and the statistical evidence across three committees and sixty bills has been consistent and compelling. It is not surprising, then, that the behavioral importance of those advantages appears when we move to the context of floor politics. For instance, the standing rules of committees and the House give committee and subcommittee leaders special advantages in managing legislation from their panels on the House floor, as well as special access to leadership deliberations over the timing of floor action and the rules that will govern it (Bach and Smith 1988; Kingdon 1989, 86; Oleszek 1984, 148–51).[4]

Probably more important, however, is that by the time that bills reach this stage of the process, the information costs of most panel members have been

---

4. However, there may also be a countervailing tendency against committee members' participating on the floor. Committee members who have been successfully involved at the committee level in, say, getting particular amendments or provisions into the committee report, need not repeat the effort on the chamber floor.

largely paid; the "spade work has been done," as one staffer put it. They are more likely to be the ones who "have sat through the hearings and are acquainted with the legislation" and who know what's at stake politically (Kingdon 1989, 85). By comparison, the average backbencher comes to the floor knowing almost nothing about the minor bills that are up for consideration and typically is ignorant of the details of even the most salient (Kingdon 1989, 96–99). Hence, as another of Kingdon's respondents commented, "You always turn to someone on the committee for information" (Kingdon 1989, 85). Kingdon also found that the alternatives that came up for floor consideration were often prefigured by prior committee deliberations. At the moment of decision on the House floor, the actions and cues of committee members figure prominently as representatives file in and decide how to vote. Kingdon quotes one member regarding the importance of even short speeches made by committee colleagues during the debate, "Their five minutes represents months of study and work" (1989, 86; see also 85–88, 140–41).

To a lesser extent, the informational advantages attributable to membership on the committee of official jurisdiction should also extend to members of panels that deal with closely related policy concerns. Such members may benefit from none of the parliamentary prerogatives enjoyed by the reporting panel, but they should be more likely than the typical backbencher to come to the floor with a plentiful supply of political and policy-related information and an experienced staff to assist them in assessing floor options and formulating an optimal strategy. Members of the House Appropriations subcommittee ultimately charged with funding the program whose authorization is the subject of a bill should fall into this category. Some select committees and standing subcommittees enjoy no formal legislative jurisdiction over the bill under consideration on the floor but provide exposure to closely related matters and programs. To be sure, such exposure should not prove as valuable as that provided by the committee of jurisdiction; as Kingdon concluded, members look for information and leadership on the floor "not just from someone who knows a given field in general, but also from someone who knows the specific piece of legislation," and "such a person is most likely to be sitting on the committee" (1989, 87). Still, membership on a related panel should give a member a comparative advantage vis-à-vis the typical committee nonmember.

Although disparities in panel participation may appear between members and nonmembers, however, strong conclusions about the "structuring effects" of panel membership are almost certainly premature. The principal problem in drawing inferences from such patterns is one we have faced before. While formally bestowed institutional positions provide important parliamentary rights and resources to the member, they also reflect the member's legislative interests. As Shepsle (1978) has shown for committees and I have shown for subcommittees, the assignment process in Congress tends to match members' institutional positions to their political interests, especially over the course of two or more congresses. In short, panel membership is but a summary indicator of several theoretically quite different factors that might plausibly affect a member's calculations about whether to become active in legislative action on the House floor. Moving beyond the description of aggregate patterns, I attempt in the following sections to better evaluate the importance of such factors in the context of a more fully specified behavioral model.

A Model of Floor Participation

The general outline of the floor participation model has been mostly anticipated in the preceding chapters. Our task is to explain why some members more than others become active on a given bill when it comes to the floor and, by extension, why one set of members will do so on one bill, and an altogether different set on the next. Adapted to the floor context, then, the basic story is this: the House floor, like the House committee, presents the individual member with a set of ways in which she might use her legislative time and resources to pursue her objectives, something like a set of political investment opportunities. Which ones she chooses, which ones she forgoes, will depend on her estimates regarding their relevance to her various interests and the likely political returns of each; the legislative resources she has to invest by comparison with other actors, and hence her expectations that her investment is likely to achieve the results she seeks; and the information and transaction costs that she will pay — calculations that may vary dramatically member to member and bill to bill.

Each of these abstract factors, of course, is inherently unobservable, but they are related to observable factors that we can identify and measure. As noted in the last section, the information, staff, and other resources available to the member, and the barriers to entry into a particular legislative game, should be directly related to the member's formal positions and memberships — these serve as something like a portfolio of informational and institutional subsidies to her enterprise. Full- and subcommittee leadership positions and membership on the subcommittee of jurisdiction should thus prove important at the floor stage; in addition, full-committee membership and related panel membership warrant attention. The results, in turn, will tell us a good deal about the behavioral importance of legislative organization — the value that we might attribute to the chamber's assignment of special parliamentary rights and resources.

In a similar vein, the House floor, perhaps more than the committee mark-up, is an important place for the practice of opposition politics, where the minority can exercise its right to obstruct, while the majority can exercise parliamentary prerogatives to counter minority tactics. Indeed, the minority's increasing tendency to exploit such opportunities in the early 1980s gave rise to the majority's increasing use of restrictive rules, a tactic about which the minority loudly complained. But even under an open rule, strategic use of agenda power should enable the majority leadership to mitigate opposition activism by favoring legislative vehicles that cross-pressure minority members, while avoiding those which cross-pressure the majority party's own.

Other, older questions of behavioral cause extend to floor politics as well. What of specialization, deference, and apprenticeship at this stage? If specialization of the sort characterized in the earlier sociology of Congress (as well as in latter-day theories of legislative organization) still operates, subcommittee membership should have a strong, independent effect on members' floor presence. Likewise, if the older norm of deference is alive, it should appear in the tendency of committee chairs to stay out of their counterparts' business on other (unrelated) committees.

Finally, the floor under the open rule should provide a somewhat difficult test for the claim advanced in earlier chapters regarding the importance of freshman status. Unlike its reported demise in committee, the death of prescriptive apprenticeship on the floor has been accompanied by a wealth of evidence, even a well-documented coroner's report. "The apprenticeship norm has disappeared," Smith concludes in his comprehensive study of floor politics over four decades. "In both chambers, manifest differences in rates of participation eroded during the 1960s and virtually evaporated in the early 1970s" (1989, 139). Undeterred on theoretical grounds and emboldened by the empirical results of the last two chapters, I stay with the argument advanced in Chapter 3 about the behavioral effects of freshman status. While it may not be now (if ever it was) a vigorous beast, apprenticeship is not dead. Rather, I reiterate, it has been misclassified as a sociological species. And lacking a fully developed model of participation against which to examine it, political scientists have found its vital signs hard to detect.

The task that will occupy us in the following sections, therefore, is formulating a basic behavioral model for floor decision making under an open rule. Unfortunately, matters of measurement become considerably more complicated with 435 observations per case, especially the measurement of the several purposes that proved important for our understanding of participation in committee. The next section takes up such problems with some care. The subsequent section presents and interprets the statistical estimates of the model for the six bills in the floor sample. The main conclusion I will draw is that the behavioral model developed here is a fairly general one, capable of illuminating important features of member behavior at the subcommittee, committee, and floor stage. But at the same time, the comparative-case nature of the floor analysis permits us to explore several issues that the committee analysis did not. In particular, the interests associated with race, ethnicity, gender, and age, as well as the class-based nature of constituency influence, come more clearly into view.

THE PURPOSES OF FLOOR PARTICIPATION
Interests Within the District

In the literature assessing the strength of constituency influence in Congress, the valid measurement of constituents' interests and opinions has been a matter of considerable import. For instance, the original Miller-Stokes study suffered from serious problems of district-level sample size, problems inherent in the survey-based study of a representative system partitioned into 435 member-district dyads. Other studies have relied on general demographic characteristics to capture the interests of the constituencies to which members might respond. Hence, it is sometimes difficult to know what to make of the variously weak or mixed findings of constituency influence that such studies produce. Are they due to a feeble underlying relationship between the member and the constituency? Or are our measures of constituency simply inadequate?

In past chapters, such problems were circumvented by research design. The constituency that a member represents, Fenno has told us, is the constituency that she sees; the interview-based design of the committee analysis permitted us to measure the issue-specific interests of constituencies at the level of members' perceptions. In this chapter, the focus on floor proceedings forces us to revisit the problems that have confronted several generations of legislative scholars. Concentrating on a small number of specific bills, however, makes good measurement more manageable; with a little extra labor, it is possible to tailor a set of constituency indicators closely to the issues under investigation. To the extent that is possible, we should be able to make more confident inferences about the underlying member-district relationship. And we will also be able to explore less abstractly the nature of the constituencies represented.

The indicators I use to tap constituency interests for the six bills in the floor sample are shown in the first column of table 7.2. In the case of the two agriculture bills, the measurement was uncomplicated; if anything, agriculture is probably the policy jurisdiction most likely to be viewed through the lens of the impact that programs have on district economies, so that industry-specific economic data should be reasonably valid. Likewise, both Education and

Labor bills entailed concrete and visible, if highly variable, consequences for district constituents. As I have noted, the Job Training Partnership Act was a major policy initiative, designed as a long-term solution to the problem of structural unemployment at a time when the national rate had reached postwar highs. For members representing areas with large numbers of workers in depressed industries, in particular, employment policy was probably the single most important matter in the 97th Congress. To capture such interests, I use the percentage of district workers unemployed in the previous year for fifteen weeks or more, as measured by the U.S. Census. Although it addressed far less salient issues and was far more modest in its potential economic effects, the reauthorization of the Older Americans Act dealt with programs designed to improve the quality of life for the low-income elderly throughout the country. Low-income elderly citizens are not distributed evenly across congressional districts, however. Thus, they are not likely to have equal importance in different members' electoral constituencies. In order to measure the importance of such programs to district constituents, I use the percentage of individuals in the district over sixty-five who were below the poverty line.

Like the Older Americans Act, the Weatherization Bill expanded a program intended exclusively to assist low-income Americans, through relatively modest home-improvement subsidies. A secondary purpose of the bill was to create new, publicly funded jobs in the housing and insulation industry. The focus on energy conservation and costs, however, meant that the program benefited areas with high heating costs almost exclusively, a theme that was consistently articulated in both the committee report and the floor debate. To accurately capture the importance of the program to particular districts, then, required some simple manipulations of data. I first gathered district-level data on both the poverty and unemployment rates and combined them to create an economic "misery index."[5] I then multiplied the index by the number of heating days in the district in excess of the national mean, as calculated from district climate data. The result is a measure of district interest that is well tailored to the nature of the program. It reflects, first, that the district stake in the weatherization bill is small if energy consumption associated with heating is low — however poor or unemployed the residents of Watts might be, this program is not designed to help them. It reflects, second, that a district's stake in the bill will be slight if poverty and unemployment are low — however high the

5. The combination of the two indicators to create a misery index was necessary because they are so closely related that introducing them separately into the equation created serious problems of multicollinearity. By adding them together, I create an index reflecting that if poverty, unemployment, or both are pervasive in the district, the district stands to gain from this program.

Table 7.2   *District Interests and Members' Policy Backgrounds*

District interest indicator	Policy Background Indicator
Peanuts Title, 1981 Farm Bill	
Peanut Production	Peanut producer
	Consumer advocate
	Director or staffer, consumer affairs agency
	Member, state legislative committee on consumer affairs
Dairy Title, 1981 Farm Bill	
Number of dairy cows	Dairy/livestock producer or owner, dairy products business
	Holder of degree in dairy husbandry
	Consumer advocate
	Director or staffer, consumer affairs agency
	Member, state legislative committee on consumer affairs
Older Americans Act Amendments	
Percent 65 or over in poverty	Administrator, nursing/mental health facility
	Administrator/social worker, human resources agency
	Official, state or local agency on aging
Job Training Partnership Act	
Unemployment rate, fifteen weeks	Labor union leader/labor lawyer
	Official, state manpower/employment agency
	Administrator or teacher, vocational institute
Weatherization and Employment Act	
Economic "misery index" × annual heating days	Social worker
	Member, state energy conservation council
	Official, city or state housing authority
Universal Telephone Preservation Act	
Percentage of rural households	Member, state legislative committee on utility rates
Percentage of communications workers	Member, communications workers' union
Percentage of below the poverty line	Regulator, state utility commission
	Consumer advocate
	Director, consumer affairs or protection agency
	Staffer, state legislative committee on consumer affairs

Note: Entries in the first column are the measure of interest within the district for each bill, based on district-level census data. Entries in the second column are examples of members' bill-relevant policy background, culled from the biographical sketches of House members. The presence of one or more background activities generated a value of one on the relevant bill-specific dichotomous variable for members' personal policy interests.

heating bills of Kennebunkport residents might get, the program is not designed to help them either.

Finally, the Universal Telephone Preservation Act included provisions likely to affect district interests along several very different dimensions. One purpose of the bill was to subsidize service to high-cost rural areas, a purpose that generated considerable attention to the bill's interstate redistributive effects; a second purpose of the bill was to establish a "lifeline" program that would subsidize minimal service to low-income households as local telephone rates and flat access charges rose in the aftermath of the AT&T divestiture; a third purpose was to establish regulations that would protect communications workers affected by divestiture (House Committee on Energy and Commerce 1983b). I attempt to capture each of these interests with the indicators shown in table 7.2.

The interests within the constituency affected by these six bills are thus diverse, important, and variable. Despite the limited empirical focus, we should be in a good position to explore whether members, in setting their legislative priorities and allocating their resources, are likely to register the intensities of very different types of interests within the constituency. That is, we should expect the political interests described above to have a direct, positive effect on members' floor participation.

At the same time, these tendencies should reflect strategic considerations. In particular, the highly visible floor is less likely to provide a good forum for the minority member to pursue constituency interests. Control of the floor agenda is squarely in the hands of the majority, so bills that go to the House floor should be more likely to aid majority than minority electoral constituencies. And in those instances where minority constituents are helped, the minority member is more likely to suffer from the cross-pressures of constituency and party (and perhaps ideology). Should she go to the floor to support or strengthen the legislative package before the House, her expected gain will be less at the margin; should she go to the floor to oppose it, in turn, she stands to do herself political harm. By comparison with the typical majority member, then, the minority member should be more inclined to pursue an issue-avoiding than a credit-seeking strategy when bills come to the floor that are relevant to her district. If the theory is correct, we should see a pattern of consistently negative coefficients on the interactions between minority status and the variables tapping constituency interests.

House Members' Policy Interests

Once one moves beyond matters of district economics and distributive benefits, imputing interests to members becomes increasingly difficult but remains no less important for understanding purposive behavior and its consequences. At the very least, the committee-centered analysis of the previous two chapters suggests that members have different personal policy interests, of differing intensities, for which the floor may provide an excellent forum for meaningful expression and perhaps happy pursuit.

Fenno's interviews suggest that members' policy interests are often related to their previous occupational background or personal experience (1973a, 11), a tendency that was confirmed in my interviews with committee members and their legislative assistants. Absent interviews of my own with members outside the committee of jurisdiction, I thus rely on data coded from members' biographical sketches. The second column of table 7.2 provides examples of the biographical entries that were coded as relevant to each bill. Note that the policy backgrounds coded as relevant vary in nature even for specific bills.[6] For instance, three bills in the sample raised issues of direct relevance to consumers of a product subsidized or regulated by the bill. The background indicators thus reflect whether a member had experience in general matters of consumer protection.

The use of such background information to gauge members' policy interests is, of course, imprecise, in part because of the incomplete and inconsistent nature of members' biographical sketches. Still, these data did permit me to draw rough distinctions between members on the basis of their precongressional interests. More than one-fourth of the House members' biographical entries reflected an interest in at least one of the six bills under study. Those entries provide the basis for a reasonably valid, dichotomous indicator of whether a member was personally interested in the subjects of the six bills.[7] My hypothesis is that this variable should be positively related to a member's floor participation in each case. On the floor, as in committee, the hypothesis of single-minded reelection seeking remains a matter for empirical investigation, not convenient assumption.

Group Identification and Members' Policy Commitments

As the committee interviews hinted as well, personal policy interests and commitments cannot be neatly traced and thus cleanly reduced to members'

---

6. Once again, interest in a bill in itself says nothing about the member's position on it, so I deliberately mean *not* to imply that while active members may be interest-intensity outliers, they are thereby positional or preference outliers.

7. Such variables, I should also note, may tap not only the member's personal policy interests but her knowledge of the policy area as well. Given that many of the major impediments to participation on the various issues that come before the House are informational, previous experience in the area may also reflect the member's lower information costs. In this respect my results reinforce a central theme of Krehbiel 1991. I return to this issue in Chapter 9.

professional and political background. A second set of factors underlying policy interests derives from members' personal identification with particular groups. Probably the most deep-seated of these of these are member race and ethnicity.

The view that her race and ethnicity matter to the representation a legislator will provide is a matter of considerable controversy and substantial importance in both legal and academic quarters. Since the 1962 landmark ruling in *Baker* v. *Carr,* the U.S. Supreme Court has held that legislative reapportionment schemes whose effect is to dilute minority voting strength violate the Equal Protection clause of the Fourteenth Amendment. At stake, the Court ruled, is the abstract principle of democratic consent, embodied in the egalitarian standard of one person, one vote, a principle more clearly codified in the Voting Rights Act of 1965 (VRA). But three decades of reapportionment strategy, legal challenges, and case law have defined the issue in more concrete terms. Rulings have focused on the extent to which the electoral voting strength of minority groups translates directly and effectively into more of their members being elected to legislative seats (Hall and Heflin 1995). In the fight over the 1992 congressional reapportionment, for instance, the explicit goal of such groups as the American Civil Liberties Union, the Mexican American Legal Defense Fund, the NAACP, and the Lawyers' Committee for Civil Rights Under Law was the drawing of congressional district boundaries to increase the number of African-American and Hispanic representatives in the House (Barnes 1991; Cohen 1991). Such groups, in turn, were also active in defending successful reapportionment plans in the wake of *Shaw* v. *Reno,* a 1993 case in which the Supreme Court questioned its own historical support for VRA-sanctioned racial gerrymanders and set the precedent for subsequent Court rejections of such schemes.

Were it the case that the race or ethnicity of the representative mattered little for what she did once elected, of course, such efforts would appear badly misdirected. Yet within the political science literature, considerable evidence indicates that this is precisely the case. The effect of a member's racial or ethnic identification on her roll call voting, for instance, appears mixed or negligible in the majority of studies. In the most prominent and comprehensive study of African Americans in Congress, for instance, Carol Swain (1993) concluded that the substantive representation of black interests in Congress will benefit as much from the election of white Democrats sympathetic to the liberal social agenda of the black community as it will from the election of black candidates per se.

Roll call studies, however, are biased on methodological grounds against finding race- or ethnicity-based differences, should they exist. The simple point is that the very proposals that might distinguish the preferences of white and nonwhite legislators rarely see a roll call vote; such expressions of preference are censored from the sample of observations available for the political scientist to analyze (Hall and Heflin 1995). Perhaps more important to such research, moreover, is the distinction between revealed preferences and revealed intensities. In voting on a censored set of issues, minority members may frequently take positions that appear similar to those of white Democrats from similar districts. But are whites committed to the issues with the same intensity? Are they as willing to invest their scarce time and legislative capital in issues that directly reflect the political interests of the minority communities?

If members of Congress are simply seeking reelection and their behavior is based on rational calculations about how to garner votes, then the white Democrat representing a district with a substantial minority population should act the same as a black one, ceteris paribus. But what the white representative almost certainly lacks is an identification with and hence commitment to the interests of the larger group from which such constituents come. She may well see their electoral strength in her district and respond to it. But she is less likely to see their political weakness beyond her district, born of past discrimination and current underrepresentation in the larger legislature, and try to compensate for it. Stated somewhat differently, the personal identifications of African-American and Hispanic legislators should predispose them to represent their extradistrict constituency, too.

Some evidence for this hypothesis appears in the unity and strength of the Congressional Black Caucus, the expressed purpose of which is to provide a "black perspective" on major legislation moving through Congress (Cohadas 1985b, 676). Other evidence comes from interviews with black representatives describing their role in the House. As Representative Louis Stokes summarized the extradistrict role of the black representative: "We're carrying the load for 25 million black people" (Cohadas 1985a, 675).

But claims about the behavioral importance of race and ethnicity in Congress require more systematic evidence. Up to this point, our investigation of such questions has been limited by our committee-centered focus. Because blacks and Hispanics were already underrepresented in the House and partitioned into committee subsets, the number whose behavior one could study at the committee stage before 1993 was minuscule — in fact, the three committee samples analyzed thus far contained a total of only four blacks and one Hispanic. An additional advantage of turning to participation on the floor in this chapter, then, is that it provides an opportunity to better study the importance of race and ethnicity as indicators of the policy interests and commitments of individual legislators.

Three of the bills in the sample contained provisions that when fully implemented would provide disproportionate benefits for minorities. With a rapidly worsening economic recession in the period under study here, black and Hispanic leaders counted unemployment as the single most important domestic issue before Congress, and both groups stood to be affected in important ways by the declining federal commitment to antipoverty programs during Reagan's first term. The racial and ethnic basis for these concerns is validated by the relevant economic statistics of the period. During the early 1980s, the incidence of unemployment among Hispanics was half again as high as the rate for whites, while the unemployment rate for blacks was twice that of whites. Likewise, the poverty rates for blacks and Hispanics were strikingly higher than for whites, with this gap growing in the early 1980s. Given its billing as the centerpiece of federal employment policy for the next decade, the Job Training Partnership Act should thus evoke the interests of disadvantaged minorities and thereby incite political entrepreneurship on the part of African-American and Hispanic representatives. To a lesser extent, in turn, the universal telephone and weatherization bills were also relevant to the interests of underrepresented minorities. Unlike the job training bill, neither held the potential to significantly affect the long- or short-term financial status of low-income blacks or Hispanics; their program benefits were both smaller and more widely dispersed. But each bill included redistributive provisions; each thus stood to benefit members of underrepresented groups disproportionately.[8]

The argument just advanced about the importance of race and ethnicity in shaping the revealed intensities of House members has its theoretical parallels in questions regarding the behavioral importance of gender (see Kathlene 1994; Thomas 1994) and, to a lesser extent, age. Women, like blacks and Hispanics, are badly underrepresented in the House. In 1980 women counted for more than 50 percent of the population, but in the congressional elections of that year they won only 5 percent of the House seats, and they made only incremental gains through the remainder of the decade. And while women are far more heterogeneous than blacks and Hispanics in their professional background, geographic location, and economic class interests, the emergence of a "gender gap" in public opinion over the past two decades suggests that women

8. For instance, U.S. District Court Judge Harold Greene summarized the effects of the FCC regulation that the universal telephone bill would reverse: "91 percent of all households now have telephones. As the FCC's access fee reaches $7, as it will in a few years, this is estimated to drop to 60 percent for very poor blacks, 65 percent for very poor living in rural areas, and 58 percent for very poor young people. That hardly sounds like universal service" (quoted in the *Congressional Record* 1983, 9644).

as a group hold somewhat different opinions and have somewhat different interests from men. To the extent this is true, women representatives should be more inclined toward entrepreneurial activity on matters that are likely to have distinct consequences for women (Thomas 1994).

This tendency finds expression, too, in the descriptions that women legislators give of their jobs. "Because there are so few women in Congress," Representative Barbara Mikulski observed, "we have a responsibility for representing American women as congressmen at large." Similarly, Republican Representative Claudine Schneider noted that although she had not initially run for Congress as "a champion of women," she had soon taken on that role: "I now feel I have a greater responsibility beyond my district concerning women" (Cohadas 1983, 784).

None of the issues in the sample focused squarely on matters of gender, but several were relevant to the interests of women in significant and discernible ways. Like blacks and Hispanics, women suffer disproportionately from insufficient training or outdated job skills, so that unemployment and poverty among female heads-of-household were considerably higher than among males. Moreover, there was growing attention in this period to findings that traditional countercyclical employment policies, so often geared to stimulating construction and other male-dominated industries, only exacerbated such inequities (Cohadas 1983, 781-83). Hence, the job training, weatherization, and universal telephone bills should have disproportionate importance to individuals who evaluate public policies through the lens of gender. The demographics of age suggest that the Older Americans Act should be of special concern to women as well.

Finally, I test for the effect that a member's age has on interest in the single piece of legislation that focuses directly on the quality of life among the elderly — the Older Americans Act. In doing so, I do not mean to suggest that the elderly, like women or minorities, have been systematically underrepresented in the House. But if group identifications matter in the formation of members' policy interests, it should follow that a member's proximity to retirement age — measured here as the number of years over sixty — will heighten her sensitivity to the policy interests of the elderly.

Administration Agents on the House Floor

The analysis of the preceding chapters revealed an important way in which presidential influence is exerted in a decentralized Congress. The legislative strategies of presidents and their staffs have as their object not simply the development of voting coalitions but the mobilization of legislative supporters who might serve as administration agents in the formal activities of committee markup and the informal activities of agenda development and staff-level negotiation. Such strategies should also prove important on the House floor. Chief legislator he may be, but the president has no parliamentary right to participate there. For his preferences to have an effect in the collective deliberations of the chamber, he requires agents to articulate his positions, offer and defend his amendments, execute parliamentary strategy, and, for those decisions where majority votes are likely to be decisive, lobby the wavering loyalist.

Of the six bills in the floor sample, four were high on the administration's agenda and all four contained significant provisions with which the president strongly disagreed. In the dairy, job training, universal telephone, and weatherization bills, the administration had a particular agenda to prosecute; in those cases, we should expect that Republicans otherwise inclined to support the Reagan agenda — measured here by using the district vote for Reagan in the previous election[9] — should be more likely to go to the floor on his behalf.

Explaining Members' Floor Participation

With the components of the floor model now in place, what remains is the empirical assessment of their importance. As members decide whether to take action on the House floor, to what extent are they responsive to the interests of their constituents? How strategic are their choices? To what extent too do their own policy interests and commitments matter? How important are the structuring effects of institutional position? To what extent, that is, does the assignment of special parliamentary rights and resources affect important behavioral patterns on the House floor? These and other questions relevant to the larger processes of collective choice in Congress become answerable in the context of this model.

The dependent variable in the analysis is the floor participation of member i on bill j, where floor participation is measured in a fashion analogous to that of the scale for committee markup participation, with the notable exception that the floor index is truncated at the lower end. Attendance on the floor is simply not recorded. To do so would be to report publicly what a vacant place the chamber is, that its own long-standing procedural requirement that a

---

9. Of the several measures of members' interests, this is undoubtedly the weakest. An alternative measure, one that has a different set of problems, is the member's presidential support score. Estimations of the six models using this alternative measure, however, produced similar results; with neither measure does "presidential" loyalty exhibit consistent effects on floor participation.

quorum be present to conduct business is honored only in the breach. And while floor roll calls are recorded, participation in them is nearly universal and what little variation there is typically derives from random or idiosyncratic factors, such as illness, the timing of trips home, scheduling conflicts, and the like. When members are in town and able to attend, that is, they try hard not to miss a vote. Hence, attendance and voting are not included in the floor index; the measure captures only members' participation in more demanding sorts of formal action, such as speaking, amending or procedural maneuvering, and agenda setting. The floor scale, then, covers the following seven-point range (see also Appendix F):

o   Took no formal action on House floor (other than voting)
1   Made insertion into *Congressional Record*
2   Acted as minor participant in floor debate
3   Acted as major participant in floor debate
4   (Co)Authored technical amendment or engaged in procedural action
5   (Co)Authored substantive first- or second-degree amendment
6   Engaged in agenda action.

As with the committee analyses, the dependent variable and each of the non-dichotomous independent variables was first transformed to a 0 to 1 scale, based on their minimum and maximum values. The results of the floor analysis are presented in tables 7.3 to 7.5.[10] For the most part, the results confirm (1) that participation on the House floor is purposive in precisely the ways hypothesized; (2) that it is strategic in the sense that members do not actively pursue their preferences when such action is likely to do them political harm; but (3) that it is subsidized and procedurally privileged by the institutional arrangements of jurisdiction and position. The theory developed and applied to the understanding of committee behavior, that is, turns out to be a fairly general one, finding support at a different legislative stage with a different population of actors, using qualitatively different data and less precise measures of some of the key independent variables. At the same time, its application to the floor permits the examination of several specific hypotheses about the nature of legislative participation.

10. Sorting out the several effects hypothesized by the floor model presents some apparent problems of statistical estimation. Reflecting an important fact of floor participation, the dependent variable in both cases is bounded and exhibits limited dispersion, with a large number of observations clustered at zero and the remainder spread across the other six points of the scale. I reestimated each model with two maximum-likelihood estimators, exponential Poisson regression and Tobit, and have presented those results in previous drafts of the chapter. Both estimators had the effect of improving the statistical significance of several of the coefficients, but neither supported inferences less favorable to my hypotheses than those presented here.

Table 7.3   Explaining Participation on the House Floor: Two Bills from House Agriculture

Independent variable	Dairy Title 1981 Farm Bill		Peanuts Title 1981 Farm Bill	
Intercept	.10	(.01)	−.01	(.01)
Political interests				
District commodity production	.62***	(.11)	.62***	(.10)
Minority district interaction	−.15	(.13)	.18*	(.10)
Marginality of district	.02	(.02)	.02**	(.01)
Presidential loyalty	−.06**	(.03)	—	—
Related policy background	.06*	(.05)	.30***	(.05)
Sex (female)	−.00	(.03)	.44**	(.02)
Race/ethnicity (nonwhite)	.00	(.03)	−.01	(.02)
Institutional positions/resources				
Member, reporting committee	.14***	(.03)	.06***	(.02)
Member, reporting subcommittee	−.00	(.04)	−.01	(.04)
Leader, reporting committee	.32***	(.09)	.44***	(.08)
Leader, reporting subcommittee	.68***	(.10)	.60***	(.08)
Member, related panel	.01	(.04)	.01	(.02)
Member, minority party	.02	(.02)	−.01	(.01)
Seniority/status				
Years of cumulative service	.05	(.04)	.02	(.03)
Freshman status	−.01	(.02)	−.03**	(.01)
Chair, other standing committee	−.04	(.03)	−.02	(.03)
Number of observations	434		434	
R^2	.40		.39	

Note: Parameter estimates are OLS coefficients, with standard errors in parentheses. (See text and Appendix F for definition and measurement of variables.)

*Statistically significant at .10, one-tailed test. **Statistically significant at .05, one-tailed test. ***Statistically significant at .01, one-tailed test.

CONSTITUENCY INFLUENCE ON THE FLOOR:
REPRESENTATION WITHOUT A LOWER-CLASS ACCENT?

As we noted in Chapter 3, the influence of constituencies on legislators' Washington behavior has been a matter of controversy for several decades. This is for good reason: the extent of such influence is an operational test of the health of representation, at least insofar as this concept has been defined by most congressional scholars studying the subject. The evidence in the literature to this point on the extent of constituent influence, however, has focused largely on a single form of legislative behavior — members' votes on floor roll calls — and the evidence is mixed. But what of members' participation in legis-

Table 7.4   Explaining Participation on the House Floor: Two Bills from House
Education and Labor

Independent variable	Job Training		Older Americans	
Intercept	−.01	(.03)	−.01	(.03)
Political interests				
District benefits	.18**	(.10)	.08	(.08)
Minority district interaction	−.18	(.17)	−.04	(.05)
Marginality of district	.04**	(.02)	.02*	(.01)
Presidential loyalty	−.07*	(.05)	—	—
Related policy background	.02	(.03)	.04**	(.02)
Race/ethnicity (nonwhite)	.10**	(.05)	−.03	(.03)
Sex (female)	.18***	(.04)	.05*	(.03)
Age (years over sixty)	—		.12**	(.06)
Institutional positions/resources				
Member, reporting committee	.20***	(.04)	.15***	(.03)
Member, reporting subcommittee	.13**	(.08)	.25***	(.10)
Leader, reporting committee	.70***	(.14)	.67***	(.10)
Leader, reporting subcommittee	.53***	(.15)	.54	(.13)
Member, related panel	.09**	(.04)	.05**	(.03)
Member, minority party	.10**	(.05)	.05	(.05)
Seniority status				
Years of cumulative service	−.06	(.06)	−.05	(.05)
Freshman status	−.02	(.03)	−.08***	(.02)
Chair, other standing committee	.01	(.05)	.00	(.03)
Number of observations	433		434	
R²	.32		.39	

Note: Parameter estimates are OLS coefficients, with standard errors in parentheses. (See text
and Appendix F for definition and measurement of variables.)
    *Statistically significant at .10, one-tailed test. **Statistically significant at .05, one-tailed
test. ***Statistically significant at .01, one-tailed test.

lative action on the House floor? The results of the floor analysis, like the
results at the committee and subcommittee level, provide a reasonably clear
answer: the stronger the interest of a district subconstituency in the legislation,
the more active will their representative be in the legislative mix. The coefficients in all six cases are correct in sign, and in four of the six — and all three of
the major ones — the substantive effects are large, moving a member from 15
to more than 60 percent along the floor participation scale.

    The importance of constituent interests appears especially dramatic in the
two Agriculture bills, a result consistent both with conventional wisdom and

Table 7.5   Explaining Participation on the House Floor: Two Bills from House Energy and Commerce

Independent variable	Universal Telephone		Weatherization	
Intercept	−.08**	(.03)	.03*	(.02)
Political Interest				
District benefits V1	.15***	(.04)	.05	(.06)
District benefits V2	.20***	(.08)	—	
District benefits V3	.01	(.08)	—	
Minority district 1 interaction	−.15**	(.07)	−.12**	(.08)
Minority district 2 interaction	−.37***	(.08)	—	
Minority district 3 interaction	−.04	(.13)	—	
Marginality of district	.02	(.02)	.03**	(.02)
Presidential loyalty	.07*	(.05)	—	
Related policy background	.14***	(.05)	.03	(.03)
Race/ethnicity (nonwhite)	.02	(.04)	.03	(.03)
Sex (female)	.03	(.04)	−.02	(.03)
Institutional Positions/Resources				
Member, reporting committee	.27***	(.03)	.05*	(.03)
Member, reporting subcommittee	.10**	(.06)	.05	(.06)
Leader, reporting committee	.34***	(.12)	.25**	(.11)
Leader, reporting subcommittee	.27**	(.14)	.58**	(.24)
Member, related panel	.18*	(.13)	.04**	(.02)
Member, minority party	.21**	(.09)	.08**	(.04)
Seniority/Status				
Years of cumulative service	.06	(.05)	−.02	(.02)
Freshman status	−.03*	(.02)	−.02	(.02)
Chair, other standing committee	−.03	(.04)	.05	(.04)
Number of Observations	433		433	
R^2	.37		.14	

*Statistically significant at .10, one-tailed test. **Statistically significant at .05, one-tailed test. ***Statistically significant at .01, one-tailed test.

with the analogous findings for participation in the committee politics on House Agriculture. In itself, the presence of substantial district dairy production is likely to have a striking effect on a member's floor activity, turning her from a bit player into an actor in a leading role. When it comes to representing cows, if not constituents, House members can hardly be called unresponsive. Among the thirty-some members active in a floor fight over administration-sponsored cuts in the dairy program, for instance, were Gunderson, Kastenmeier, Obey, Petri, and Roth. Among these five, only Gunderson was an Agriculture Committee member, and one of the most junior at that; but all five were from Wisconsin and represented the top five dairy-producing districts in the country, and three were Republicans opposing the president of their own party during his first year in office. Also vigorous in the program's defense were Jeffords of Vermont and Hagedorn and Weber of Minnesota — all three Republicans representing top-twenty dairy-producing districts. For this bill in which billions of dollars of discretionary domestic spending were at stake, members' distributive impulses were powerful and bipartisan. Thus do we see that while the coefficient on minority-district interaction is of the predicted sign (negative), it is considerably smaller than the direct effect of district dairy production.

The behavioral impact of commodity interests is remarkably similar in the peanuts case. Like the dairy title, the peanuts title faced a program-threatening challenge from the floor, and in like fashion, the members from high-production areas came out in force. Active in the battle, for instance, were Democrats Hatcher of Georgia, Stenholm of Texas, and Fountain of North Carolina, and Republican Dickinson of Alabama. Together, the districts of these four accounted for almost half of the country's peanut production. We see in this case that minority status actually enhanced constituent influence on participation, an effect that materialized probably in part because the Reagan Administration chose to support rather than oppose this bill, despite its costs and despite the fact that it represented a major federal intervention in one sector of the economy, to control both supply and prices.

In sum, the results from the two Agriculture cases show that for both a major and a minor bill — one that involves producer interests in 351 districts in addition to one that involves producers in only 70 — the constituency component of the model proves at once powerful, stable, and bipartisan. On some nontrivial measures, we can conclude, the distributive impulses of members have considerable behavioral punch.

Although the effects may be less dramatic and somewhat less certain, there is good evidence of constituent influence on members' legislative participation in bills from the Education and Labor and Commerce committees as well. In the case of universal telephone, in fact, the results of table 7.5 demonstrate that a single bill can evoke the interests of very different subconstituencies, and they suggest that various election-minded legislators may participate on the same issue for substantively quite different reasons (reasons likely to imply very different preference directions). In a reflection of the potential harm that the AT&T divestiture threatened to cause rural telephone rates and availability, members from heavily rural districts (District VI) were far more likely to go to the floor, and their comments revealed that they were nearly unanimous in their support for the bill's protections for rural telephone companies and consumers. Likewise, members were more likely to participate if they represented districts with large numbers of communications workers (District V2), many of whom stood to lose or gain job security and other benefits, depending on the outcome of the legislative battle.

So too do we find clear evidence of constituency influence in the major bill selected from the Education and Labor Committee sample — the Job Training Partnership Act. Important matters of national economic policy were certainly central to this legislation, but unemployment and hence the benefits of employment programs varied considerably across districts. As the district benefits associated with JTPA increased, so did the legislative investment of the member in activity on the House floor.

For the minor bills from Education and Labor or Energy and Commerce, respectively, the coefficients for the constituency variables are correct in sign, but the null hypothesis regarding constituent influence cannot be rejected even at generous levels of statistical significance. However, the relative importance of constituency across the six cases reveals a pattern consistent with long-standing accounts regarding the conditions under which members will respond to some constituencies more than others. The proposition that lower-class interests will suffer from relatively weak representation in the American political system dates at least back to E. E. Schattschneider's *The Semisovereign People* (1960).

Such a class-contingent pattern of constituent influence is evident when one compares the results from the several cases under study here. While we cannot draw firm conclusions from an examination of six bills, the results of tables 7.3 to 7.5 reinforce Schattschneider's lament that interests already advantaged in the economic realm (and hence better organized) will find better expression in the political realm. For instance, the clearest constituency effects are those of district business interests — those of well-organized and well-financed dairy or peanut producers. In the telephone case, likewise, the communications workers constituted a relatively well-paid and largely unionized group; and the rural telephone subscribers likely to be affected were directly represented by rural local telephone companies whose interests they shared. In contrast, the incidence of poverty in a district (District V3) had no similar effect on members' involvement in the universal telephone case, this despite the fact that a widely touted purpose of the bill was to transfer millions of dollars in telephone revenue to guarantee that low-income households would have affordable telephone service. Likewise, one cannot safely conclude that the incidence of low-income households in areas with high heating costs had any discernible effect on members' involvement in the weatherization case, despite strong conservative opposition to the bill on the floor. Nor is it possible to conclude that the incidence of low-income elderly had a significant behavioral effect on the deliberations on the older Americans amendments, despite the tendency for elderly people to be more active in electoral politics and better organized nationally.

An apparent exception to this tendency appears in the case of the job training bill, where table 7.4 indicates that the number of unemployed workers in the district had a discernible effect on the behavior of legislators during floor consideration of the Job Training Partnership Act. Several factors complicate the conclusion that legislators are very responsive to the interests of unemployed workers per se. First is the fact that unemployment at the time of House consideration of the bill had reached postwar highs — in excess of 10 percent nationally, with many districts exhibiting rates two to three times the national average. Unemployment was the most salient issue on the domestic agenda in 1982, and JTPA was the only significant bill on the legislative agenda to address it. Hence, this bill constitutes something of a limiting case: if the incidence of unemployment doesn't affect members' behavior in this instance, it is unlikely to matter on employment or labor legislation that arises under less pressing conditions. Second, JTPA, unlike the expiring CETA program it would replace, set up a public-private partnership through which the federal government would directly subsidize employment and training in the private sector, managed through what were labeled Private Industry Councils. No government jobs would be created under JTPA. By representing the interests of long-term, unemployed workers in this case, then, legislators were acting to promote business interests and private economic development within their districts as much as to alleviate unemployment per se.

In sum, the results of the floor analysis suggest that the interests of district subconstituencies find their way into the decisions that members make to actively support or oppose legislation that comes to the House floor. The results thus reinforce my conclusion in the previous two chapters that the influence constituents exert extends to bills that are very different in character and arise from the jurisdictions of very different committees. But at the same time, the exploration conducted here provides clues about the conditions under which constituencies will be more or less influential. While one should not make too much of inferences drawn from six bills, the individual-level behavioral patterns reinforce the worry that American pluralism has a disturbing underside. Schattschneider's lament (1960) primarily focused on the underrepresentation of the lower class in the pressure group system, but the results of tables 7.3 to 7.5 suggest that this tendency extends to, perhaps gives rise to, uneven representation in the revealed intensities of elected officials as well.

STRATEGIC BEHAVIOR ON THE HOUSE FLOOR:
PLAYING IT SAFE

Members tend to walk onto the House floor to pursue the interests of (nonpoor) constituents likely to be affected by the matter under consideration. Considerably less consistent evidence indicates that members will sometimes walk off the floor (or stay away to begin with) to avoid alienating those constituents. As the account of strategic behavior elaborated and tested in previous chapters would predict, minority party members are far more likely than majority party members to be faced with the dilemma of disliking a bill on partisan or ideological grounds when the effect of the bill is to send government benefits to or is otherwise favored by their constituents. In some cases at least, such cross-pressures appear to matter a good deal. In four of the six cases — and all the major ones — minority members are less responsive than majority members to the constituency interests evoked by the legislation that comes to the House floor. As I note above, the two Agriculture bills constitute probably the two most difficult tests for this hypothesis, given that constituency interests were clear, compelling, and compatible across partisan lines. Thus do we find a statistically insignificant (but substantively nontrivial) effect in one case, the Omnibus Farm Bill dairy title, and an anomalous result in the other, the peanuts title.

In the other four cases, however, the minority-district interaction is consistently negative, suggesting that minority status at least partly mitigates members' inclination to exploit floor opportunities to represent the intensities of district subconstituencies. In three of the four cases, in fact, the negative effect of the interactive variable equals or exceeds that of the analogous direct constituency effect.

The account here thus provides both theoretical underpinning and empirical evidence to explain the frustration that Republicans expressed with increasing vigor prior to their takeover of the House in 1995 about the partisan use of the majority's agenda powers on the floor. A majority's strategic use of its prerogatives not only makes it harder for a minority to accomplish its policy objectives — never a good bet in any case — but also diminishes minority opportunities for constituency representation on the floor. And if, as Mayhew (1974) suggests, such Washington activities constitute good exercises in credible credit claiming, which in turn enhance an incumbent's subsequent political support, minority members are electorally less advantaged.

Finally, strategic considerations on the part of marginal members find little support at the floor level, any more than they did in committee and subcommittee. If the marginal member is, as others have suggested, inclined to allocate her time and effort to work in the home constituency rather than in

Washington, the consequences of the apparent tradeoff do not find their way into her participation. On the contrary, we find consistent evidence for the opposite hypothesis: the marginal member is more likely to participate, other things being equal. The coefficient on electoral insecurity is positive in all six cases and is statistically significant at the .10 level in four.

A plausible explanation, however post hoc, can be given to these results that renders them consistent with the claim that members allocate their time and energy to floor deliberations rationally and strategically. Marginal members, like car-rental companies second in market share, "try harder" than their relatively more secure colleagues. That is, marginal members, like most of us in the expansionist stage of our careers, see their level of effort as front-loaded. They invest heavily early on, believing that the investment will pay dividends in securing their position in the longer run. The tradeoff between home and Washington work is thus translated into a tradeoff with regard to career stages. Moreover, the greater visibility of the floor for advertising, position taking, and credit claiming should make it especially attractive to the marginal member trying to secure the favor of her constituents.

POLICY INTERESTS AND FLOOR ACTIVISM

Few "Mr. Smiths" may have gone to Washington, but good evidence from various literatures suggests that member behavior on the floor is driven in part by deeply felt policy interests and commitments. For instance, the importance of ideology, while hard to measure and assess, is widely thought to affect members' voting decisions on the floor, the arguments of some economists notwithstanding. More generally, Kingdon found that members "have their conception of good public policy, and act partly to carry out that conception" (1989, 246). Likewise, numerous case studies exist wherein the activism of some legislative entrepreneur — Edmund Muskie on the Clean Air Act (Asbell 1978), Pete Domenici on inland waterways policy (Reid 1980), William Ford on the Clinton National Service Plan (Waldman 1995) — is driven by personal or ideological commitments, beliefs about justice and fairness, or some general concern that the public interest is being sacrificed for political gain.

I have no method for measuring such (more or less) public-spirited intentions here, but the results of the floor analysis do recommend the more modest but related claim that members' motivations, even in such visible political forums as the House floor, are not reducible to calculations of electoral self-interest or politically expedient credit claiming. More specifically, a decision by members to go to the floor is clearly and consistently related to personal, precongressional interest in the policy area, independent of whether some district subconstituency also has a stake in the matter at hand. Despite the problems of measurement, this finding holds for four of the six bills spanning the three committees. For instance, the involvement of House members in floor action on the Older Americans Act was directly affected by whether they had occupational experience in social work, senior citizens' causes, or charitable organizations (see table 7.4). More noteworthy is the positive effect of the member's age; for issues concerning their own age cohort, members nearing or past conventional retirement age tend to be more active than younger members (independent of the chamber seniority they enjoy and the number of elderly constituents affected). Similarly, involvement in the weatherization bill was related to members' experience in community low-income housing programs and energy conservation. Such findings are hard to square with the simple assumption of legislative self-interest, electoral or otherwise, unless one so expands the meaning of self-interest that it explains nothing in explaining everything. The better interpretation is that these members have personal interests and commitments regarding the welfare of low-income households, whether those households are within the district or beyond; that these personal values are important components of their utility calculations; and that they thus pursue such interests in their legislative work.

Nor are these interests collinear with or often especially related to the character of the district that the member represents. For instance, while it is true that members from largely agricultural districts are more likely to have agriculture-related backgrounds, recall that the policy background coded relevant to the peanut bill included consumer protection interests or experience. Indeed, in a subsidiary analysis where the member's agricultural and the consumer backgrounds were differentiated and included separately, the consumer background was both positive and statistically significant, exceeding relevant agricultural background. An almost identical pattern appeared in the universal telephone case as well. Given that consumers of peanut butter and local telephone service are neither geographically concentrated nor politically well-organized, this, too, is a behavioral tendency not reducible to constituency-based explanations.

REPRESENTING THE UNDERREPRESENTED

Other important evidence in the floor analysis reveals the importance of members' personal policy commitments. Specifically, we find some support for the hypotheses about the behavioral importance of race, ethnicity, and gender. Recall the specific nature of those hypotheses: we should not expect a positive and significant effect for these attributes on all issues. Clearly, not all issues will evoke equally the larger interests of the underrepresented national groups.

And, of course, African-American, Hispanic, and female members must suffer under the same resource constraints as everyone else, more or less, so they cannot be more involved in everything. But there should be a predictable pattern of the issues where the representatives from each particular group invest more, other issues where they would invest less. For instance, the demographics of age and the economics of agriculture lead us to expect that the Older Americans Act and agricultural price supports should not disproportionately evoke the policy interests of minority members, at least insofar as their interests derive from a commitment to represent an extradistrict constituency. If anything, we should see less activity on these bills, as minority members concentrate on concerns more relevant to minority group interests. But the incidence of poverty and unemployment in the larger, extradistrict black and Hispanic communities should affect the revealed intensities of the minority representative on the Job Training Partnership Act, given its promise of multibillion dollar benefits to the unemployed, and to a lesser extent, on the Weatherization and Employment Act and the Universal Telephone Preservation Act.

The Behavioral Importance of Race and Ethnicity

The bills analyzed in this chapter were considered in the early 1980s, a period in which the small number of Hispanics in the House made it difficult to estimate the effects of each minority group separately in the analysis; I thus collapse the two groups into a single variable reflecting minority group identification. As shown in the first column of table 7.4, behavioral analysis applied to the Job Training Partnership Act clearly supports the hypothesis regarding the behavioral importance of race and ethnicity. The effect of member race or ethnicity, that is, is large and statistically significant for the single issue in the sample that was most relevant to the interests of minorities, the Job Training Partnership Act of 1982.

Of course, black and Hispanic members are also likely to represent districts with high numbers of black and Hispanic constituents and thus with far higher unemployment rates. On district constituency grounds, members of color should have been disproportionately active in the legislative action on the Job Training Partnership Act. And in fact they were, at both the committee and floor stages. Representative Augustus Hawkins (Democrat from California) was the principal author of the original bill, William Clay (Democrat from Missouri), Harold Washington (Democrat from Illinois), and Baltasar Corrada (Democrat from Puerto Rico) were all members of Hawkins's Employment Opportunities Subcommittee and were all significant players in drafting the bill as it moved through several stages of committee negotiation. Hawkins managed the bill on the floor, while four different black members offered a total of eight substantive amendments and more than half of the minority group representatives participated in the floor debate (three times the ratio of whites). Structural unemployment in each of these members' districts was far above the national average.

But if minority group members should be especially active in the employment and training area on behalf of their constituencies, the substantial coefficient on the member's race or ethnicity tells us something more and different. Members of color disproportionately represent high unemployment areas, but unemployment is controlled for in the equation. Black representatives were disproportionately represented on the originating committee, and a black member happened to be subcommittee chair (and thus floor manager); these factors too are controlled for in the equation. In short, the minority group identification of the member was responsible for increasing her involvement in this area, independent of the otherwise important effects of constituency and institutional position.

Not controlled for in the analysis of the Job Training Partnership Act, however, is the racial composition of a member's district. It is possible, for instance, that members of color might be inclined to participate more in legislation on employment opportunities because of the greater support it might generate within their predominantly nonwhite, liberal districts. If that is true, the effect of race that we observe in the job training case might actually reflect the responsiveness that an election-minded white Democrat representing a predominantly nonwhite district would exhibit as well. That is, regardless of race, the member representing such a constituency should follow the laws of political ambition.

In fact, however, the data of this case suggest that the opposite conclusion is closer to the truth. Table 7.6 provides the relevant results from a reestimation of the floor participation model for the Job Training Partnership case where I control for the racial composition of the member's district.[11] This alternative specification actually increases rather than attenuates the size of the coefficient on race, reinforcing the finding that the race of the member does make a difference in the legislative priorities he sets, especially for a black member from the South. Moreover, the coefficient on the racial composition of the district (with unemployment and the race of the representative controlled for) proves slightly negative (though insignificant). Judging from this case, then, we might rather conclude that the interests of black and Hispanic constituents actually figure little in the legislators' behavioral calculations, rather than that

11. All of the other coefficients in the model not reported in table 7.6 were virtually identical to the original estimates reported in table 7.4.

Table 7.6   The Importance of Race, Ethnicity, and Constituency for Floor Participation: The Job Training Partnership Act

Independent variable	Original Model		Reestimated Model	
Intercept				
Unemployment, fifteen weeks or more	.10**	(.05)	.25***	(.11)
Percent black in district	—	—	−.12	(.10)
Percent Hispanic in district	—	—	−.02	(.09)
Region (South)	—	—	.01	(.03)
Member race (black)	—	—	.11*	(.07)
Member ethnicity (Hispanic)	—	—	.03	(.10)
Member race/ethnicity	.10**	(.05)	—	
Member race/region interaction	—	—	.71***	(.19)
R^2	.32		.35	

Note: The only coefficients shown are those that changed in the reestimation of the original model (see table 7.5).

*Statistically significant at .10, one-tailed test. **Statistically significant at .05, one-tailed test. ***Statistically significant at .01, one-tailed test.

minority interests command electoral responsiveness from whoever represents them. Given that citizens of color have been systematically ignored in the practice of representative politics, that they operate in the political process from a position of economic disadvantage, and that (for these reasons and others) they exhibit relatively low levels of political mobilization, this should not be a surprising result. Whether it holds up under the scrutiny of future analysis, however, is a matter of substantial importance for understanding and evaluating the practice of representation in Congress.

The other cases are less well suited to testing the behavioral importance of color, and the results suggest as much. The Older Americans Act and the Agriculture bills exhibit negative but statistically insignificant coefficients, consistent with the fact that blacks and Hispanics occupy disproportionately small subsets of the national groups most affected by these three bills. The signs on the coefficients for race and ethnicity in the weatherization and universal telephone cases are positive, as predicted. But in both of these cases the coefficients are small and statistically insignificant.

In sum, though I would not emphasize the point too much, the pattern of coefficients across the six cases suggests that the behavioral importance of race and ethnicity varies directly with the impact that a bill might have on minorities nationally. If the tendency does hold up to further scrutiny, it will only reinforce the view that efforts to redress the racial and ethnic imbalance in Congress are likely to have substantive legislative consequences. Alternatively, as the Supreme Court continues the line of doctrinal development outlined in *Shaw* v. *Reno* (1993), the behaviorally relevant diversification of the House set in motion by the 1992 elections may well be short-circuited.

A Woman's Place Is in the House

The results of the floor analysis provide new and different evidence regarding the legislative importance of gender as well. In three of the six bills, the effect of gender on a member's participation was substantial and significant, including on the two bills that were most directly related to issues on the agenda of the Women's Caucus. As predicted, the importance of gender appears strongest in the Job Training Partnership Act. The coefficient is, by almost any comparative standard, substantial — clearly greater than the coefficient on subcommittee membership and nearly as great as that on subcommittee leadership. An almost identical result appears in the case of the Older Americans Act, suggesting that women in the House disproportionately invest their legislative energies on behalf of women over 65 below the poverty line.

Evidence of the effect of gender on members' participation also appears in the peanuts title of the 1981 Farm Bill, a result I did not predict, but for which a reading of the floor record provides a plausible if post-hoc explanation. The record suggests that in an important way, the peanuts title did evoke the concerns of low-income women — concerns that were altogether submerged in policy development in this area prior to 1981. None of the women who participated on the House floor represented peanut-producing districts and none spoke in support of peanut producers; rather, all of them called attention to the program's effect on the price of peanut butter and hence the cost to the care providers for low-income children. For instance, Representative Millicent Fenwick observed during floor debate, "Anything that raises the price of peanut butter, which is a staple in low-income families, particularly those with large numbers of children, is a tragedy for them" (*Congressional Record* 1981a, 24169). Similarly, Representative Margaret Heckler charged that the peanut provisions in the committee report represented an "unconscionable effort to soar up the price," noting specifically that the increase in the peanut price support would produce a 31 percent increase in the price of retail peanut products paid by consumers (*Congressional Record* 1981a, 24718–79.)

Underrepresented in the House, women, like blacks and Hispanics, appear motivated to take compensatory action, pursuing issues that are more likely to appear relevant to members of their group. In this way, they transcend district boundaries and represent the interests of a historically underrepresented constituency. By extension, such findings suggest that improving the balance of

race, ethnicity, and gender in the House is likely to have identifiable consequences for congressional policy making. In the prevoting processes of agenda
setting and legislative drafting, the behavior of women and minorities is not
likely to be the same as that of white males who represent similar districts,
have similar backgrounds, and have similar institutional positions (Thomas
1994). As more representatives of these underrepresented groups are elected
to Congress, in short, different issues are likely to receive greater weight.

PROSECUTING THE PRESIDENT'S AGENDA ON THE FLOOR

In contrast to the findings at the subcommittee and committee level, no
consistent evidence indicates that the incentives associated with carrying the
administration's water have discernible effects on members of the president's
party — at least not that I was able to predict. Each of the major bills was
identified by committee staffers as a relatively high-priority item on the president's agenda. These three allowed investigation of the hypothesis. For one
bill, the Universal Telephone Preservation Act, the coefficient on the presidential loyalty variable is, in fact, positive and statistically significant at .10. But in
the analysis of the other two bills, the dairy title of the 1981 Farm Bill and the
1982 Job Training Partnership Act, the coefficient is similar in size and statistical significance but opposite the predicted sign.

Several speculations and one important inference can be drawn from these
results. First and most simply, the results of the prefloor analysis do not extend
to the floor stage, and consequently we are led to question the generalizability
of this part of the model. Second, the main agent of the administration on the
floor is invariably the subcommittee or full-committee leader acting as the
party's floor manager; if such leadership variables are already included in the
model, the distinctive effect of presidentialist activism is difficult to disentangle statistically. Third, whatever behavioral effect this factor may have, it is
conditional in a way that the theory does not capture. For instance, students of
presidential success in Congress have pointed to such conditions as presidential popularity, the condition of the economy, and other factors that may cause
the influence of a particular president to rise and fall over time and across
issues (Bond and Fleisher 1990; Forshee 1994; Peterson 1990).

In any case, the best inference to be drawn here is that the findings of this
study are different for floor and prefloor forums. It may well be that the floor,
as Kingdon has suggested in his study of floor voting, is where the member's
behavior is most constrained by various actors in her field of forces, and that
relatively little room is left for presidential influence (Kingdon 1989, 20, 177–
80, 253–54). The results here suggest that presidential influence may be more
evident at earlier, typically more important stages, stages that have been

largely ignored by students of presidential-legislative relations. Thus should we conclude that future work in this area should encompass action at each stage in a sequential process. Indeed, Forshee (1992) has found that any inferences drawn solely from floor analysis systematically underestimate the influence of the executive in legislative decision making.

INSTITUTIONAL POSITION AND RESOURCES

If members are motivated to participate by their different interests, the importance of institutional position is also clear in the results from the floor analysis. The leadership and committee membership variables, in particular, are highly associated with the extent to which a member gets into the mix on the floor; the variables are large, positive, and significant in almost every instance. The procedural prerogatives and various informational resources that these positions command are centrally important for understanding who takes part on the House floor.

In contrast, the results of tables 7.3 to 7.5 provide less support for the behavioral importance of subcommittee position — this in an era of alleged "subcommittee government" (Davidson 1981; Hardin, Shepsle, and Weingast 1983; Dodd and Oppenheimer 1985). For instance, there is a clear disparity between the coefficients on subcommittee membership in the multivariate estimates and those in the bivariate estimates. Subcommittee members were consistently several times more active in floor action than other members, regardless of the specific activity or case one examines. But the multivariate analysis suggests that subcommittee membership per se often has little to do with that. In only three of the six bills does this variable both prove positive and pass statistical muster, and in one case it is incorrect in sign.

The inconsistent results may occur in part because much of the subcommittee's action on the floor is carried out by the subcommittee leaders, who serve as agents for subcommittee members of their respective parties. But controlling for leadership position, there is still a strong bivariate relationship between subcommittee membership and participation, one that is significantly attenuated in the estimation of a more fully specified model. Rather, much of what might be read by the congressional observer as the behavioral importance of subcommittee position simply reflects the disproportionately high level of issue-specific interests among subcommittee members. For four of the six bills, for instance, there is a strong relationship between district interest and subcommittee membership, but in three of those cases, the importance of subcommittee membership is insignificant in the multivariate model.

Finally, the results for minority status suggest that the factor of political party may have quite different behavioral effects, depending on the form of legislative behavior under study. Party may be important for understanding members' voting decisions and important in a different way for understanding decisions about how active to be. What matters most is not party identification per se but majority or minority status. Smith finds some evidence that minority members are disadvantaged in their ability to offer amendments under restrictive rules (1989, chapter 5). I find the complement here. Under open rules, at least for bills dealing with programs that divide the parties, minority status increases members' participation. Whatever substantive effect such minority participation may have on the outcomes of floor decision making, this finding suggests that the open floor provides opposition members with the opportunity to have their views represented in the chamber's debate. (This is true even when we control for whatever loyalty the minority member feels toward the president of her own party—a factor that exhibits inconsistent effects in the six cases studied here.) For those interested not simply in power and policy but in the representativeness of legislative deliberations, this is not a minor point.

The Sociology of the House Floor

We conclude the discussion of the floor results by revisiting the several hypotheses that derive from the sociological approach to legislative behavior, an approach that enjoys a rich if now somewhat distant tradition in the literature but stands in stark contrast to the theory of purposive behavior that I have articulated.

The first inference we can draw is that apprenticeship on the House floor is not altogether dead. Although the statistical tests are not conclusive, we find here, as we found in the analysis of committee participation, that freshmen do not participate as much as their senior colleagues, even when we control for the fact that freshmen members are less likely to be assigned to committees and subcommittees that interest them and that they are far less likely to be panel leaders. In all six cases, freshman status has a negative effect on floor participation, and in three of the six, the coefficient is statistically significant. But here as in earlier chapters, such results should not be interpreted as a challenge to the view that the prescriptive norm about being "seen and not heard" is at work.

The results of the six cases give reason to doubt the behavioral importance of other prescriptive norms as well. Even after members' interests, background, and committee assignments are controlled for, there is no consistent evidence that seniority per se provides any advantage in floor politics. In fact, the effects of seniority on floor behavior are as likely to be negative as positive, and no obvious logic is discernible in the pattern. Nor do I find evidence of mutual noninterference treaties between jurisdictions, treaties that members tacitly understand and respect. Committee membership is an important predictor of participation, but significant numbers of committee nonmembers were also active on the floor in every case. The most telling evidence on the weakness of the prescriptive norm of deference appears in the coefficients for the variable that captures whether a member is chair of some other (unrelated) standing committee. If such a norm is still alive, it should certainly constrain the chair of one committee from interfering in the business of another. But again, there is little evidence that that is the case. The coefficient is negative in only one of the six cases, and a reading of the floor record revealed several instances in which chairs from other committees used the floor to oppose the recommendations of the floor manager. Absent a more comprehensive study, of course, we cannot know for sure whether such instances are common; but they do call into question the idea that committee chairs will defer to their jurisdictional peers when interests incline them to do otherwise.

Conclusion

The analysis of participation on the floor has permitted us to accomplish several objectives. First, it has allowed us to assess the optimization theory of participation articulated and tested in earlier chapters at a third, qualitatively different stage of the legislative process. Though no precise scientific comparisons between the results of the various stages are possible, we are led to the conclusion that the theory is a fairly general one, capable of comprehending the legislative participation of different populations of members acting on different samples of bills in quite different institutional contexts.

A second objective accomplished by the floor analysis is closely related to the first: it has enabled the systematic assessment and refutation of an older, alternative theory of legislative participation, one based on the sociology of group decision making.

Third, in the floor analysis I concentrated in depth on six specific cases, which allowed closer examination of the nature of the various interests underlying members' revealed intensities. The results reinforce the results for committees and subcommittees regarding the importance of members' policy interests that are independent of constituency concerns, despite the representatives' greater visibility on the floor. One of the most important if still tentative inferences is that the race, ethnicity, and gender of members affect the intensity with which they pursue their preferences on the floor. In sum, the problems of measuring the various interests of 435 members end up being something of a blessing in disguise. In a way that the interview instruments of earlier chapters could not, the objective measures used here more clearly differentiate the subconstituency and policy interests that affect members' willingness to pay the costs of participation.

PART **III**

Extensions and Implications

8

Back to the Future:
Participation in the 1990s and Beyond

All the world's a stage, and all the men and women merely players; They have their exits and their entrances; And one man in his time plays many parts.
— William Shakespeare, *As You Like It*

Upon rereading *Congressional Government* fifteen years after its original publication, Woodrow Wilson warned his readers that recent trends and events "may put this whole volume hopelessly out of date" (1956 [1885], 23). In the preface to the fifteenth printing, Wilson emphasized that the original text described "a living system . . . subject to constant subtle modifications," and that his earlier account was no longer fully accurate in "matters of detail" or "matters of substance" (19–20).

Few scholars before or since have exhibited such gracious and public self-criticism. I will certainly exhibit no good Wilsonian grace here, preferring to invoke self-servingly the timeless wisdom of William Shakespeare. Specifically, my purpose in this chapter is to suggest that the theory of legislators' "exits and entrances" advanced in these pages extends not only back to the early 1960s (as I show in Chapter 6) but forward to the 1990s, and that it applies not only to the House of Representatives but to the U.S. Senate as well. None of this is to deny, of course, that institutions undergo change — often subtle and incremental, sometimes dramatic and episodic — nor that such changes are relevant to the behavioral choices of institutionalized individuals such as congressmen. Indeed, the House of Representatives enacted significant reforms in 1995, several of which should play out in the participation choices of individuals. The theory developed here, I will simply suggest, provides the framework for understanding the behavioral changes we should most expect.

Back to the Future: Participation in the Early 1990s

One of the limitations I noted in the opening chapter is that the detailed data I analyze come from congresses and members of the 1980s. Were my principal purpose contemporaneous description, the reader should rightly take that to be a damning matter. But my purpose was not to catalogue who participated in specific bills at a particular time; rather, it was to explain why those who did did, why those who didn't didn't.

But to what extent is selective participation yet evident in the deliberations of the contemporary Congress? And how well does the theory explain the participation choices we currently observe?

A full-blown analysis of these questions is beyond scope of this work. Rather, I will argue on theoretical grounds why the account of legislative participation developed in Part 1 and tested in Part 2 should in the main be generalizable to other congresses. I will briefly replicate some of my earlier analysis, which focused on the early 1980s, using identical data gathered from the same three committees during the early 1990s (1993–94). I will then offer speculations on the behavioral implications of the institutional changes of the mid-1990s and otherwise suggest potentially fruitful directions for future work on legislative participation.

THEORETICAL CONSIDERATIONS

Insofar as abstract matters of theory go, there is no development in positive logic, cognitive psychology, or neurochemistry to suggest that members of Congress should prove less rational or strategic in their allocation of legislative time and resources over the course of several congresses. Of course, the elections of 1992 and 1994 caused more than a little turnover — far more than average for a typical election in the postwar era. Thus do we have an altogether different pool of optimizers. But there had been far greater turnover and far greater changes in Congress and country in the twenty years spanning the 87th and 97th Congresses, and the behavioral model nonetheless worked consistently well in the particular respects I was able to test.

With respect to the factors that render important the abstract concept of constraint, neither is there reason to believe that these have diminished in importance over time. If anything, members complained only more loudly in the 1990s about the grueling demands of the job and the poor quality of life. As the number and sophistication of private and public, intra- and extra-district interest groups grew, so too did the demands on members' scarce legislative time and attention (Birnbaum and Murray 1987; Jackson 1988). As the cost of the typical campaign grew, so too did the demands on the members'

Table 8.1   Selective Participation on Three Committees: The 1990s and 1980s Compared

	Agriculture		Education and Labor		Energy and Commerce	
	97th	103rd	97th	103rd	98th	103rd
Players in bill-specific games						
Players (%)	33.5	24.1	26.2	34.7	30.9	19.7
Nonplayers (%)	66.5	75.9	73.8	65.3	69.1	80.3
Sample of members	32	49	29	39	33	44
Sample of bills	21	15	17	16	20	20
Number of observations	672	730	493	619	660	924

Source: Markup minutes and transcripts from the 97th, 98th, and 103rd Congresses. (See Appendixes A and B.)
Note: Number of committee members shown for the 97th and 98th Congresses are from dense, stratified samples of the committee populations. (See Appendix A.) Number of members shown for the 103rd Congress are the full populations of members from each committee.

fundraising responsibilities (Magleby and Nelson 1990). And as constituency service and casework grew, so too did the demands on the typical member's enterprise (Fiorina 1989), which became still more overburdened in the wake of significant staff cuts in the mid-1990s.

PARTICIPATION IN COMMITTEE DECISION MAKING, 1993–1994

I analyze in this section behavioral data in the same way as I do in the previous chapter, from the records of the same three committees for the (pre-Republican) 103rd Congress (1993–94), in an attempt to reevaluate many of the earlier inferences.

Table 8.1 reports on behavioral patterns in committee comparable to those reported for the early 1980s. The basic finding of Chapter 2 remains intact. Even on panels to which most members seek assignment, their postassignment participation in panel deliberations is mostly a sometimes thing. On House Agriculture, the selectivity of participation proved more noticeable in the 103rd, with the average number of committee players dropping from one-third to one-fourth. (Identical thresholds were used.) A drop-off appears in the participation rate of Commerce Committee members as well.[1] On Education

---

1. I do not mean to make much of the absolute differences in participation rates for a given committee across congresses, only to establish that committee participation remains highly selective. Committee agendas change, sometimes dramatically, from one congress to another, and we know from work on national agenda formation that actors

and Labor, the aggregate participation rate appears somewhat higher during 1993–94, but the verbatim transcripts of committee and subcommittee mark-ups failed to reveal that members of this committee were bona fide players in much more than one-third of the cases.

The bill-level patterns of behavior for the 103rd Congress can be broken down in a fashion similar to the analysis of the 97th in Chapter 2. Again, some differences emerge from a comparison of the pattern of one committee in the early 1990s with that of the same committee in the early 1980s. In two of the three committees, the size of the active subsets — what Carroll has referred to as the efficient committee — appears smaller. For well over half the bills considered in the Agriculture and the Energy and Commerce Committees during the 103rd Congress, fewer than 25 percent of the nominal members were players. Only on Education and Labor, where the majority's agenda in the 103rd was reinvigorated by a Democratic president, were more than a handful of members active in committee deliberations on a majority of bills. On none of the three committees did the number of active players exceed 50 percent for as many as a fifth of the bills marked up in the 103rd Congress.

It is also possible to disaggregate the patterns of table 8.1 to compare the breadth of participation by individual committee members in the two periods. Again, the story of Chapter 2 remains mostly the same. Rare is the member who can reasonably be considered a player in half the legislative gambits before his committee in any given congress. This conclusion remains valid, regardless of the congress under study. About half the eligible members of the three committees during both periods were active on less than a quarter of the bills. The rates of absenteeism and absentee voting on the three committees, likewise, were just as high in the 103rd Congress as they were in the 97th and 98th.

In sum, the participation remains highly variable across members and bills. This despite the fact that the processes of (constrained) self-selection onto legislative panels had not noticeably changed. This despite the fact that many of the same sorts of external changes that Wilson described for the 1880s and 1890s transpired during the 1980s and 1990s: during the 97th Congress, party unity in Congress was on the wane; as the 104th Congress began, party unity neared postwar highs (Ornstein et al. 1996, 208). The 97th and 98th Congresses spanned a period of divided government, with the presidency and

---

outside Congress have much to do with the issues that particular committees take up in any particular year (Kingdon 1984; Baumgartner and Jones 1993). Neither are committee boundaries static institutional facts; committee jurisdictions are themselves inconstant, even in the interregna between major jurisdictional reforms (King 1994).

Senate controlled by the Republicans and the House by the Democrats; the 103rd was a period of unified government, with Democrats controlling both institutions. In the early 1980s, the country was still focused on the national security threat posed by the Soviet Union; by the early 1990s, the Soviet Union was no union at all, and attention was more squarely focused on domestic concerns. In the earlier period, the economy was weak, with unemployment and interest rates reaching postwar highs; in the later decade, the economy was strong, with the country enjoying low unemployment and interest rates close to post-OPEC lows. President Reagan, in turn, was generally considered a strong executive and President Clinton a weak one.

As much as things have changed in the national government and political agenda, in short, the behavioral patterns that form the point of departure for this study have stayed much the same.

EDUCATION AND LABOR ACROSS THREE DECADES

As noted, a full-blown reestimation of the behavioral model is not possible. Although data on bill-specific participation and members' attributes were available for the most recent congress, I did not try to redo the 100-plus interviews necessary to generate comparable data on members' interests. I thus cannot get at questions of participation and *purpose* in the more recent period. Nonetheless, this analysis does provide considerable leverage on several hypotheses that I derived and tested in earlier chapters. I conducted such an analysis in the final section of Chapter 6, where I analyzed the participation of Education and Labor members during the 87th Congress. I here extend the analysis to behavior on Education and Labor three decades later.

The last column of table 8.2 presents the multivariate estimates of participation on Education and Labor for the 103rd Congress. The middle two columns bring forward the results reported in table 6.8. A comparison of the several sets of results offers solid reassurance that the model is stable, even when applied to different samples of members and bills from different congresses. The coefficients on the variables tapping institutional position are smaller in the 103rd than the 97th, but they reinforce the relevant findings from earlier chapters. While critics may have exaggerated the importance of subcommittees (and while the relevant coefficients reported here may be inflated due to the omission of variables on members' interests), subcommittee membership implies lower information and transaction costs relative to the nonmember, such that subcommittee members are better able to get more involved in legislative games originating from their panels. If the member occupies a subcommittee leadership position, in turn, his enterprise will receive greater subsidies. And majority full- and subcommittee leaders enjoy significantly greater subsidies to pay the relevant participation costs than their minority counterparts.

The coefficients on seniority and status likewise change little under the light of more recent data. If anything, the results of the 103rd Congress appear more similar to those of the 87th than they do the congress in between. But the sociological hypotheses embedded and tested in this part of the model founder across all three congresses, before and after the democratizing reforms of the 1970s. Even in the latter-day 103rd, freshman status still has a significant and negative behavioral effect — this during a congress that included one of the largest cohorts of freshmen in decades. Seniority by itself exhibits no direct effect either, independent of institutional position. Neither is there evidence of deference, the observational equivalent of cross-panel logrolls, even in the behavior of those from whom you would expect it most. A subcommittee chair who does not sit on the panel of jurisdiction is as likely to get into the mix of legislative deliberations as any other committee member. If subcommittee chairs go along with each other's bills in order to gain greater autonomy within their own domains, I find no evidence of such cross-jurisdictional cooperation.

House-Senate Comparisons

To what extent and why do members of the U.S. Senate participate in the issues that come before them?[2] So far in this study I have focused on the House, where scholars have long observed that the higher membership and more numerous standing panels permit more specialized work. U.S. senators, by contrast, must cover roughly the same legislative territory with only a hundred members to divide the legislative labor.

If anything, then, the demands placed on them are even more severe than those confronted by the typical member of the U.S. House. With few exceptions, senators represent much larger and more heterogeneous constituencies to which they have incentives to respond. They receive (sometimes suffer from) greater media and interest group attention. And they must spend more time per year raising funds for a typical reelection campaign. The greater legislative demands are reflected most clearly in their committee assignments. In the 100th Congress, for instance, the average number of committee and subcommittee assignments for House members was 6.6; for senators the average number was 11.1 (Ornstein et al. 1987, 130). As one Senate staffer noted, the multiplicity of assignments produces scheduling conflicts that are a major

2. This section is adapted from Hall 1989, 1993.

Table 8.2 Participation on House Education and Labor Across Three Decades: Multivariate Analyses

	87th Congress (1961–62)		97th Congress (1981–82)		103rd Congress (1993–94)	
Intercept	.35***	(.02)	.27***	(.07)	.37***	(.06)
Marginality	.04*	(.03)	−.01	(.04)	−.01	(.03)
Institutional position						
Full-committee chair	.24***	(.05)	.43***	(.10)	.34***	(.08)
Ranking full-committee member	−.03	(.06)	.27***	(.10)	.25***	(.08)
Subcommittee chair	.51***	(.06)	.54***	(.08)	.35***	(.09)
Ranking subcommittee member	.02	(.06)	.30***	(.08)	.22***	(.09)
Subcommittee member	.11***	(.03)	.12***	(.02)	.12***	(.03)
Minority party	.01	(.02)	.02	(.05)	−.02	(.03)
Seniority/status						
Committee seniority	.04	(.09)	−.07	(.09)	.02	(.08)
Freshman status	−.15***	(.04)	−.13***	(.05)	−.11**	(.05)
New transfer	−.01	(.03)	—		−.05	(.06)
Chair, other subcommittee	.09*	(.06)	−.04	(.05)	.04	(.05)
Number of observations	773		493		619	
Adjusted R^2	.21		.25		.18	

Source: Minutes of House Education and Labor Committee markups, 87th Congress; 97th Congress; 103rd Congress.

Note: Parameter estimates are OLS coefficients. Standard errors appear in parentheses. Education and Labor had no new transfers in the 97th Congress. Data are missing for two observations from the 87th samples and five observations from the 103rd sample.

*Statistically significant at .10, one-tailed test. **Statistically significant at .05, one-tailed test. ***Statistically significant at .01, one-tailed test.

source of frustration. Members' avarice in expanding their assignment port-folios at the beginning of a congress comes back to haunt them during the day-to-day work of committee decision making: "[Scheduling conflicts] happen all the time, and it's a major pain. [The senator's] almost always got more than one hearing going on at the same time. Or he'll need to be on the floor, and there'll be a committee markup. The staffer has to monitor the thing, leave the room, and get on the phone and track him down. [The senator] just has to make on-the-spot decisions about where to be and how much to do. It really gets crazy sometimes."

The problems of time management and scheduling at the committee level became so severe in the mid-1980s that the Senate, with self-conscious appre-ciation of the irony involved, formed a select committee to study them. Named for Dan Quayle, then a junior senator from Indiana, who chaired it, the

Quayle Committee received a litany of complaints that senators "have work-loads which the hours of the day make it impossible to faithfully execute," are "burdened by a mass of obligations on [their] limited time," and face multiple "responsibilities [that] are often directly in conflict" (U.S. Senate Select Committee to Study the Senate Committee System, 1984, 41). Testifying before the committee, Senator Daniel Evans (Republican from Washington) summarized the prevailing view: "We would all agree that there is member inconsistency regarding participation, disappointment regarding performance due to conflicting committee assignments, frustration with committees scheduled at similar or the same times, ineffectiveness due to the oversized membership of some committees, and sometimes member disincentives to participate . . . at the maximum level."

Not surprisingly, patterns of truancy in Senate committees are as bad as if not worse than those reported for the House. Several senators who testified before the Quayle Committee noted the frequency with which committee or subcommittee chairs have trouble getting the 50 percent of the membership on hand to establish a quorum. At the commencement of its hearings, in fact, Chairman Quayle noted that "of the 12 members that are on this Select Committee, 9 of us have conflicts this morning with other committees and subcommittees in where we are supposed to be." My own examination of the hearing record revealed that only three members of the select committee showed up for both days of its hearings, while five of the twelve did not appear even momentarily at either meeting.

SELECTIVE PARTICIPATION IN HOUSE AND SENATE COMMITTEES

Table 8.3 provides a House-Senate comparison of participation in committee decision making. The sample contains only ten bills but spans several congresses (97th to 100th), cuts across the respective jurisdictions of three House and three Senate committees, and contains a mix of major and minor bills. The table shows the percentage of committee members actively involved and reveals, bill by bill, considerable variation in the breadth of participation across the eligible committee membership, both within and across committees.

More specifically, two patterns evident in table 8.3 warrant mention. First, the statistics suggest that participation is at least as selective in Senate as in House committees. In only half of the ten bills could even a third of the respective House or Senate committee members be counted as full-fledged players in their panel's decision making.

Second, the bill-specific percentage of players in Senate committee deliberations very closely tracks that for the comparable bills in the House. The rank-order correlation is .81, statistically significant at .01 with only ten cases. It

Table 8.3   Participation in Committees: A House-Senate Comparison

Policy area/bill	Percentage of Committee Members Active During Prefloor Consideration	
	House	Senate
Human resources		
Job Training Partnership Act of 1982	59	75
Older Americans Act Amendments of 1981	31	31
Head Start Reauthorization of 1981	28	19
Commerce		
Universal Telephone Service Preservation Act of 1984	64	41
1984 Amtrak/Railroad Amendments	24	18
1983 Textile Labeling Act	21	12
Agriculture		
Farm Credit Act Amendments of 1987	65	68
Wheat, soybeans, and feed grains, 1981 Farm Bill	56	71
Conservation title, 1985 Farm Bill	44	33
Cotton title, 1981 Farm Bill	28	29

Source: Hall 1993.
Note: Entries are the percentages of committee members who (1) offered at least one amendment during committee or subcommittee markup; (2) were major participants in markup
debate; or (3) were cited in staff interviews, secondary accounts, or official records as having
played a significant role behind the scenes.

would seem, then, that in the Senate as in the House, no stable set of norms or
structural arrangements can well explain members' decisions to participate. In
a single congress and on a single committee, the number of participants for
one bill can be three or four times that for another. Clearly, something about
particular bills, or more accurately, something variable about the interests that
particular bills evoke, must be at work in the Senate, as in the House.

PARTICIPATION AND PURPOSE AMONG SENATORS

Qualitative evidence from several sources suggests that just such interest-driven participation operates in Senate committees. Not surprisingly, serving constituency interests is a common theme in these calculations.[3] "Gas and

3. In her masterful study of the transformation of the U.S. Senate, Sinclair conducted
open-ended interviews in the offices of eighteen senators in the mid-1980s, reporting that
in only two cases did senators' priorities appear to be wholly dominated by constituency
considerations (1989, 144). Her interviews did not gauge issue-specific variation relevant
to members' various interests, however (1989, 144–46; see also Evans 1991).

oil, those are crucial to the economy of the state," one Democratic Senate staffer explained, "so that's where we spend most of our time." With respect to the grain commodity provisions of the most recent farm bill, a staffer to an Agriculture Committee Republican observed: "We go all out on wheat, and I mean all out. It's our number one cash crop . . . so everything else gets pushed aside." But considerable qualitative evidence suggests that members' personal policy interests are also important in setting legislative priorities. In 1987, freshman senator, later to become Senate minority leader, Thomas Daschle (Democrat from South Dakota) sought assignment to Agriculture, whose jurisdiction was crucial to the economy of his state, and to the Senate Finance Committee. One of his aides explained the latter choice: "When Daschle came to the Senate, it was the first time in his political career that he didn't have to worry about reelection two years down the road. . . . He could go after a committee that he didn't feel he had to be on for political reasons. Finance gave him the chance to get involved in all of the big issues he's interested in. Trade, tax, health — it's all right there." Similarly, an aide to Finance Committee member Bill Bradley (Democrat of New Jersey) observed: "Bradley's got certain interests. He's really got burning interests in trade, third-world debt, and tax. He's on the trade subcommittee, he chairs the one on international debt, and all the tax stuff gets handled at full committee. He just doesn't get that involved in the rest of it. He doesn't have the time, or at least he doesn't think he has the time, to go into other things."

Various case studies suggest that a similar mix of interests drives senators' participation decisions. Reid (1980) describes how junior senator Pete Domenici (Republican from New Mexico) concentrated much of his time and energy on a single issue, an inland waterways user fee, because of the strong conviction that government subsidies to the barge industry's right of way were indefensible on the grounds of either budgetary or economic efficiency. At the same time, Reid describes how Domenici met strong opposition from key Senate committee members, such as Russell Long of Louisiana, who had long fought such taxes because they would affect costs for his state's substantial and thriving barge industry. So too does Asbell (1978) describe how Senator Edmund Muskie's strong personal policy commitments led him to champion congressional budget reform, then labor long and hard to implement the reforms in the mid-1970s. And so too does Waldman (1995) describe the importance of personal policy interests for Senator Claiborne Pell in compromising and Senator Edward Kennedy in pushing President Clinton's 1992 National Service Bill.

SENATORS' RESOURCES

Participation in Senate committees tends to be interest-driven, but few senators have the time and resources to pursue their interests on more than a few bills with any efficacy. In this fundamental respect, senators face the same constraints as their House counterparts. If anything, senators are even more limited, given that participation on the floor is typically more important and more accessible in the Senate than the House. Hence, senators are more likely to be lured by opportunities to participate on bills outside their own committees' jurisdictions (Davidson 1981; Sinclair 1989).

With the few differences I will note, the allocation of resources in the Senate follows roughly the same pattern as the House. In both chambers, committee and subcommittee leaders enjoy more staff, better access to information, important lines of exchange and communication, and some procedural prerogatives not available to the typical backbencher. Given the wider range of issues that come before their panels, senators may be even more dependent on staff than are House members, and staff allotments come (in varying degrees) with formal institutional position. One aide to a senator from the majority party explained why his boss did so little to pursue his interests in the federal nutrition area during the 100th Congress, despite being well positioned to do so: "Well, it's not so much the political risks as it is the resources that we have to work with. [Senator] Kennedy's been working on this for years. So has [Representative] Panetta — his staffer is really sharp, really knowledgeable on the details. For my boss to take the lead on, say, something comprehensive in the hunger/nutrition area would take me years, given how little our office has to work with. . . . Notwithstanding the criticism of Hill resources, there is not a lot of staff around here."

At the time of this staffer's observation, Kennedy was the chair of the Senate Committee on Labor and Human Resources and enjoyed a huge and experienced staff. Representative Panetta was chair of the House nutrition subcommittee and thus could afford a full-time staffer devoted solely to nutrition issues.

Another staffer commented on the barriers to entry that thinly spread senators confront when faced with issues that are complex or esoteric in nature. In such instances, the important roles tend to be played by the chair and ranking minority members of the relevant panel. The staffer remarked, about committee members' involvement in one of the most salient, expensive, and important policy areas of the day:

> There are really only a couple of senators who are really interested in Medicare — interested enough to understand it — and that's [Health Subcommittee chair] Mitchell and [subcommittee ranking member] Durenberger. The others are intimidated and bored by it — intimidated because the discussion quickly progresses beyond their level of comprehension. It's such a technical program. I remember one day I was sitting alone in the anteroom while Medicare hearings were going on. [One senior senator] walks out and says to me, "You

Table 8.4   Institutional Position and Committee Participation: A House-Senate Comparison

	Percentage of Members Active During Markup	
Institutional position	House	Senate
Formal leaders		
Subcommittee	100	75
Full committee	80	70
Committee rank and file		
Subcommittee members	65	49
Subcommittee nonmembers	24	24
All		
Subcommittee members	72	58
Subcommittee nonmembers	29	32

Source: Hall 1993.
Note: Entries are the percentages of committee members in the row category who (1) offered at least one amendment during committee or subcommittee markup; (2) were major participants in markup debate; or (3) were cited in staff interviews, secondary accounts, or official records as having played a significant role behind the scenes.

> know, my eyes just glaze over when they start talking Medicare this and Medicare that, Part A this and Part B that. I don't understand any of it." Not ten minutes later, another senator walked out and said to me, he was clearly being sarcastic, "That Medicare is really interesting stuff, isn't it?" It's not that senators don't care—at one level they have to care. But they're not really interested. Mitchell and Durenberger, maybe [committee chair] Bentsen, are the only ones who have any real influence.

Several Senate staffers noted, however, that while subcommittee leaders and members tend to participate more than subcommittee nonmembers, subcommittee position is less important in the House than the Senate. I have already noted that the behavioral importance of subcommittee membership may well be exaggerated by students and observers of the House; subcommittee members may participate more not so much because of their position but because of the interests that led them to select their subcommittee positions in the first place. If anything, this is probably truer in the Senate, where most bills forgo a subcommittee markup altogether.

In table 8.4 I use data from the ten bills listed in the previous table to compare more systematically the participation of differently positioned members of Senate and House committees. The first two rows demonstrate the frequent involvement of full- and subcommittee leaders. The statistics from this sample for the House tell us nothing new; they closely mirror the statistics reported in earlier chapters from much larger samples of bills. But table 8.4 does reveal House-Senate differences in behavioral patterns associated with institutional position. In particular, the descriptive statistics confirm that sub-committee position is more closely associated with participation in commit-tees of the House than in those of the Senate. Subcommittee leaders counted as principal actors in 100 percent of the House bills, 75 percent in the Senate. Taking leaders and backbenchers together, in turn, 72 percent of House sub-committee members were active across the ten bills, compared with 58 percent in the Senate.

Once again, I would emphasize that such statistics cannot help disentangle the importance of position per se, as distinguished from the interests that lead members first to seek and acquire assignment, then to exhibit involvement in matters before the panels that they have sought. In the Senate as in the House, members usually can choose the subcommittees on which they will sit, and subcommittee sizes often fluctuate in response to member demand.

After the Revolution of '95: Legislative Participation in a Centralized House

In the elections of 1994, House Republicans seized the majority for the first time in four decades and quickly went about recasting the committee system, congressional staff and caucuses, and the standing rules of the House to their own liking. Most participants and commentators described such re-forms as prolegomena to dramatic changes in the structure and processes of House decision making. At least some of that description can be attributed to emotions of the "revolutionary" moment, but several reforms warrant atten-tion here. To what extent might such changes affect our expectations about member participation in the decision making of future congresses? The theory elaborated in previous chapters should provide a guide for informed specula-tion.

A central tenet of earlier chapters was that much of the important legislative action occurred in behind-the-scenes deliberations among actors on or con-nected to the relevant panels of jurisdiction. Several centralizing reforms en-acted by the 104th House, however, created new forums in which majority party leaders and their agents could better participate. In particular, the Speaker's office and Speaker-created task forces handled a number of legisla-tive matters high on the majority party's agenda during the 104th Congress, effectively bypassing the committees of jurisdiction (Ornstein 1995; Aldrich and Rohde 1996). On the basis of cases in the immediate aftermath of a transition forty years in coming, it would be a bit premature to report the impending death of the committee system. Even in the 104th moment, most bills (including many of the most important ones) progressed through the House in typical prereform fashion, and only a few of the fifteen ad-hoc task forces took any significant action. But the reforms of the mid-1990s do reinforce the more general theoretical argument regarding the behavioral importance of institutionally enhanced opportunities and constraints. To the extent that the reforms survive in the deliberative practice of future congresses, research on legislative participation should focus greater attention on the formal and informal forums populated by leaders and agents of congressional parties as well as leaders and members of committees.[4]

Other factors affecting members' capacity to participate changed as well. As we have seen in several forums, the staff available to pay the information and transaction costs is especially important to members' ability to invest in more than a few legislative matters. In particular, I emphasized the comparative staff advantages associated with committee and subcommittee positions. Such advantages did change appreciably in the mid-1990s. Staff cuts passed by the 103rd Congress had already pushed staff levels for members close to those of the decade before. The Republican-controlled 104th enacted cuts in House staff by an additional 30 percent, and the House moved toward the Senate practice of centralizing formal control of committee staff in the hands of committee leaders. Hence, for most members, staff allocation choices should prove all the more important inside the representative's enterprise. If my claim regarding the importance of staff to members' participation decisions is correct, for instance, the redistribution of such resources from subcommittee to committee should prove discernible in the behavioral tendencies of leaders and members of these two groups.

A noteworthy but less visible reform implemented by the 104th House was the elimination of proxy voting in committee and subcommittee. As members of what long appeared to be a permanent minority, Republicans had objected to proxy voting for decades, repeatedly proposing changes in House and committee rules to ban the practice. Such proposals followed from the frustrating but frequent experience wherein Republicans constituted a sitting majority in markup yet found themselves powerless to amend legislation when the panel chair wielded the proxies of absentee colleagues. For the Democratic majority, in turn, the practice of proxy voting had allowed members to miss markups in

4. In fact, theoretical work on the partisan basis of legislative organization that predates the 104th Congress implies the value of just such a focus. See especially Cox and McCubbins 1993; Rohde 1991. To date, however, there has been no systematic research on legislative participation in party organizational forums.

the face of competing demands on their time, without endangering legislation proposed by their more interested colleagues.

In light of the larger account of legislative participation developed in these pages, at least one noteworthy consequence should follow from the abolition of this longstanding practice: member attendance and voting will almost certainly increase in the House. That is, participation at the lower end of the formal participation scale will go up, even if more labor-intensive and more important forms of participation do not. This tendency will be reinforced by other reforms, such as those mandating the publication of committee roll calls and the elimination of rolling quorums, whereby chairs could hold open votes on final passage of a bill, to allow members to vote in person at their own convenience. Thus will truancy and nonvoting in committee become more publicly visible, hence politically more hazardous.

At the same time, however, the conditions enumerated in Chapter 2 that gave rise to such truancy — and selective participation more generally — have not been appreciably diminished by the reforms of the 104th House. The reforms redesigned the committee system by cutting the number of committees and subcommittees on which members sit, but they did so only by consolidating jurisdictions, not by paring back the scope of their agendas. Members may have fewer panel assignments, but the number of issues and other demands on their time (in relation to the size of their enterprise) have, if anything, increased. The agenda of a party long frozen in minority status spontaneously thawed, sending forth scores of legislatively viable proposals scarcely mentioned during the congress before.

With the number of competitive House seats dramatically enlarged in the aftermath of 1994, finally, the "money chase" that beleaguers members should only hasten. The some seven dozen Republican freshmen will, like most freshmen, anticipate the need for greater funding to consolidate their position for future elections that may not exhibit favorable political tides. So too should incumbents feel the need to expand their fundraising efforts. Among those who felt electorally safe before the 1994 election, only a naive few should feel complacent after it. House incumbents of the 103rd Congress committed the time necessary to raise on average more than five thousand dollars each week of their two-year term. Over the course of the 104th Congress and beyond, such extralegislative demands on members' time should only increase.

In sum, the House reforms of the mid-1990s are as likely to exacerbate as alleviate the conditions that give rise to the selective participation in legislative decision making analyzed in this book. While the party in the majority has changed, the majority party continues to have most of the staff, budget, and strategic advantages that their colleagues across the aisle formerly enjoyed. To the extent that the new majority has diminished those advantages, however, I would expect practice if not procedure to regress to something like its former state. For instance, proxy voting, rolling quorums, and restrictive rules were, as Republicans had long pointed out, useful tools of the majority even if they were infringements on minority rights. They permitted the majority to prosecute its agenda in the face of the competing demands on its members' time. In the steady state of a House run by a new party, especially one whose majority is small or whose core is imperfectly cohesive (Dion 1995), such tools (or their practical equivalents) should reappear in the practice if not the publicly acknowledged principles of the majority party.

Organizational reforms in the Senate were much more incremental in the aftermath of the 1995 Republican takeover than those in the House. In particular, no similar centralization of majority party power occurred. Proxy voting in Senate committees and subcommittees was limited but not abolished. The number of standing committees and subcommittees dropped only slightly. And cuts in Senate committee budgets were approximately a third those implemented by the House majority. In any case, a Republican-controlled Senate is not so dramatic a turn of institutional events, given that the Republicans held the Senate from 1981–86, a period that spans most of the cases sampled for my comparative House-Senate analysis.

In both chambers, then, reforms have not diminished the fact that members and their staff are constantly pulled between the interest-driven lure of legislative opportunities and the limits on what they can do. None can afford to invest in every issue; indeed, most members must select just a small number of issues for inclusion in the portfolio of enterprise priorities.

Whither the Study of Legislative Participation?

Changes in institutional arrangements and other developments in the political environment of the contemporary congressman thus suggest that, while the basic model of legislative participation may be robust in most important respects, it is certainly not exhaustive. The study of legislative participation — I not only concede but strongly hope — should help to answer numerous other important questions, questions that I implicitly or explicitly bracket in this book.

First, some of the best scholarship on congressional policy making in recent years has focused on the importance of legislative entrepreneurs. Such actors are crucial, Kingdon (1984) claims, for they seize opportunities to push particular policy proposals onto the legislative agenda. Arnold (1990) refers to these individuals as coalition leaders and places them at the heart of his account of the logic of congressional action. But neither of these award-winning authors attempts to explain why and under what conditions some members and not others choose to invest so heavily in a single issue that they adopt an entrepreneurial role. For instance, Arnold (1990, 89) notes the lack of research on the subject and consciously excludes the question from the scope of his study.

The systematic study of participation provides guidance regarding this important but poorly understood form of legislative behavior. Entrepreneurship or coalition leadership on a given issue is simply a special case of participation, one where the individual ranks at the high end of the formal and informal participation scales. The unresolved theoretical matters relate to whether the factors examined here explain participation equally well at various ranges — specifically, the higher range — of the participation continuum. For instance, entrepreneurship can be conceptualized as a dichotomous choice — whether to invest the enterprise heavily enough to exceed some high threshold of issue-specific participation — by, say, authoring a bill, working aggressively in negotiating and building support for a proposal behind the scenes, or planning and executing obstructionist tactics (see Arnold 1990, chapter 5). The analysis presented here suggests that institutional endowments will figure prominently in the explanation. I furthermore suspect that understanding this form of participation will require more careful reasoning and more sophisticated modeling of how members' interests structure their behavior. For instance, it may well be that the choice, especially for backbenchers, to invest in entrepreneurial activity is not a function simply of interest intensity but also of the confluence of and interaction between several different interests evoked by a single bill.

A second promising direction for research on legislative participation follows from the issues already raised regarding the changes in Congress in the mid-1990s. One reading of the legislative aftermath of the 1994 elections is that a new partisan period has been ushered into the House, if not the Senate. To the extent that this change proves episodic rather than incremental, the behavioral importance of majority-driven strategies discussed in Chapter 3 may increase, at least for a time. Likewise, to the extent that institutional reforms placed significantly greater sanctions and rewards in the hands of the House Speaker, the factor I have here labeled prosecuting the administration's agenda might be better recast as prosecuting the agenda of the party leadership. Future work on legislative participation should thus more carefully explore the ability, in the form of tangible incentives and resources, of party leaders to engage members in the prefloor politics of prosecuting the party's agenda. However transitory the party-related changes of the mid-1990s prove to be, in any case, the growing currency of partisan theories of legislative organization (for example, Aldrich 1995; Cox and McCubbins 1993; Rohde

1991, 1995) recommends that the investigation of party importance in Congress extend beyond the traditional analysis of revealed preferences (that is, voting coalitions) to the partisan factors that shape members' revealed intensities.

A third and what I take to be an especially promising line of inquiry is the extent to which and the ways in which public and private interest groups mobilize legislators to serve as active agents on the groups' behalf. Elsewhere Frank Wayman and I (Hall and Wayman 1990) have observed that political strategists of moneyed interests contribute most to candidates most likely to support group positions (absent any group contribution). That tendency should be considered more than a little irrational, in light of the widely held view that contributions and lobbying are intended to affect members' revealed preferences — that is, their votes (see, for example, Austen-Smith and Wright 1994; Kau and Rubin 1982; Grenzke 1989; Wright 1985, 1990; but see also McKissick 1995). Why would political action committee (PAC) strategists operate in this ostensibly irrational fashion? The answer we develop is that the purpose of rational PAC allocations is rarely to change members' minds but much more frequently to induce sympathetic legislators to participate actively on issues that the group cares about. The high organizational price that both public and private groups frequently pay for lobbying activity is likewise intended not to persuade but to subsidize the participation of the sympathetic member's enterprise by supplying it with policy-relevant information, political intelligence, and legislative arguments and language — even speeches and talking points that might enable the group's legislative agent to do better at persuading potential members of a winning coalition to support the group's point of view.[5] In short, we need to know much more about the influence of campaign contributions and lobbying on legislative coalition building than the further analysis of roll call voting can tell us.

There are, I believe, other important areas of legislative research to which the study of legislative participation might contribute, questions that bear on larger matters of representation, legislative organization, and collective choice in Congress. Such matters I have mentioned at various points along the way, but I explore them more fully in the final chapter.

5. In this indirect way, then, lobbying and contributions to sympathetic members may have an indirect effect on the voting decisions of some members. Paradoxically, however, the effect would be most likely to appear in the behavior of members whom PAC strategists and lobbyists did not specifically target. The full effects of interest group investments in legislative voting would thus go undetected in conventional models of roll call voting. See Hall 1994b for a fuller discussion.

Participation, Representation, and Legislative Choice

> It is not necessary that the interested bias should extend to the majority of the assembly. In any particular case it is often enough that it affects two or three of their number. Those two or three will have a greater interest in misleading the body, than any other of its members are likely to have in putting it right. The bulk of the assembly may keep their hands clean, but they cannot keep their minds vigilant or their judgments discerning in matters they know nothing about: and an indolent majority, like an indolent individual, belongs to the person who takes most pains with it. — John Stuart Mill, "Considerations of Representative Government"

Mill was writing of the British Parliament in the nineteenth century. But in the glint and glare of the behavior examined in this book, Mill's words reflect a timeless and intercontinental concern regarding the deliberations of legislative assemblies. One need not (I do not) subscribe to an *ad hominem* harshness regarding member indolence; the common problem is that the typical member of Congress has too much to do, not that she does too little. But the pith of Mill's lament is central to our understanding of the contemporary Congress. In any particular case that comes before her chamber, each legislator must make essentially two decisions: what position to take and how active to be. In any particular case, we have found, the bulk of the assembly is anything but vigilant. Indeed, in any particular case that comes before even the small subset of institutionally designated committee or subcommittee members, much the same can be said.

What are we to make of such behavior? What does it mean for our assessments of Congress as a decision-making institution and the representativeness of legislative deliberations? Does selective participation necessarily imply that Mill's "interested bias" infects congressional decision making? More generally, what implications does the variable participation of members have for our understanding of legislative organization and collective choice in an ostensibly majoritarian assembly? I have touched on such themes at different points in earlier chapters, but certain implications warrant closer elaboration. Depending on the level at which the analysis is pitched and the assumptions about member purpose one is willing to make, the findings of this study suggest to the student of democratic institutions potentially quite different assessments.

Revealed Intensities and Delegate Representation

The first implication is that at one level, that of the principal-agent dyad, the practice of representation in Congress appears to be in excellent health. In light of the substantial literature on this subject, this is no minor matter. Since Miller and Stokes (1963) published their famous essay on the influence of constituencies on Congress, more than three decades ago, students of the institution have spilled considerable ink over the question of whether members act like good delegates, adopting positions in their chamber that reflect the views of their respective districts. Miller and Stokes gave good reason to doubt that members did so in any consistent fashion. The social science literature since then, in turn, has generated a more heartening body of evidence about members' responsiveness. In what remains a classic work on the subject, for instance, Kingdon found that "by several measures used in this study, constituency does appear to be quite important" (1989, 67). Others have elaborated the theoretical basis and found clear support for constituency influence on members' voting (Fiorina 1974; Jackson 1974; Jackson and King 1989). Still, the corpus of work does not unequivocally point to this conclusion. One reviewer unenthusiastically concludes that "some degree of constituency influence, generally varying by issue, has been found in many of these studies" (Jewell 1983, 119). Another, more comprehensive review summarizes the literature thus: "Constituencies do not control the policies adopted by their representatives; they have some influence over what those policies are, but members are by and large free to adopt what they think best" (Bernstein 1989, 104).[1]

However one reads the roll call voting literature, the results of the present study are quite consistent with respect to member responsiveness to district

---

1. My own view is that the best work on this subject never suggests that constituencies will "control" member voting. Rather, the influence of a constituency is conditional in ways that theoretical scholars have examined (see Fenno 1978; Fiorina 1974; Jackson 1974; Jackson and King 1989; Kingdon 1977, 1989). The constituency-relevant hypotheses I develop regarding participation build directly on that scholarship.

interests. The key distinction on which these results turn is between members' revealed preferences and their revealed intensities, between their public positions and their public and nonpublic participation. Whatever the relation may be between opinions within the district and the members' positions, the relation between interests within the district and members' participation is quite clear. To the extent that members perceive a particular issue as relevant to constituents' interests, they invest more of the scarce time and resources of their enterprise in relevant legislative action. This tendency is predictably mitigated in cases where high-profile activity is more likely to incur constituency blame than to bring credit; yet the finding that district interests influence members' participation decisions holds true across qualitatively different policy domains — Agriculture, Energy and Commerce, Education and Labor, and other specific policy areas that these jurisdictions subsume. It holds true across decision-making forums — behind-the-scenes negotiations, public debate. And it holds true across several stages in a sequential legislative process — subcommittee, committee, floor. For those who worry about the responsiveness of representatives to constituents at a time when cynicism about "out-of-touch" incumbents runs high and term limit proposals are the reform of choice, these findings should give a little pause.

I say "a little pause" in that, as Fenno has said, the constituency a member represents is the constituency he or she sees. To this point I have elaborated the corollary, following Dahl (1956), that the constituency a member represents is the minority whose intensity he or she feels. Thus I do not mean this to be a sanguine conclusion. Indeed, there is evidence in the results of Chapter 7 that the cynicism about out-of-touch incumbents is more justified when the relevant subconstituency is unorganized, underclass, or different in race or ethnicity from the typical white citizen. Unfortunately, such evidence is as unremarkable as it is disturbing. In his classic essay written mid-century, *The Semisovereign People*, E. E. Schattschneider (1960) said precisely this. And there is little evidence and less logic developed since then to suggest that the incentives of electoral accountability lead legislators to pay much more attention to poor, unorganized, and nonwhite segments of their constitutional constituencies as the century comes to a close.

The Representativeness of Legislative Deliberations

As I suggested in the opening chapter, the dyadic-delegate standard of representation by no means exhausts what we need to know about the meaning and practice of representation in Congress. Even were one to assume that the practice of democratic elections somehow worked to preserve egalitarianism in members' responsiveness to district constituents, the responsiveness of members to their districts does not a representative assembly make. The standard more appropriate to the evaluation of an institution is what Chamberlin and Courant (1983), following Mill, refer to as the "representativeness of deliberations."[2] Central to this standard is the view that the electoral connection between members and their districts is less an end in itself than it is a means to a larger institutional end — the creation of an assembly that roughly resembles the larger population in the interests and opinions that might find expression in parliamentary deliberation and debate. As Mill puts it:

> Representative assemblies are often taunted by their enemies with being places of mere talk and *bavardage*. There has seldom been more misplaced derision. I know not how a representative assembly can more usefully employ itself than in talk, when the subject of talk is the great public interests of the country, and every sentence of it represents the opinion either of some important body of persons in the nation, or of an individual in whom some such body have reposed their confidence. A place where every interest and shade of opinion in the country can have its cause even passionately pleaded . . . is in itself, if it answered no other purpose, one of the most important political institutions than can exist anywhere, and one of the foremost benefits of free government. (Mill 1975 [1861], 227)

Mill's statement may seem melodramatic to our cynical contemporary tastes, but the issue he raises warrants renewed attention in the study of Congress. Representation, Mill suggests, is something like a process of citizen participation once removed, and it is important in two senses. First, the participation of citizens' elected agents in legislative decision making is not simply instrumental. In the course of any deliberation, some views will be expressed that the chamber may ignore, even actively repudiate. But such expressions should not therefore be derided as "mere talk." Rather, the expression of what subsequently prove to be minority opinions is central to the practice of democratic consent. Participation is what obligates minorities to outcomes they do not like (Herzog 1989). It is the solution of liberal democracy to the puzzle, How is it that free agents can agree *to* something they do not agree *with?* Thus did Mill hold that members' "indolence" in the assembly's deliberations inherently undermines the practice of representation; that is, one need repair to no argument or evidence that the legislative outcome has been affected. In principle, an assembly may arrive at a popular end without regard to democratic means — but rare is the democratic theorist who would accept that an end thus produced is, by itself, good enough.

2. The interested reader may want to contrast this standard to the notion of collective representation elaborated by Robert Weissberg (1978).

At the same time, Mill is not so unpragmatic as to focus solely on matters of process. The selective participation of members in legislative decision making should also be viewed with suspicion, for it may subvert democratic ends. The decision making of the assembly may be infected with an "interested bias."

Participation, Bias, and the Practice of Legislative Organization

Mill's writings thus raise an empirical question of considerable importance for students of the contemporary Congress. To what extent do members who actively participate in legislative deliberations exhibit the interested bias to which he refers or, alternatively, to what extent are the active few themselves representative of the chamber on whose authority they act? The important theoretical task, in turn, is to understand the conditions under which Mill's bias is likely to characterize the participants in a multistage deliberative process.

Thus does the behavioral focus of this book bear directly on important issues in the recent literature on the nature and purpose of congressional institutions (see, for example, Shepsle and Weingast 1995). Central to this literature are questions about the composition of committees and hence the distributive or informational roles they play in legislative choice (Krehbiel 1991; Shepsle and Weingast 1987a, 1995; Weingast and Marshall 1988). The implication here is *not* that committees are typically composed of preference outliers, as distributive theorists of legislative organization have long contended. But neither is it that committees are rarely composed of preference outliers, as more recent informational theorists assert. Rather, the principal implication is this: the formal theoretical debate about institutional arrangements has begun with the wrong question, or, more accurately, it has not begun with the right one. The right question is this: Who are the principal participants in a given policy area? The profoundly important but implicit and unexamined assumption of institutionalist theory is that the answer is institutionally given, namely, that the membership rolls of standing committees (or subcommittees) determine the identities of those whose preferences warrant our attention.

I have shown that assumption to be largely inaccurate. The "division of labor" in Congress is no structural feature, no matter of organizational design, rational or otherwise, that is somehow imposed and maintained. Rather, it bubbles up from the day-to-day decisions of individual members as they decide how to best allocate the time, energy, and other resources of their enterprise on the numerous issues that arise both within and beyond the panels to which they are assigned. Moreover, even their assignments are not delegated in a way faithful to principal-agent principles. Rather, the membership rolls at the subcommittee as well as the committee level themselves reflect a significant measure of self-selection. Stated somewhat differently, the study of whether committees or even subcommittees are preference outliers is somewhat beside the point. Closer to the point is whether what Carroll once referred to as the "efficient" committee — the issue-specific subset of behind-the-scenes and public players — harbors the "interested bias" to which Mill referred.

THE MEANING OF INTERESTED BIAS

Before we can determine the degree of interested bias in congressional deliberations, we must first break Mill's notion down into its components, *interestedness* on the one hand and *bias* on the other. Translated into the terms of this book, the former refers to a maldistribution in actors' underlying intensities, and the latter refers to a maldistribution in their underlying positions. The only inferences one can draw from the analysis thus far relate to interestedness, not bias. Other things being equal, the more or less self-selected subsets of members who act on specific matters tend to be unrepresentative in the first respect; they tend to be interest-intensity outliers.

Given that interestedness characterizes behavior at each stage of a multi-stage process, does it necessarily imply bias, where *bias* refers to a maldistribution of the policy positions that players hold? The simple answer is no. The simple justification is that members may be "interesteds," to use Shepsle's language (1978), but there is no logic I know that implies that members with similarly intense interests in an issue will automatically have mutually compatible positions (Hall and Grofman 1990; Krehbiel 1991, 134–37). Both Democrats and Republicans may feel strongly about abortion funding and federal Aid to Families with Dependent Children; both white Republicans and black Democrats may feel strongly about affirmative action and civil rights legislation; both energy-consuming Northerners and energy-producing Southerners may feel strongly about oil and natural gas deregulation. But in none of these cases would one impute similar positions to the respective sets of interested legislators.

The conceptual conundrum thus before us is this: What substantive meaning do we have in mind when we speak of legislators' preferences?[3] We know what the concept of preference looks like on the graph paper of the formal economist, where ideal points can be mapped in Euclidian space. But preference in a real-world sense is better captured by Mill's two-dimensional notion

3. For a fuller discussion, see Hall 1995, on which this section directly draws.

of interested bias than it is by the political scientist's comparison of different groups of members on some voting index. Translating Mill's idea back into abstract economics, one needs to know not only which of two legislative goods individual members prefer but their willingness and ability to pay as well. Preferences (even with respect to a single issue) are vectors — psychological phenomena with both direction and force.

It is a contested matter whether roll call votes accurately reveal members' sincere positions — the direction of their preferences. But in any case roll call votes in Congress do not reveal force, the intensity of their preferences (Hall 1995; Krehbiel 1990). One cannot recover from the voting record a member's willingness to pay. Votes are not fungible assets; when the roll is called, a member either uses her vote or loses it. She cannot abstain and save her yea or nay for some later use, thereby allowing her to spend more on issues she cares more about. And if there are differences in members' ability to pay for some particular legislative outcome, as I have argued in this book, neither can those differences be recovered from the behavior of members at the only moment in the legislative process when all members are equally endowed.[4]

SELECTIVE PARTICIPATION AND DELIBERATIVE BIAS: AN EXPLORATION

The challenge for the study of representative deliberations, then, is this: How can we capture both legislative intensities and policy positions — the twin components of Mill's interested bias? My hope is that framing the empirical study of legislative preference in this way will generate conceptually more clear and hence more productive work in the interplay between the wonderings of graph-paper theory and the wanderings of empirical research.

Undoubtedly many of the methodological and measurement problems ahead are beyond my ability to anticipate. But nonetheless I feel obliged to make a brief if reckless exploration into the wilderness before I quit the book. The exploratory path I take is not theoretically blind, however. Bernard Grofman and I have argued elsewhere (Hall and Grofman 1990) that the existence of an interested bias on the relevant panels of actors turns on two highly variable factors: the extent to which particular issues involve geographically concentrated benefits and widely dispersed costs (or vice versa) and, more

---

4. The theoretical exception to this is that members engage in ad-hoc logrolling, something like a barter system in votes. I have little doubt that such arrangements sometimes affect legislative decisions in important ways. But absent a commonly recognized (changing) rate of exchange (even were there an exogenously given institutional enforcement mechanism), it is not apparent how one uses votes to get at preferences in a sense that has substantive meaning in the world.

specifically, the extent to which the prospective beneficiaries have mutually compatible positions. I extend that logic here to the "efficient" as well as the official committee. The empirical path I take is to return to the six bills analyzed in Chapter 7 in an attempt to track the interested bias of which Mill speaks.

The intensity that members reveal in bill-specific deliberations, I have argued, is reflected in their participation — the investments of their time, staff, and legislative energy in the legislative action. The question thus becomes, to what extent do participants in a multistage process of deliberation exhibit bias in the issue-specific policy positions they hold?

To gain some initial insight into this question, I employ the simple distinction I have used before between participants and nonparticipants, between players and nonplayers in particular legislative games. In addition, I employ admittedly problematic indicators of members' positions on the policy dimension underlying each bill. The first of these indicators relies on roll call voting indexes. Above and elsewhere (Hall and Grofman 1990), I have criticized the use of voting indexes to get at members' sincere preferences, so it is best I be clear about their use here. I use them to get at members' public positions, not their preferences. Second, I use the available voting index most relevant to the issue under investigation, and I correct for measurement error following the procedure described in Hall and Grofman (1990, 1154–55). Finally, I should note that roll call voting indexes are inherently conservative with respect to any finding of difference between the chamber and subsets of real or presumed participants (Hall and Grofman 1990; Londregan and Snyder 1994; Snyder 1992).

Because of such problems, I also return to the district-level demographic characteristics that I used to measure issue-specific district interests in the floor analysis of Chapter 7. Again, I do not mean to imply that measures (of one type) of interest can be easily interpreted as indicators of members' positions (Hall and Grofman 1990, 1157–58). The key assumption I must make, one that deserves close critical scrutiny, is whether the issue-specific demographic characteristic indicates not simply greater district interest but a greater likelihood that the district's representative will support the program at hand. Such indicators are valid to the extent that one can reasonably assume that interests and positions are positively correlated (Jackson 1973). To the extent such an assumption is reasonable, the indicator of district interest is well suited to testing whether Mill's interested bias is present among the nonindolent few.

In sum, my purpose is to investigate whether members whose revealed intensities are high, namely, those who actively participate — for whatever purposes, enjoying whatever resources, burdened by whatever constraints — are

Table 9.1　Position, Participation, and Bias in Agricultural Deliberations: The 1981 Farm Bill, Dairy Title

	N	NFU Score		Dairy Cows in District	
		Mean	T-Test	Mean	T-Test
Committee nonmember	391	48.8		21.9k	
Committee member	43	64.4	5.03	52.5k	4.21
Committee actor	12	70.8	3.67	89.7k	5.08
Subcommittee member	14	68.1	3.45	86.6k	5.25
Subcommittee actor	5	79.0	3.28	159.2k	6.91
Floor Nonactor	393	49.5		19.2k	
Floor Actor	41	58.9	2.92	80.6k	8.83

Source: National Farmers Union 1982a, 1982b; U.S. Department of Agriculture 1981.
Note: T-test statistics are from a difference-in-means test between the mean of the italicized category and the subsequent categories of each group. (For details of measurement, see Appendix F.)

Table 9.2　Position, Participation, and Bias in Agricultural Deliberations: The 1981 Farm Bill, Peanuts Title

	N	NFU Score		District Peanut Production (Bushels)	
		Mean	T-Test	Mean	T-Test
Committee nonmember	391	48.8		5.2m	
Committee member	43	64.4	5.03	28.5m	2.69
Committee actor	11	67.0	2.80	107.6m	6.46
Subcommittee member	10	66.9	2.68	120.2m	6.98
Subcommittee actor	5	68.9	2.11	235.3m	10.54
Floor nonactor	404	49.8		2.2m	
Floor actor	30	57.9	2.17	79.1m	7.99

Source: National Farmers Union 1982a, 1982b; U.S. Department of Agriculture 1981.
Note: T-test statistics are from a difference-in-means test between the mean of the italicized category and the subsequent categories of each group. (For details of measurement, see Appendix F.)

unrepresentative of their parent committee or parent chamber in the public positions they adopt.

Interested Bias in Agricultural Policy Deliberations

Tables 9.1 and 9.2 present the results of this exercise for the two agricultural bills analyzed in Chapter 7, the dairy and peanuts titles of the 1981 Farm

Bill. The tables report conventional difference-in-means tests between different categories of members using the voting index of the National Farmers Union (NFU), an organization known for its support of federal agricultural subsidies and other governmental interventions to boost farm income. Table 9.1 reports the same tests using the number of dairy cows in the district to indicate not only the district's interest in the program but also the electorally minded members' incentives to support legislation friendly to dairy producers and related business interests. Likewise, Table 9.2 uses district peanut production to indicate members' incentives to support acreage allotments and other USDA interventions to control supply and thus bolster the income of district peanut producers and people in related occupations.

Agricultural programs such as these, of course, are classic examples of cases where benefits are concentrated and costs dispersed, with little cause for conflict among the attentive constituencies. They are thus cases where we should most expect Mill's interested bias to operate. And that is precisely what we find. Note first that the committee and subcommittee of jurisdiction are outliers on both measures, as the distributive institutionalist would predict. But the more striking and important finding is that post-assignment participants are biased — indeed, significantly more biased than nominal members of the respective panels.

In the case of the dairy legislation, a bill that would generate more than five billion dollars per year in subsidies for dairy producers, the evidence of an interested bias infecting the deliberations is apparent at each stage (when either measure is used). Participants in the dairy subcommittee deliberations average more than thirty points higher on the NFU index than the committee nonmember, while participants in committee deliberations average more than twenty points higher. On average, the subcommittee participant represents a district with over seven times as many dairy cows as the committee nonmember, and the committee participant average is well more than four times as great.

While the difference between actors and nonactors on the floor is not as great, the tests show that even during consideration of a multibillion dollar program under an open rule, the floor actors were far more biased than nonactors toward the program. Indeed, neither committee nor floor muted the enthusiasms of the dozen or so participants representing districts with some of the highest levels of dairy production in the nation. The multibillion-dollar dairy title was passed by the House in a year of budget-cutting fever and ultimately signed into law by one the most conservative, market-oriented presidents in the postwar period.

Evidence of Mill's interested bias is at least as strong in the case of the 1981 peanuts title. In this case, too, it is important that we look at participants and

*Table 9.3   Position, Participation, and Bias in Education and Labor
Deliberations: The 1982 Job Training Partnership Act*

| | N | AFL-CIO COPE Score | | Percentage Unemployed in District, Fifteen Weeks | |
		Mean	T-Test	Mean	T-Test
Committee nonmember	401	49.9		6.7	
Committee member	33	61.4	1.85	7.0	.90
Committee actor	21	65.7	2.07	7.2	1.09
Subcommittee member	9	62.8	1.59	8.4	2.35
Subcommittee actor	5	68.8	1.59	8.8	1.93
Floor nonactor	355	48.0		6.5	
Floor actor	79	63.0	3.54	7.5	3.49

Source: Kirkland 1982a, 1982b; U.S. Bureau of the Census 1981.
Note: T-test statistics are from a difference-in-means test between the mean of the italicized category and the subsequent categories of each group. For details of measurement, see discussion in text and Appendix F.

not simply panel memberships. According to the NFU index, participants were more favorably disposed at every stage to farmer-friendly interventions by USDA than were nonparticipants. But the most striking evidence of behavior-driven bias appears in the district peanut production of participants and nonparticipants. Again, the data suggest that members of both the committee and subcommittee of jurisdiction are outliers, but the mean district peanut production of the committee actor was four times the average for all committee members. And the mean peanut production of the subcommittee actor was twice that of all subcommittee members and eight times the average for all committee members.

When the peanuts title reached the House floor, it faced a challenge from consumer-oriented members who were exercised by a recent, drought-induced, triple-digit inflation in the price of peanut butter and other peanut products. Even so, the program supporters far outnumbered the challengers, such that floor participants were significantly more farmer-friendly according to the NFU index and their districts exhibited levels of peanut production thirty-five times that of nonparticipants. In the end, the USDA peanut program easily survived the challenge, despite the fact that a peanut grows neither in Brooklyn nor in 80 percent of other U.S. House districts.

Interested Bias in Employment Policy Deliberations

Table 9.3 presents a similar analysis of bias in the multistage deliberations over the 1982 Job Training Partnership Act (JTPA), perhaps the single most important domestic program enacted during President Reagan's first term. As I described in Chapter 7, JTPA would replace the expiring Comprehensive Employment and Training Act. The latter subsidized job experience in the public sector; the new program would subsidize private-sector experience and training: local governing councils would work with local industry to tailor the program to private-sector needs. At the same time, JTPA would concentrate federal benefits in some districts — namely, those hardest hit by the recession — more than others, and benefits would accrue not only to the unemployed but to local businesses and industries as well.

Table 9.3 produces somewhat less striking results than the two earlier cases. Nonetheless, we can safely conclude that, according to the AFL-CIO's Committee on Political Education (COPE) score, committee and subcommittee members were more likely than other members of the House to adopt positions supporting spending on federal employment and training. The same pattern appears in the district data as well; subcommittee and committee members represented districts with higher levels of interest in programs addressing problems of structural unemployment.

More important, participants at each stage exhibit higher levels of unemployment than nonparticipants. In particular, subcommittee actors represented districts with the highest unemployment levels of any subset, more than two points higher than the average for committee nonmembers and almost two points higher than that for committee members. Again, the clear implication is that the comparison of mere members and nonmembers tells us too little of what we need to know. When we get to the floor stage, in turn, the differences between actors and nonactors in floor deliberations is striking according to both measures, with the average for actors fifteen points higher on the COPE index and a full point higher on the district indicator of structural unemployment.

In sum, for the first three bills under examination, there is good reason to worry that the interested bias of locally minded members infected legislative deliberations. To put the point somewhat differently, the interesteds who acted as if they were legislative agents of the chamber were not representative of the chamber's legislators, even applying inherently conservative tests. Whatever the legislative end, the deliberative means appears to have fallen short of Mill's standard.

Representative Deliberations? The Other Three Cases

The results of identical tests using analogous data for the other three bills project a less disturbing silhouette of the deliberative process. If the bias of an interested few sometimes subverts the will of an indolent majority, this is not a robust empirical regularity insofar as I am able to determine. Again, we

Table 9.4   Position, Participation, and Bias in Education and Labor Deliberations? The 1981 Older Americans Act Reauthorization

	N	AFL-CIO COPE Score		Percentage of Elderly Below Poverty Line in District	
		Mean	T-Test	Mean	T-Test
Committee nonmember	401	49.9		1.6	
Committee member	33	61.4	1.85	1.5	(1.07)
Committee actor	12	58.8	.82	1.6	.05
Subcommittee member	4	47.3	(.20)	1.6	(.09)
Subcommittee actor	3	55.3	.23	1.5	(.34)
Floor nonactor	395	49.6		1.6	
Floor actor	36	62.2	2.17	1.6	(.09)

Source: Kirkland 1982a, 1982b; U.S. Bureau of the Census 1981.
Note: T-test statistics are from a difference-in-means test between the mean of the italicized category and the subsequent categories of each group. (For details of measurement, see Appendix F.)

must repair to specific conditions regarding when and where we should expect Mill's bias to appear.

The Older Americans Act did not concentrate benefits in particular geographic locales. Elderly constituents are widely distributed across congressional districts, and this program targeted for benefits mostly the low-income elderly, who are less likely to vote or otherwise mobilize in ways that matter to an election-minded member. In table 9.4, we do find that Education and Labor is biased, as far as the COPE voting index goes. But additional analysis prevents us from making a strong and probably incorrect inference about bias in legislative deliberations at the prefloor stage. Subcommittee members actually scored lower on the index than did other members of the House. And we cannot conclude with statistical confidence, even applying generous thresholds, that either committee or subcommittee participants on this bill were more predisposed to support AFL-CIO positions than their ill-positioned colleagues.

Moreover, the issue-specific indicator of constituency-induced positions suggests that panel members and nonmembers on the one hand and bill participants and nonparticipants on the other are as like one another as one could reasonably expect to find. So too with comparisons between floor actors and nonactors. Participants on the floor for the Older Americans Act score thirteen points higher on the COPE voting index, yet the two groups are nearly identical in terms of the district benefits targeted to the low-income elderly. Neither

Table 9.5   Position, Participation, and Bias in Energy and Commerce Deliberations? The 1983 Universal Telephone Service Preservation Act

	N	ADA Score Mean	ADA Score T-Test	Rural (%) Mean	Rural (%) T-Test	Poverty (%) Mean	Poverty (%) T-Test	Communications Workers (%) Mean	Communications Workers (%) T-Test
Committee nonmember	391	48.6		27.0		12.5		2.9	
Committee member	42	52.7	.75	22.4	(1.22)	11.4	(1.18)	3.0	1.08
Committee actor	14	51.6	.30	20.7	(.95)	11.0	(.89)	2.9	.28
Subcommittee member	14	68.4	2.20	15.6	(1.81)	12.7	.21	2.9	(.14)
Subcommittee actor	8	68.1	1.50	15.2	(1.4)	12.6	.09	2.8	(.51)
Floor nonactor	368	48.3		25.3		12.4		2.9	
Floor actor	65	52.9	.99	33.1	2.53	12.4	.01	3.0	.67

Source: Americans for Democratic Action 1984, 1985; U.S. Bureau of the Census 1981.
Note: T-test statistics are from a difference-in-means test between the mean of the italicized category and the subsequent categories of each group. T-statistics in parentheses indicate that the difference was the reverse of the expected direction. (For details of measurement, see Appendix F.)

is there evidence in the floor record of significant divisions between participants and nonparticipants on the panel and the floor, the COPE differences notwithstanding. It remains possible that either a liberal or conservative outlier at some stage sneaked an unpopular provision into the bill, but the evidence that the deliberative process was roughly representative is about as good as one might find in data of these kinds.

I will treat more briefly the two bills that emerged from House Energy and Commerce. Suffice it to say that in these two cases the evidence regarding bias is mixed at best. With respect to the Universal Telephone Service Preservation Act, subcommittee actors appeared more predisposed toward federal regulation as an instrument of equity, at least as this dimension is captured by members' ADA scores. But Commerce Committee actors were virtually indistinguishable from the larger chamber membership; one might reasonably conjecture that committee actors had both the ability and the willingness to "mute the enthusiasms" of the Telecommunications Subcommittee. The other, more issue-specific indicators also lead one to doubt that a nontrivial bias infected committee deliberations. Using three different indicators, most of the difference-in-means tests yield results opposite in sign to the prediction of the outlier hypothesis. Oddly enough, if a deliberative bias appears, it does so during open consideration of the bill on the House floor, where actors tended to represent more rural districts, which would benefit most from regulatory interventions of the act. So, too, in the Weatherization and Employment Act. There is no clear

Table 9.6   Position, Participation, and Bias in Energy and Commerce Deliberations? The 1983 Weatherization and Employment Act

	N	ADA		District Heat/ Unemployment Index	
		Mean	T-Test	Mean	T-Test
Committee nonmember	391	48.6		4.8	
Committee member	42	52.7	.75	4.3	(.48)
Committee actor	7	48.6	.03	5.4	.26
Subcommittee member	11	55.7	.67	2.8	(1.05)
Subcommittee actor	4	29.4	(1.16)	4.7	(.06)
Floor nonactor	368	48.1		4.6	
Floor actor	65	54.1	1.33	5.9	1.85

Source: Americans for Democratic Action 1984, 1985; U.S. Bureau of the Census 1981.
Note: T-test statistics are from a difference-in-means test between the mean of the italicized category and the subsequent categories of each group. T-statistics in parentheses indicate that the difference was the reverse of the expected direction. (See Appendix F for details of measurement.)

evidence of a proprogram bias among either panel members or participants, using either indicator. But the data suggest that some proprogram bias may enter floor deliberations, in that floor participants are distinguishable on both measures from the "indolent" majority of their colleagues.

PARTICIPATION, RESPONSIVENESS,
AND REPRESENTATIVE DELIBERATIONS: A SUMMARY

While there is significant variation we can attribute to other factors, there is little doubt that members of Congress, in choosing how to allocate their resources and set their legislative priorities, systematically respond to constituency interests. Pitched at the dyadic-delegate level, representation is strong, even though the district constituency the member represents is the subconstituency whose intensity she feels.

But as the exploratory analysis in this chapter clearly suggests, it does not follow that representativeness in legislative deliberations is a natural consequence of responsiveness to the constituency. Paradoxically, the reverse is closer to the truth: the more strongly members represent intense constituency interests in their participation decisions, the less likely are the deliberations of the chamber to approximate Mill's standard of representativeness.

Reform-minded critics of congressional committees and subcommittees have frequently invoked a similar worry (Hardin, Shepsle, and Weingast 1983), but the implication here is that institutional reforms reform institutions; they have no necessary, much less predictable, effect on interest-driven behavioral tendencies. Thus did we see in the first three cases that the unrepresentativeness of the committee and subcommittee memberships was magnified by the constituency-driven participation choices of individuals. In the other three cases, where concentrated district benefits were not at stake, evidence of a behavior-induced bias was not discernible in the prefloor deliberations, even when generous standards were applied. In short, we observe different patterns under identical institutional arrangements, suggesting that theorizing about institutions with little more than a highly stylized theory of individual behavior may impede our understanding of both.

Legislative Choice and Democratic Consent

From the foregoing discussion if not the thrust of this book, several other implications for our understanding of legislative choice and democratic consent follow.

Before we can understand how collective decisions emerge from games played by players with (imputed) preferences, we must first understand why members decide to become players. Baldly put, a theory of behavioral choice must precede a theory of collective choice, and the theory of behavioral choice must entail something more than and different from a theory of voting. The theory of collective choice, in turn, requires something more than and different from the premise, penned on constitutional parchment, that a majority of formally equal members rules.

In the study of legislative choice, of course, a version of minority rule is evident in the large literature on the distributive Congress.[5] As they have developed over the past two decades, however, distributive theories of legislative choice begin with the premise and ensuing puzzle of one member, one vote majority rule. Focused on the theoretical instability of unstructured majoritarianism, the most prominent works have concentrated on the institutional and procedural arrangements to explain minority-driven, distributive policies —Kenneth Shepsle's notion of structure-induced equilibrium leading the way (1979, 1986). With respect to specific policy domains, a relatively uninterested majority trades away its constitutional right to decide, while its members, in return, anticipate legislative advantages in domains of their own choosing. The self-selection of interested members onto committees, the allocation of

5. For recent reviews, critiques, extensions, and challenges to this literature, see Krehbiel 1991 and the papers published in Shepsle and Weingast 1995. Part of the discussion in this section is adapted from Hall 1993 and 1995.

agenda power and other parliamentary rights, the assignment of restrictive rules to bills in the House, and the procedural advantages awarded to committees at the postfloor stage, in turn, restrain agents of nominal majorities from undoing, bill by bill, the cross-committee logrolling arrangements that redound to the electoral benefit of alternating minorities. Policy benefits, then, are distributed to members whose districts value them most.

As I noted earlier, distributive impulses undoubtedly characterize the process through which important legislative decisions are sometimes made. Specifically, we should expect such impulses (which occur with highly variable frequency across bills situated in many different jurisdictions) to be prominent when program benefits are geographically concentrated but costs are not. Under such conditions, however, a bill exhibiting distributive bias might well succeed not because of institutionalized logrolling but because of rational abdication by the large majority of members busy with what, to them, are more important matters. Hence, what appear to be gains from trade hold together on the floor because they are behaviorally "self-enforcing," not because of institutionalized arrangements or enforcement mechanisms. A majoritarian maverick may well have the incentive and the opportunity to make mischief. But under such conditions she is unlikely to have the willingness and ability to pay the information and transaction costs that serious mischief making entails. Mounting a viable challenge requires far more than simply offering an amendment that echoes on the floor, especially when the majority (whose votes the maverick needs) is, if not indolent, simply uninterested, and the mere costs of credibly communicating to 217 other members are nontrivial, if not prohibitive.

When concentrated and compatible constituency interests are less evident, legislative choice is less likely to exhibit a clear distributive character. Indeed, considerable evidence presented here suggests that those conditions may not be terribly common; as Krehbiel (1991) has forcefully argued, the distributive nature of Congress may be overblown in recent institutionalist theory. Whatever interests drive committee self-selection, we have found that the interests driving subcommittee self-selection and selective participation are several and qualitatively different. Even on House Agriculture, members' personal policy interests are at work in both choice processes, independent of their constituency interests. And there is no logic of which I am aware that implies that members active on issues due to their personal policy interests or ideological commitments will tend to have closely compatible issue positions. Even on an Agriculture committee, then, constituency interests and hence distributive impulses vary (Hall and Grofman 1990). On other committees, such cross-issue variance is even greater.

Still, the absence of a distributive character in a program-benefits sense does not imply that the legislative choice process or the choice itself will be majoritarian. The patterns of behavior revealed in this book suggest that minorities of interested members usually govern the legislative process. Their interests may differ and their positions may conflict, but the typical game is nonetheless played by the few, not by the many. The notion of an "act of Congress" or, similarly, the idea that "Congress acts" is thus seldom more than textbook myth, legal fiction, or logical fallacy. Some small, largely self-selected subset acts in the name of Congress, and that subset is rarely a majority of equal members. Acting in the name of Congress, that subset nonetheless fashions the host of specific provisions that constitute the typical act, which in the end enjoys the constitutional imprimatur of both legality and legitimacy. Thus do courts invariably repair to the statements, amendments, and other determinations of active players whenever interpretations of "legislative intent" are contested.

Of course, the full membership is empowered through one or another procedural means to monitor, modify, or reject what some interested subset proposes (Krehbiel 1987). To the extent that interested actors are heterogeneous in their positions, in turn, an "informationally efficient" process of legislative signaling may induce outcomes that approximate majority rule (Krehbiel 1991). One might say that a majority of minimally attentive members thus provide their "consent" in some abstract sense. But if majoritarianism (remote or otherwise) is to be thereby imputed, the age-old issues of explicit and tacit consent must be reexamined in the context of Congress.

The results of this book suggest that explicit consent is perhaps as rare in Congress as it is in nonmythical accounts of democratic politics, popular sovereignty, or constitution building. When the issues are salient and the choices clearly defined, most members of Congress may well get into the deliberative mix or at least engage in perceptive signal seeking. But such cases do not make for a good "stylized" account of individual decision making upon which a theory of collective choice can confidently rest. Only a small number of the specific decisions that go into the construction of a particular bill are ever subjected to a vote of any kind, nor are the preferences of most members anticipated by those who act as the principal legislative entrepreneurs. For the theorist to rightly register members' preferences on an abstract graph, members must invest substantial time, energy, or legislative capital. Most members most of the time do not do that; they rationally abdicate. And if you do not appear at least somewhat vigilant and discerning, to embellish Mill, you cannot assume that others will treat you as if you were.

More accurately, those who do invest do so in varying degrees. Members' choices about when and to what extent they will participate are the principal means of registering the intensity of their positions in the legislative process.

If legislative majorities do not explicitly consent, can we plausibly assume that, despite their inaction, they tacitly consent? Democratic theorists have long thought the concept of tacit consent a dubious notion, something of a fig leaf to cover the embarrassment of liberal democracies where political participation is low.

My view is that tacit consent is no less slippery in a legislative context, even though participation in floor roll calls, unlike participation in elections (and constitutional foundings), is nearly universal. This is not to say, however, that all members must be equally involved in every decision. Nonparticipation does not inherently imply abdication; rather, it can reflect a process of delegation by the chamber (or party) to some subset of members who act as its agents (see Kiewiet and McCubbins 1991; Krehbiel 1991). Public bodies, like private organizations, can achieve substantial gains in efficiency by implementing a division of labor that brings expertise to bear on complex matters in a timely fashion (Krehbiel 1991). Indeed, I suspect that informational processes of this kind are no small part of the collective-choice process most of the time. No one would assert — I certainly do not — that panels of members or subsets of players can do whatever they want in the name of the chamber. But neither would one make such a claim about a dictator in the name of the state. Even indolent members can be roused to revolt when intense minorities prove guilty of gross malpractice in their nominal role as chamber agents. There are always some limits.

But because of the competing demands on the mass of legislators, we have seen, those limits in most cases are fairly broad. Hence, the student of democratic assemblies must worry that the focused few will bring an interested bias into the decisions of the organization in a way that is not easily checked. One cannot simply assume that reputed specialists will act as delegates of the district delegates, the practice of representation thus a process of citizen participation twice removed. This assumption becomes especially troublesome in light of the consistent findings in this book that reputed specialists are largely self-selected rather than formally delegated and that the costs of monitoring what they do are invariably high. To put the point in Mill's terms, it is as true in Congress now as it was in the House of Commons two centuries ago that members cannot "keep their minds vigilant or their judgments discerning in matters they know nothing about." And about most provisions in most bills (and about many provisions in prominent bills), we know, most members of Congress have neither the time nor the interest to know much, still less participate in a meaningful fashion. At best, they receive simple signals or quick cues from colleagues who presumably know something more than they (Kingdon 1989; Krehbiel 1991; Matthews and Stimson 1970). And even then, they receive and respond to more or less informative signals only in those (selected) instances when an interested entrepreneur emerges who is willing to invest heavily in contesting (or credibly threatening to contest) a provision by offering an amendment and forcing a roll call vote on the floor.

Majoritarianism in Congress, then, is a behaviorally contingent thing, the constitutional and institutional rules governing legislative games notwithstanding. Whether and to what extent a minority of players produces policy choices that resemble what a fully engaged, egalitarian assembly would do are questions to which we should expect no categorical answers. Rather, one need look to the behavioral conditions, explored in this book, that transform Mill's indolent majority into a relatively numerous and representative set of legislators who engage in the deliberations of any given legislative game.

Appendixes

Appendix A: Samples of Members and Bills

The data for the core empirical chapters of this book are drawn primarily from bills considered before three House committees: Agriculture, 97th Congress (1981–82); Education and Labor, 97th Congress (1981–82); Energy and Commerce, 98th Congress (1983–84). In Chapter 6 I analyzed identical committee markup data that were collected for one committee, Education and Labor, for a single congress (the 87th, 1961–62) a decade before the democratizing reforms of the 1970s. Finally, the analysis in Chapter 8 relies on identical markup data from the same three committees in the early 1990s (the 103rd Congress, 1993–94). Here I describe the samples of bills and members that constitute the various datasets analyzed.

SAMPLES OF MEMBERS, 97TH AND 98TH CONGRESSES

In general, the samples of members and bills that I analyzed in the central empirical chapters (Part 2) contain almost the full populations of all three committees in the respective congresses during the period of the study. My initial strategy was to gather the appropriate data from committee records (see Appendix B) and staff interviews for every member of each committee who held membership for the entire two-year congress. To the extent that this proved impossible, I made a special effort to interview sets of departed staffers in order to achieve a sample of members that was roughly stratified according to party, seniority, and subcommittee membership. I was successful in these efforts, although seven former staffers ultimately had to be interviewed by phone, with the interview supplemented by a mail questionnaire. In the end, I collected both interview and archival data on 79 percent of House Agriculture members, 88 percent of Education and Labor members, and 79 percent of Energy and Commerce members.

SAMPLES OF BILLS

For each committee, I selected dense samples of bills. In choosing the samples, I attempted to make the number of bills included from the various subcommittees roughly proportionate to the number that were reported for full-committee action, but I generally excluded those bills that committee records revealed to be trivial. In the end, the samples — twenty-one bills for Agriculture, seventeen for Education and Labor, twenty for Energy and Commerce — included more than half of the bills for which legislative markup at the full- or subcommittee level was more than perfunctory.

In short, the respective samples of bills include a good mix of major and minor bills, as well as bills reported from each of the nonoversight subcommittees. If there is any bias in the samples, then, it is a self-conscious one against minor or noncontroversial legislative actions. A complete listing of all the bills used in the analysis of the several congresses examined in this book is available on request.

In Chapter 6 I took advantage of the access I had obtained to records of Education and Labor markups for the 87th Congress in order to better evaluate the several competing hypotheses that derive from the older sociological theory of participation and to support the alternative theory that I develop in this book. The markup minutes for this earlier Congress were kept in identical form by the same person who kept the markup records upon which I relied for the 97th Congress. I used the same sampling and measurement strategies for the 87th Congress that I used for later congresses. Participation data were collected for all members who served on the Education and Labor Committee for the entire 87th Congress.

In Chapter 8 I employ identical committee markup data and measures for the 103rd Congress. In this dataset as well, all members who sat on the committee for the entire congress were included. Bills were sampled according to the same criteria described above.

Appendix B: Committee Records and Markup Participation

The unpublished records on file in committee and subcommittee offices provide the political scientist with an embarrassment of riches with respect to committee decision making in general and member participation in particular. These records — which were unavailable to committee scholars before the early 1970s (see, for example, Fenno 1966; 1973a; Manley 1970; Price 1972) when most markups were held in closed executive session — should prove invaluable to the progress future scholars might achieve. The records, of course, are not equally helpful across all committees and subcommittees; a few committees do not permit full public access.

But most House and Senate panels now maintain detailed records of their markups and make them available to scholars.

THE RECORDS OF THREE COMMITTEES ACROSS TWO CONGRESSES

The relevant records of the House committees on Agriculture and Education and Labor were detailed and complete. This was due in part to the fact that the people responsible for keeping the records over most of the postwar period were extremely sensitive to the importance of the historical record. It is also due to the fact that the full and subcommittees in Agriculture and the full committee in Education and Labor kept two different but overlapping kinds of records of the markup sessions. One was a verbatim account of the markup proceedings, transcribed by a professional stenographer. The other was a separate set of detailed minutes, compiled by a committee clerk or secretary from notes taken in person. In the case of House Agriculture, these minutes were published by the committee — the only committee in either chamber to do so to date. Unfortunately, record keeping by Education and Labor subcommittees was less routinized: some subcommittees kept minutes, some did not. Indeed, for several of the bills studied here, the subcommittee records were altogether missing — hence the diminished number of subcommittee markup observations for this committee. The records for House Agriculture were maintained in the same way for the 103rd Congress as they were for the 97th. By the 103rd, Education and Labor had stopped distilling the markup events into minutes, but it did maintain a verbatim transcript of every markup for this congress, including records of attendance and roll call votes.

Energy and Commerce did not allow public access to the markup transcripts I sought. But the full- and subcommittee minutes are centrally maintained in the full-committee office and were kept in the same way for both congresses studied here. These minutes were very detailed, especially in rough-draft form (minutes are abridged and formatted before being permanently bound and placed in the committee anteroom). These drafts were especially helpful because they provided brief summaries of the issues at stake and the participants in markup debates, enabling me to reconstruct the speaking participation with sufficient accuracy for my measurement purposes — that is, I could distinguish between minor and major speakers. For both the 98th and 103rd Congresses, I relied on the draft minutes.

THE MARKUP DATA

From the available committee and subcommittee records, then, I gathered the following data:

Attendance: For every full-committee markup, the minutes note which members attended. Members, of course, often come in and out of meetings, so that a member may be listed as attending even though he or she missed a substantial part of the meeting. I have only a dichotomous indicator, then, to the effect that the member either did or did not show up at some point.

Voting: I collected data on participation in recorded roll call votes from the markup minutes. For reasons discussed in Chapter 2, members whose votes were cast by proxy were recorded as not having voted. In several cases, a member who missed a markup asked at a subsequent meeting for unanimous consent to have his vote changed from a proxy to a personal vote. Even when such approval was given, I coded him as not having voted.

Speaking: I captured participation in the markup discussion by counting the number of transcript lines attributed to each member. As discussed in Chapter 2, however, considerable care was taken to eliminate speeches that were clearly inconsequential to the bill. Administrative remarks of the chair (or other member serving as presiding officer) that had no substantive relevance to the collective deliberations were not counted. And remarks by other members that were not germane to the bill as well as their responses to roll calls and quorum calls were likewise excluded. In the case of all Energy and Commerce and two Education and Labor subcommittee markups, however, the minutes provided the best records available. In these cases, I counted as a minor speaker anyone who was recorded as saying anything other than a response to a quorum call or roll call vote. Individuals who were also mentioned as speakers in the summaries of the minutes of the markup debate were designated major.

Amending and Procedural Action: I gathered data on members' offering of amendments from the markup minutes or, when necessary, from the verbatim transcripts. Although it was impossible to assess each amendment's relative importance to the shape of a bill, the records are sufficiently detailed to allow me to distinguish what are normally referred to as technical or grammatical amendments from those that would have a substantive effect. In order to be placed in the former category, an amendment had to meet two conditions: first, it had to be explicitly referred to as technical, grammatical, or minor and noncontroversial; second, it had to pass without controversy or opposition. The second condition was necessary to screen out amendments that were described by their author as technical or noncontroversial simply as a ploy to disguise their substantive but potentially unpopular effect on the bill. Thus the author's label had to be confirmed by the absence of opposition to it: no objections were raised, no controversy followed, and the matter was decided either by unanimous consent or by voice vote.

So too with motions to insert language into the committee report. While a parliamentary move of this kind has no direct effect on the statutory language, the meaning of a bill to committee outsiders invariably depends on more than statutory language. Other members, executive officials, and especially the courts consider the committee reports in applying and interpreting legislative intent.

Procedural motions were also assumed to be nontrivial, in that they can and often do reflect strategic maneuvering, obstructionist or dilatory tactics, and the like. These were also subsumed in the grammatical-technical-minor category, including moving the previous question, points of order, or motions to table or adjourn. I excluded clearly trivial motions, such as unanimous consent requests to insert something into the record, striking the last word, or taking back one's time.

Agenda-Setting: This variable is intended to capture whether a member played a role in setting the agenda for the committee markup deliberations. A member was coded as having played a significant agenda-setting role if she (1) called up or was otherwise responsible for drafting the bill used as the original markup vehicle, or (2) offered an amendment as a substitute to the vehicle. The author of a substitute was obvious from either the markup minutes or verbatim transcripts, but the markup transcripts invariably revealed the original bill's authors as well. The primary author on the majority side normally calls up the bill or is the first person recognized to explain its contents; if there are (majority or minority) coauthors, they would normally be acknowledged or recognized to give statements before actual markup of the legislation began. The coding of the agenda setting was validated and where necessary modified by information gained from committee staff interviews.

MEASURING PARTICIPATION

Throughout this book, I have tried to describe the coding and measurement strategies used so that the reader could evaluate them in the context of the interpretations I was making. Still, the details regarding the construction of the formal participation scales warrant further discussion. The measure used here was generated using a simple Guttman scaling technique, which confirmed the hierarchical order that seems intuitive in terms of the time and energy required for each of the types of activity and is, in part, inherent in the nature of the data. The measurement scale was developed and applied in the pilot study for the project, whose results are reported in Hall (1987).

I tried several variations on the cut points and components included in the scaling exercise, but all were so highly correlated (all correlations between the trial scales exceeded .95) that they made little difference in the analysis of the pilot study on House Education and Labor (Hall 1987). I then employed the same scale in my analysis of the other two committees for the early 1980s and again in the analysis of the 1961–62 and 1993–94 data.

Using any of these scales, of course, results in the loss of a nontrivial amount of information. A member's amending activity, for instance, is reduced from the number of amendments she actually offered to whether she offered any at all. Hence, a member who offered a single amendment is treated the same as one who offered five. But with the exception of the speaking and amending data, the other activities tended to be either dichotomous or trichotomous, so that more sophisticated scaling was difficult to apply. I thus opted for a method of data reduction that captured several different kinds of decision-making action, that was easily interpretable, and that permitted replication and comparison across bills in different committees and subcommittees.

MARKUP DATA ONLINE

As a final note, I would simply add that it has become increasingly possible to replicate, adapt, modify, or improve by remote means the markup-participation measures used here. For instance, the online service *Legi-Slate* now includes a data base that contains minutes of committee and subcommittee markup sessions. These records usually include descriptions of the bill and its author(s), descriptions of amendments and their authors, roll call voting data, major procedural action, and often brief summaries of the principal issues and the identities of the advocates on each side. (Not surprisingly, however, the more salient, controversial, or lengthy the markup, the more detailed the online markup minutes become.) In short, much of the behavioral data gathered and analyzed here can now be acquired from afar (even from places as distant from Washington as Pasadena or Palo Alto) via the Internet.

Appendix C: Committee and Subcommittee Staff Interviews and Informal Participation

As discussed in Chapter 2, I used face-to-face interviews with committee and subcommittee staff for tapping behind-the-scenes participation in committee decision making and acquiring other information relevant to deliberations on particular bills. Chapter 2 contains a general discussion of these interviews. Here I provide a more detailed description of the interview process and the schedule and measurement of behind-the-scenes participation. Note that I concentrate on the analyses from the early 1980s. I did not conduct similar interviews for my analysis for the 103rd Congress (reported in Chapter 7).

DECIDING WHOM TO INTERVIEW

The first task I faced at this stage of the field research was identifying the individuals who had primary responsibility for staffing each of the bills in the sample at both the subcommittee and the full-committee level. This was accomplished with the generous help of the majority and minority staff directors. They directed me to the most knowledgeable people for each of the bills on my list. I then interviewed each of these staffers (although in some cases this entailed tracking the staffer to a new job that was not on Capital Hill), during which interview I requested the names of other staffers who had been actively involved with that particular bill. This process produced a list of twenty to thirty individuals for each committee who were reported to be the key majority and minority actors at the panel staff level and who had usually played a central role in more than one bill in the sample. All but five of seventy-seven were fully cooperative, producing a response rate of 94 percent. In approximately half the cases (usually those where the staffer had handled more than one bill), either the interview could not be completed or the staffer was willing to talk further. In those cases, a second interview was arranged. In all, more than ninety meetings were held with committee or subcommittee staff.

Different staffers may work on the same bill and yet hold different loyalties and have different experiences; their perceptions and recollections are thus apt to vary. For this reason, I tried to interview at least one majority and one minority staffer for each bill; this proved possible for 88 percent of the bills. Similarly, for approximately 30 percent of the bills, at least one full-committee staffer and one subcommittee staffer were interviewed. Multiple responses to questions on the same bill thus provided an opportunity to systematically check the reliability of the staffer reports. (For reliability checks on specific measures derived from staff interviews, see Chapter 2.)

THE INTERVIEW PROCESS AND SCHEDULE

A structured interview schedule introduces its own problems — the potential damage to rapport being the most important. There is always the problem that the academic's instruments will strike the elite respondent as artificial, simplistic, or awkward — the unhappy result being that the instruments will not be taken seriously. For this reason, rapport was especially important to my interview objectives. For a number of reasons, some of which I had not originally anticipated, however, rapport was not a problem. As described in Appendix B, the first stage of my research involved long hours inspecting committee records on committee premises as well as general hanging around. The unintended consequence of this was that by the time I got around to interviewing people, I was already familiar to committee and subcommittee staffers. On occasion, I was mistakenly referred to as one of the staff, an impression I did not go out of my way to correct (thus following Fenno's example; see 1978, appendix). In a pinch, I'd answer the phone, direct lost visitors to the offices, or help fix the photocopying machine. I thus met many of the staffers I was about to interview; of those whom I hadn't met, many seemed to know who I was and were comfortable talking to me. In cases where I did not know the staffer to be interviewed, one of those I did would introduce me, pave my way with a call, or simply offer, "Tell her I sent you."

In short, the first stage of my research facilitated the second. In less than a quarter of the cases did I begin a committee or subcommittee staff interview without a previous introduction or reference. This, I think, tended to overcome an otherwise natural tendency on the part of staffers to suspect academics or outsiders, though it is hard to be sure. I usually began the interview by briefly noting the research I had done and outlining what I could not discover from the records — hence, what I needed to know that I could learn only from the respondent. In addition, at the beginning of each interview I assured the staffer that her remarks were off the record and simultaneously provided her with a signed statement to that effect. I would then ask permission to record the interview. In only four instances was permission denied. In half a dozen more, the respondent showed some hesitancy, so I withdrew the request, believing that it was more important for the respondent to be at ease than to have a perfect transcript of what was said. For the interviews that were not recorded, I took notes during the interview and fleshed them out immediately after its completion.

The bulk of the interview focused the staffer's memory on the step-by-step development of the bill as it moved through the committee, with my questions mainly geared to tapping information I could not obtain from the records. In conducting the interview, I gave the staffer a list of the committee members to review as she reflected on particular questions.

MEASURING INFORMAL PARTICIPATION: RELIABILITY

The use of the interview transcripts to produce the five-point index of behind-the-scenes participation is described in Chapter 2. In creating that index for the pilot study (Hall 1987), I used two methods to assess the reliability of the measure. First, I had two separate coders (myself and a research assistant) read each transcript, apply the criteria of the index to the discursive accounts, and using these assign a numerical rating to each member for each bill. I did this for all transcripts of taped interviews for all bills in the original study of Education and Labor. Our intercoder reliability, measured by the product-moment correlation of the ratings we assigned to the staffer-bill-member observations ($n = 833$), was .95. In cases where coder discrepancy did exist, I averaged our ratings.

For bills where more than one staffer was interviewed, I also tested for interstaffer reliability. A comparison of all dyads of staffers' (coded) assessments of the informal roles played by member i on bill j, produced a product-moment correlation of .86. When the comparison was confined to majority-minority staffer dyads, the correlation was (surprisingly) nearly identical (.87). When the comparison was confined to majority full committee and majority subcommittee staffers (Education and Labor's minority did not have distinct full- and subcommittee staffs), the correlation measured .84.

Given the multiple sources of ratings, there remain several ways to calculate the informal participation of member i on bill j. I chose to average the minority staffers' responses to produce the Republican informal participation scores and the majority staffers' ratings to produce the Democrats' scores, rather than, say, simply averaging across all staffers. My assumption in doing so was that staff members interact more often with members (and members' personal staffers) of their own party, and thus they are in a better position to accurately report the role that those enterprises played. As the intraparty staffer correlation suggests, in any case, Republican and Democratic staffers did not report significantly different perceptions of members' informal participation, so that my strategy made little statistical difference.

Similar though less comprehensive reliability checks were conducted for the other two committees as well and produced similar confirmations of interstaffer reliability. Energy and Commerce provided the only noteworthy qualification, where majority full committee and majority subcommittee staffers generated ratings that correlated at .65. When the respective full- and subcommittee staffer ratings were averaged, however, they still correlated with Republican staffer ratings in excess of .8. The various reliability checks for Agriculture exceeded .8 in each case.

Appendix D: Personal Staff Interviews and the Survey Instruments

In order to assess the relevance of committee bills to individual members' bill-specific interests, I conducted face-to-face interviews with personal staffers and administered structured survey instruments. Because of their importance to the main theoretical arguments of this book, these interviews are discussed at some length in Chapter 3. Here I provide some of the remaining details about the interview schedule and its administration; in Appendix E I give evidence of the reliability and validity of the measures that the interviews produced.

DEVELOPMENT OF THE INTERVIEW SCHEDULE

I devised the interview schedule with the help of experienced legislative interviewers, congressional staffers, and a former congressman. I then subjected the schedule to a pretest, which led to several changes. Most related directly to the length of the interview. In the original interviews, I sought to elicit more detailed information about the particular groups or subconstituencies that were likely to be affected by the bill. This effort was premised on Fenno's finding in *Home Style* (1978) that House members perceive their districts in different ways. Such probes proved too time-consuming, however. During one pretest, for instance, a staffer spoke for nearly ten minutes about the attentiveness of district senior citizens to proposed cuts in the Older Americans Act. Hence, I left the notion of a bill's "district relevance" general and undefined, so that staffers could define it according to their own perception of the issue and of who constituted the relevant segment of the district constituency. As I discuss in Chapter 3, such perceptions of interest or salience vary according to the specific legislative issue, and the staffers' perceptions form the basis for the members' perceptions (and vice versa).

IDENTIFYING THE APPROPRIATE RESPONDENTS

The next task was to identify the best staffer with whom to talk about each committee member. This was facilitated by the generous help of senior committee and subcommittee staffers. Toward the end of my interviews with those staffers, I would usually describe the next stage of my project and ask them to direct me to the legislative assistants or other staffers responsible for staffing the committees for the different committee members during the congress. Without exception, they obliged. In cases where the appropriate staffer had left Capitol Hill, moreover, the senior committee staffers were helpful in providing phone numbers and addresses. In most cases, the staffers who had left Capitol Hill had remained in the Washington area and could be interviewed with a little extra effort. When this was not possible, I attempted to contact the staffer by phone and arrange a telephone interview once I had sent the staffer the structured survey instruments. I guided the staffer in filling out the surveys as part of the phone interview, much as I had in the face-to-face interviews. This alternative interview strategy was necessary only for seven of almost two hundred interviews, mainly as a means of obtaining data on members whose inclusion was important for achieving the stratified samples I sought (see Appendix A).

The strategy for identifying the best personal staffers with whom to speak worked well. As I had expected, legislative assistants in the congressman's personal office usually topped the list. But in a number of cases, the senior staffers directed me to individuals I might not have sought out — such as the member's administrative assistant or legislative director or, in several cases, someone she had appointed to the subcommittee or full-committee staff. For approximately half the members in the Education and Labor pilot study, more than one staffer was identified. In those cases, I attempted to interview each staffer. For those I could track down, the cooperation rate was almost perfect (forty-one of forty-two staffers, or 98 percent). In scheduling the interviews, I tried to speak as generally as possible about my project so not to influence staffers' responses. In most cases, it was sufficient to say that I was doing a study of decision making in the relevant committee and that I was seeking background on the member and her committee work.

THE INTERVIEW PROCESS AND THE ADMINISTRATION
OF SURVEY INSTRUMENTS

At the beginning of each interview I gave the same assurances I had offered in the committee staff interviews, but I did not record this set of interviews. Much of the information was captured through the structured surveys. I also took extensive notes during the interview, which I enlarged upon as soon afterward as possible. Interviews ranged in length from twenty-five minutes to an hour; the average interview took approximately forty minutes. I sought the same information in each interview, but I varied the order of questions. In particular, whenever two staffers were questioned about the same member, I reversed the topics covered to mitigate measurement error generated by question order.

Respondent Perceptions of District Interests: In the first round of interviews, though, I normally began with questions about the member's district, for example:

> Generally speaking, how relevant is Education and Labor's jurisdiction to the district? Which programs, if any, are especially relevant?

I would then follow up with the two-page form discussed in Chapter 3. The form listed each of the bills in my sample, including the bill number, the most commonly used short title, and a very brief description (condensed from the committee's activities report). I asked staffers to rate each bill according to its importance to the district, using one of four categories: negligible, minor, moderate, and major. The categories were listed beside the description of each bill, so that the staffer simply had to check off the appropriate category, bill by bill. Almost without exception, the staffers seemed to take the instrument seriously and filled it out carefully.

Questions about the district were the easiest for the staffer to answer. Indeed, staffers offered much more detail than I could capture in a thirty-to-fifty-minute interview.

Respondent Perceptions of Members' Policy Interests: The second part of the interview focused on the member's personal policy interests:

> I'd like to turn now from the interests of the district to the member's own personal policy interests. Generally speaking, how relevant would you say the committee's jurisdiction is to the member's personal policy interests or ideological commitments?

> Here is a list of the same set of bills [you just examined]. If you would, go

through them one more time, this time rating each bill according to its relevance to the member's own personal policy interests or ideological commitments.

I then would provide a second form, identical to the first except that the categories were defined in terms of the member's personal policy interests rather than the district's interest. Once again, staffers had little difficulty filling out the form. At times, they would digress after rating a particular bill in order to explain the nature of the member's interest. Although they could be time consuming, these digressions provided reassurance that the staffers were interpreting the form as I had intended.

Commitment to the President's Agenda: The personal staff interviews were also used to assess other possible motivations (see Chapter 3), though the strategy was necessarily different.

The individual member's general inclination to prosecute the president's agenda was elicited by the following question, which was administered exclusively to staffers whose bosses were of the same party as the president.

> During [the two-year period] the Reagan administration was aggressive on a number of issues before Congress. Generally speaking, how committed would you say [member Q] was to carrying out the president's agenda in the jurisdiction of [committee X]?

Where the response was equivocal (anything other than "very strongly committed" or "he was adamantly opposed to everything the Administration stood for"), I followed up with a probe to clarify how strong or weak the member's commitment was. The responses were subsequently coded, with numerical weights set to fit a three-point scale, equivalent to the one used in the district and policy questionnaires: 3 = unequivocal, strong commitment to Reagan administration's agenda; 1.5 = committed to administration agenda, with some qualification; 0 = not committed to administration agenda.

The measure of the member's bill-specific interest in prosecuting the president's agenda was then calculated as the product of two terms: the L.A.'s rating of her boss's commitment to the administration agenda and the administration priority level assigned separately to each bill by committee and subcommittee staffers. (On the latter, see Appendix C.)

Respondent Perceptions of Member's Desire to Make a Mark: In the pilot study for the project (Hall 1987), I also sought to measure and estimate the effects of a fourth type of member interest, one that emerged from previous scholarship on members' motivations. This was how interested a member was in making a mark, leaving behind a legislative legacy. Dodd characterized this motivation in his classic essay "Congress and the Quest for Power" (1977); Kingdon found evidence of it in his study of members' voting decisions (1989); and this motivation bears some resemblance to the legislative goal that Fenno (1973a) referred to as "power with the House."

However, subsequent analysis and posttesting of the bill-specific responses designed to tap this dimension of interest after the completion of the pilot study revealed significant problems with determining its validity. Specifically, several types of evidence suggested that the responses probably tapped a post-hoc explanation that was offered when the staffer deemed no other interest relevant. Thus measured, the fact of participation implied a desire to make a mark, thereby making it artificially easy to reject the null hypothesis when the null may in fact be true. Hence, while I believe that this type of interest is important for understanding members' priority setting and resource-allocation decisions, the data I generated from the interviews were insufficiently valid to permit me to test the hypothesis.

Appendix E: Measuring Members' Bill-Specific Interests

As I note in Chapter 3, a plausible concern about the analysis of purposive participation in this book involves the validity of the measures for members' bill-specific interests. Specifically, in rating members' levels of (different types of) interest, staffers may be themselves inferring interest from participation previously observed. To the extent that this occurs, the error term in the multivariate analysis will be correlated with the interest variables, the resulting coefficients thus upwardly biased.

I take this to be a legitimate concern, but as I discuss in the text, it was one that I anticipated and took special efforts to minimize. To briefly recapitulate that discussion, comments and asides offered during the interview provided unsystematic reassurances that staffers were interpreting the instrument properly and not simply reflecting post hoc the issues on which their boss participated. I carefully avoided mentioning my academic interest in participation until late in the interview, only after the essential items in the interview schedule had been completed.

In addition, I tested the robustness of the inferences I drew from the interview-based measures using objective measures. For instance, in the analysis reported in Chapter 6 I reproduced findings regarding participation and purpose on the House floor that were consistent with those at the subcommittee and committee level, using cruder but objective and replicable measures of members' various interests. Unfortunately, the creation of objective measures of member interest for even a few bills is a time-consuming, sometimes intractable endeavor. Hence, while the floor analysis provides some reassurance that the inferences made from the interview-based measures are robust, it does not suggest a generally applicable alternative strategy for conducting the comprehensive committee and subcommittee-level analysis undertaken here. (On a more limited scale, however, committee analysis is possible. See Hall and Wayman 1990.)

Finally, I took advantage of the cooperation and access given me by one of the congressional offices in order to test the extent to which staffer perceptions of member interests were valid reflections of members' perceptions of their own interests. I selected a sample of thirty bills from the member's three committee assignments; the structured interview schedule was therefore identical in form to the

*Table E.1   Checking the Measurement Validity of Member Bill-Specific Interests:
Member-Staffer Agreement in One Congressional Office*

	Member's Own Rating of Bill-Specific Interests	
	District Constituency	Personal Policy
L.A.'s rating of member's interests	.71	.57
L.D.'s rating of member's interests	.63	.59
Average of L.A.'s and L.D.'s ratings of member's interests	.72	.67
Number of bills	30	30

Source: Interviews with staffers and member in one congressional office during the 100th Congress (1987–88).

Note: Entries are Pearson correlation coefficients. All coefficients are statistically significant at the .001 level. The measures of staff ratings are the average of the L.D.'s and the relevant L.A.'s rating for the respective types of interst. The respective ratings are respondents' bill-specific scores that were assigned using the four-point survey instrument, administered to both staffers and member.

original but broader in scope across bills and jurisdictions. And this exercise was conducted during a different congress (the 100th) from those studied here. In sum, the exercise was independent of the analysis presented in these pages and, given the multicommittee sample of bills, it provides a somewhat demanding validity check. I administered the structured interview schedule to (1) the legislative assistant who had responsibility for each of the various bills in the sample; (2) the legislative director who supervised the legislative assistants and was central in developing and coordinating the member's legislative priorities; and (3) the member himself.

The cooperation of the member in completing the structured interview significantly assisted me in checking validity. While it is possible that staffers may impute interestedness to their boss based on their observation of his participation on a bill, no similar worry holds for the member himself. One can assume that he knows his own interests and hence need not reconstruct them from his imperfect recollections of how active he or his staff were on each of the dozens of bills that came before each of his panels over the preceding two years.

Table E.1 reports the bivariate associations (Pearson's r) between the member's own ratings of his bill-specific interests and the ratings of the staffers. The relationships are shown for both the constituency and personal policy dimensions of interest. Because the member in question was not of the same party as the president, a validity check could not be conducted for the measurement of the member's interest in prosecuting the president's agenda.

As the table shows, the district-interest ratings provided by the legislative assistants exhibit a high correlation with the member's own rating ($r = .71$), confirming my observation in the text that it is the L.A.'s job to know (or find out) the extent to which particular bills might affect district interests. The member can thus be forewarned about either possibilities for political trouble or opportunities for profitable credit claiming. Indeed, that the member and the L.A. show closely related perceptions of district interests suggests the reciprocal nature of their principal-agent relationship. Legislative assistants have strong incentives to know how the boss perceives the interests of the constituency. At the same time, the member's perceptions are based in part on district-relevant information that the staffer gathers and interprets for him.

Predictably, the correlation between the staff's and the member's perceptions of bills where his personal policy interests or ideological commitments are at stake is smaller than the comparable statistic for district interest. Nonetheless, the correlation is high and highly significant, both for the L.A.s and the legislative director. Table E.1 demonstrates the advantage of interviewing one or more staffers from a member's office, at least insofar as improving the measure of members' bill-specific policy interests is concerned. The third row of the table demonstrates that the average of the L.A.s' and L.D.'s rating on this dimension is more highly correlated with the member's than is either staff rating taken alone. Where one staffer may misperceive the policy relevance of a particular bill as her boss sees it, the other is usually likely to get it right.

Table E.2 brings more specific evidence to bear on the worry that staffers' observation and recall of their principal's bill-specific participation leads them to inflate their ratings of his bill-specific participation artificially. If this is true, there should be a discernible pattern to the mismatches between staffer and member ratings. Specifically, on bills where the boss was active, staffers should rate his interests *higher* than he does. Similarly, on bills where he was inactive, staffers should rate the interests of their boss *lower* than their boss does.

Neither of these patterns appear in table E.2. Although staffers were slightly more likely to rate the district interest of their boss higher than lower (38 percent versus 31 percent) than the member did, they were much more likely to rate his district interest higher than lower on bills where he was *not* active (41 percent versus 12 percent). On the basis of this single-office exercise, the evidence generally indicates that staffers' observation and recollection of members' (non)participation did not contaminate their ratings of their boss's bill-specific policy interests or ideological commitments. On bills where their boss was active, staffers were less likely (8 percent versus 54 percent) than he to rate his policy interests higher than he did. On bills where their boss was not active, in turn, staffers' ratings were higher than their boss's in a larger percentage of cases than where he was active.

This exercise in validity assessment may thus provide data from a single office, but it draws upon the responses of several legislative assistants, the legislative director, and the member himself with respect to thirty bills from three committees. The member's cast of legislative assistants, I should add, exhibited no greater longevity in his employment than we see in most congressional offices — about two years on

Table E.2   Checking the Measurement Validity of Member Bill-Specific Interests: Member Participation and Staffers' Ex-Post Ratings of Interest in One Congressional Office

	District Constituency	Personal Policy
Percentage of bills on which member was active player where		
Staff rating of interest was higher than member's	38	8
Staff rating of interest was equal to member's	31	38
Staff rating of interest was lower than member's	31	54
Percentage of bills on which member was not an active player where		
Staff rating of interest was higher than member's	41	23
Staff rating of interest was equal to member's	47	42
Staff rating of interest was lower than member's	12	35

Source: Interviews with staffers and member in one congressional office during the 100th Congress (1987–88).
Note: The measures of staff ratings are the average of the L.D.'s and the relevant L.A.'s rating for the respective types of interest. The respective ratings are respondents' bill-specific scores that were assigned using the four-point survey instrument, administered to both staffers and member. The number of bills was 30.

average. (The legislative director, however, had been with the member from the time he became a congressman.) Neither was the member himself atypical in any apparent way: he was a white, middle-aged, electorally secure male with close to the median length of congressional service.

The results of this exercise suggest, first, that although there are discrepancies between the staffers' and the member ratings of interest, the two sets of ratings are nonetheless strongly correlated. Second, where discrepancies occur, their patterns suggest that staffers do not systematically impute higher levels of interest to their boss on the basis of whether he was active on a bill. If anything, the reverse is more likely to be the case; if the member-staff lines of communication in this office are at all typical, the coefficients on both the district and policy variables reported in the subcommittee and committee analysis may be attenuated by my reliance on staffers as respondents.

Appendix F: Floor Data

Chapters 7 and 9 employ data that were specific to six bills that emerged from the three committees and that were considered on the House floor under open rules during the period 1981–84. The bills, described in table 7.1, were chosen with three simple criteria in mind. First, I chose two from each of the three committee samples under study in early chapters, so as to provide variance across issue areas and formal jurisdictions and provide at least some basis for comparison with the analysis of earlier chapters. Second, I chose one salient and one non-salient bill from each committee, so as to examine the robustness of the model under conditions which should, in the main, provide different incentives to members to participate.

FLOOR PARTICIPATION

Several details regarding the measurement of the floor participation of member i on bill j likewise bear elaboration. A research assistant and I independently coded the floor record, resolving the few discrepancies after each of us had reviewed the record. The coding criteria closely track those applied in measuring of committee markup participation.

First, the category of insertions into the *Congressional Record* included any speech marked by a bullet or an insertion of a speech, article, report, letter, bill, amendment, or other written material into the text of the *Record*. If a member actually spoke on the floor, her speech is automatically inserted into the *Record*, although her speech may be edited before it is printed. Hence, all members who spoke were by definition responsible for insertions in the *Record*, but many members who made insertions did not speak.

Second, a member was credited with procedural action if she made a procedural motion of any kind or if she participated in debate on the special rule that would govern floor debate on the bill. With respect to amending action, a member was given credit for a technical amendment if she (co)wrote a floor amendment that met the criteria for technical amendments that I described for committee markups in Appendix B, namely, that the amendment was labeled grammatical or technical *and* that it evoked no evidence of controversy. A member was credited with offering a substantive amendment if she either (co)authored any kind of nontechnical amendment; or was mentioned in any speech in either the *Record* or the committee record as having been involved in developing the amendment.

Third, members were credited with participating in floor agenda-setting action if they were principal authors of the bill reported out of committee; proposers of a successful amendment in the nature of a substitute to the bill reported out of committee; proposers of an amendment in the nature of substitute on the floor, regardless of whether that amendment proved successful; or advocates before the Rules Committee regarding whether a special rule should be given to the bill and, if so, in what form. (This advocacy was revealed by debate over the rule on the floor, subsequent statements by speakers in the ensuing floor debate on the bill, or secondary sources regarding the prefloor action on the bill.)

Finally, I would simply note that the floor index thus created, like the committee markup index, constitutes an almost perfect Guttman scale. The coefficient of scalability exceeded .95 for each bill.

INDEPENDENT VARIABLES IN THE FLOOR ANALYSIS

The data collection and measurement of all independent variables were based on bill-specific criteria that are described in table 7.2 and discussed in Chapter 7.

Details regarding the measurement of several of these require greater elaboration, however.

The coding of members' bill-specific policy and district interests discussed in the text is reasonably straightforward. But the variable needed to tap the district relevance of the Weatherization and Employment bill was more complicated, in that it benefited only those areas that suffered from both high heating bills and low employment. I thus required a "misery index," which was calculated by averaging the heating-day statistics for every major weather station within each district and then subtracting the average from the mean number of heating days across all districts (minimum = o). This statistic was then transformed to a o to 1 scale and interacted with the rate of district unemployment.

Among the institutional variables, a few words should be added about the category "related panel membership." Included in this category were all individuals who sat on a panel whose jurisdiction was related to the specific policy questions taken up by the particular bill in my floor sample. Given the subjective nature of such categorizations, a research assistant and I independently coded whether a panel was "related." To briefly illustrate, the House Select Committee on Aging marks up no legislation, but it had held hearings on the Older Americans Act, the amendments to which were formally marked up and reported by Education and Labor. Similarly, the Banking and Urban Affairs Subcommittee on Housing enjoyed no jurisdiction over the Commerce Committee's low-income weatherization bill, but the panel and its staff regularly dealt with a wide range of related issues covering the cost and quality of housing for the poor. The relatedness of two jurisdictions is not always this clear, however; hence the strategy of independent codings. Still, our initial codings matched for all but eight out of several hundred dyads; where we did not agree, I assumed no relevance.

VOTING INDEXES: CAVEAT EMPTOR

As I discuss in Chapter 9, the use of voting indexes to ascertain bias in official panels of members or unofficial subsets of participants is problematic. For instance, to the extent that either intergroup logrolling or rational abdication goes on, such data will inherently favor the null hypothesis regarding the existence of bias (Hall and Grofman 1990). Likewise, decisions on specific bills and provisions that reach a roll call constitute a censored sample of all decisions made in drafting and reporting bills to the floor (Forshee 1994; Londregan and Snyder 1994). The floor may monitor and attempt to mute the enthusiasms of the interested and active participants regarding the most visible and objectionable provisions, but it will have more trouble doing so on the host of relatively minor provisions that cumulatively can prove very important. To the extent that voting indexes are not jurisdiction-specific (much less issue-specific), likewise, they constitute contaminated indicators of members' underlying positions on the matters of relevance to the researcher. The best that I could do in this regard was to use voting indexes that were as jurisdiction-specific as possible, then correct the scores by eliminating votes included in each index that were obviously extraneous to matters within each committee's jurisdiction. In the end, I remain worried about the use of roll call voting indexes for tapping members' underlying positions. But the bias of such indexes in favor of the null hypothesis implies that we should be all the more confident when the null can be rejected at conventional levels of statistical significance. In addition to roll call indexes, moreover, I employ various district-level indicators of panel or participant bias. Although the assumptions involved in making valid inferences about members' underlying positions from such indicators are noted in the text (see also Hall and Grofman 1990), the triangulation of different measures should boost the reader's confidence in the inferences I make.

References

Abrams, Robert. 1980. *Foundations of Political Analysis: An Introduction to the Theory of Collective Choice.* New York: Columbia University Press.

Achen, Christopher H. 1978. "Measuring Representation." *American Journal of Political Science* 22:475–510.

Adams, Henry. 1903 [1918]. *The Education of Henry Adams.* Boston: Houghton Mifflin.

Aldrich, John H. 1991. "Power and Order in Congress." In *Home Style and Washington Work,* ed. Morris P. Fiorina and David W. Rohde. Ann Arbor: University of Michigan Press.

Aldrich, John H. 1995. "A Model of Legislature with Two Parties and a Committee System." In *Positive Theories of Congressional Institutions,* ed. Kenneth A. Shepsle and Barry R. Weingast. Ann Arbor: University of Michigan Press.

Aldrich, John H., and David W. Rohde. 1996. "Conditional Party Government Revisited: Majority Party Leadership and the Committee System in the 104th Congress." *Extension of Remarks,* December 5–7.

Americans for Democratic Action. 1984. "The ADA Congressional Voting Record." Press release, January.

Americans for Democratic Action. 1985. "The ADA Congressional Voting Record." Press release, January.

Arnold, R. Douglas. 1979. *Congress and the Bureaucracy: A Theory of Influence.* New Haven, Conn.: Yale University Press.

Arnold, R. Douglas. 1990. *The Logic of Collective Action.* New Haven, Conn.: Yale University Press.

Asbell, Bernard. 1978. *The Senate Nobody Knows.* Garden City, N.J.: Doubleday.

Asher, Herbert. 1974. "Committees and the Norm of Specialization." *Annals of the American Academy of Political and Social Science* 67:63–74.

Asher, Herbert. 1975. "The Changing Status of the Freshman Representative." In *Congress in Change: Evolution and Reform,* ed. Norman Ornstein. New York: Praeger.

Austen-Smith, David, and John R. Wright. 1994. "Counteractive Lobbying." *American Journal of Political Science* 38:25–44.

Axelrod, Robert. 1984. *The Evolution of Cooperation.* New York: Basic Books.

Bach, Stanley, and Steven S. Smith. 1988. *Managing Uncertainty in the U.S. House of Representatives.* Washington, D.C.: Brookings Institution.

Bachrach, Peter, and Morton S. Baratz. 1962. "Two Faces of Power." *American Political Science Review* 56:947–52.

Barber, James David. 1965. *The Lawmakers: Recruitment and Adaptation in Legislative Life.* New Haven, Conn.: Yale University Press.

Barber, James David. 1966. *Power in Committees: An Experiment in the Governmental Process.* Chicago: Rand McNally.

Barnes, James A. 1991. "Minority Mapmaking." *National Journal,* Apr. 4, pp. 837–39.

Baron, David P., and John Ferejohn. 1989. "The Power to Propose." In *Models of Strategic Choice in Politics,* ed. Peter C. Ordeshook. Ann Arbor: University of Michigan Press.

Barone, Michael, and Grant Ujifusa. 1983. *Almanac of American Politics 1984.* Washington, D.C.: National Journal.

Bauer, Raymond, Ithiel de Sola Pool, and Lewis Anthony Dexter. 1963. *American Business and Public Policy.* New York: Atherton Press.

Baumgartner, Frank R., and Bryan D. Jones. 1993. *Agendas and Instability in American Politics.* Chicago: University of Chicago Press.

Bernstein, Robert A. 1989. *Elections, Representation, and Congressional Voting Behavior: The Myth of Constituency Control.* Englewood Cliffs, N.J.: Prentice-Hall.

Bessette, Joseph M. 1994. *The Mild Voice of Reason.* Chicago: University of Chicago Press.

Birnbaum, Jeffrey H., and Alan S. Murray. 1987. *Showdown at Gucci Gulch: Lawmakers, Lobbyists, and the Unlikely Triumph of Tax Reform.* New York: Vintage Books.

Black, Duncan. 1958. *The Theory of Committees and Elections.* Cambridge: Cambridge University Press.

Bond, Jon R., and Richard Fleisher. 1990. *The President in the Legislative Arena.* Chicago: University of Chicago Press.

Brady, David W. 1981. "Personnel Management in the House." In *The House at Work,* ed. Joseph Cooper and G. Calvin Mackenzie. Austin: University of Texas Press.

Brady, David W. 1988. *Critical Elections and Congressional Policy Making.* Stanford, Calif.: Stanford University Press.

Brady, David W., and Charles S. Bullock III. 1985. "Parties and Factions Within Legislatures." In *Handbook of Legislative Research,* ed. Gerhard Loewenberg, Samuel C. Patterson, and Malcolm E. Jewell. Cambridge: Harvard University Press.

Browne, William P., and Won K. Park. 1993. "Beyond the Domain." *American Journal of Political Science* 37:1054–78.

Brownson, Charles B. 1982. *Congressional Staff Directory.* Mt. Vernon, Va.: Congressional Staff Directory Ltd.

Brownson, Charles B. 1983. *Congressional Staff Directory*. Mt. Vernon, Va.: Congressional Staff Directory Ltd.

Bullock, Charles S. 1976. "Motivations for U.S. Congressional Committee Preferences: Freshmen of the 92nd Congress." *Legislative Studies Quarterly* 1:201–12.

Burgin, Eileen. 1991. "Representatives' Decisions in Participation in Foreign Policy Issues." *Legislative Studies Quarterly* 16: 521–46.

Cain, Bruce, John Ferejohn, and Morris P. Fiorina. 1987. *The Personal Vote*. Cambridge: Harvard University Press.

Carroll, Holbert. 1966. *The House of Representatives and Foreign Affairs*. Pittsburgh, Pa.: University of Pittsburgh Press.

Chamberlin, John R., and Paul N. Courant. 1983. "Representative Deliberations and Representative Decisions: Proportional Representation and the Borda Rule." *American Political Science Review* 77:718–33.

Chappell, Henry. 1982. "Campaign Contributions and Congressional Voting: A Simultaneous Probit-Tobit Model." *Review of Economics and Statistics* 62:77–83.

Cheney, Richard. 1989. "An Unruly House: A Republican View." *Public Opinion*, Jan.–Feb., 41–44.

Clapp, Charles. 1963. *The Congressman: His Work As He Sees It*. Washington, D.C.: Brookings Institution.

Clausen, Aage. 1973. *How Congressmen Decide*. New York: St. Martin's Press.

Cloud, David S. 1995. "GOP, to Its Own Great Delight, Enacts House Rules Changes." *CQ Weekly Report,* Jan. 7, pp. 13–15.

Cohadas, Nadine. 1983. "New Unity Evident: Women Shift Focus on Hill to Economic Equity Issues." *CQ Weekly Report,* Apr. 23, p. 784.

Cohadas, Nadine. 1985a. "Black House Members Striving for Influence." *CQ Weekly Report,* Apr. 13, p. 675.

Cohadas, Nadine. 1985b. "Black Members: The Drive for Recognition." *CQ Weekly Report,* Apr. 23, p. 676.

Cohen, Michael, James March, and Johan Olsen. 1972. "A Garbage Can Model of Organizational Choice." *Administrative Science Quarterly* 17:1–25.

Cohen, Richard E. 1991. "Pushing for More Black House Seats." *National Journal,* Jan. 5, p. 34.

Cohen, Richard. 1992. *Washington at Work*. New York: Macmillan.

Collie, Melissa P., and Joseph Cooper. 1989. "Multiple Referral and the 'New' Committee System in the House of Representatives." In *Congress Reconsidered,* 4th ed., ed. Lawrence C. Dodd and Bruce I. Oppenheimer. Washington, D.C.: CQ Press.

Congressional Record. 1981a. Oct. 14–15. Washington, D.C.: Government Printing Office.

Congressional Record. 1981b. Nov. 20. Washington, D.C.: Government Printing Office.

Congressional Record. 1982. Aug. 4, 1982. Washington, D.C.: Government Printing Office.

Congressional Record. 1983. Nov. 10. Washington, D.C.: Government Printing Office.

Congressional Record. 1984. Jan. 24. Washington, D.C.: Government Printing Office.

Converse, Phillip E., and Roy Pierce. 1986. *Representation in France*. Cambridge: Harvard University Press.

Cook, Timothy E. 1989. *Making Laws and Making News.* Washington D.C.: Brookings Institution.

Cooper, Joseph. 1977. "Congress in Organizational Perspective." In Lawrence C. Dodd and Bruce I. Oppenheimer, *Congress Reconsidered,* New York: Praeger.

Cooper, Joseph, and Cheryl Young. 1989. "Bill Introduction in the 19th Century: A Study of Institutional Change." *Legislative Studies Quarterly* 14:67–106.

Cox, Gary, and Mathew McCubbins. 1993. *Legislative Leviathan: Party Government in the House.* Berkeley: University of California Press.

Dahl, Robert A. 1956. *A Preface to Democratic Theory.* Chicago: University of Chicago Press.

Dahl, Robert A. 1984. *Modern Political Analysis,* 4th ed. Englewood Cliffs, N.J.: Prentice-Hall.

Davidson, Roger. 1974. "Representation and Congressional Committees." In *Annals of the American Academy of Political and Social Science* 411:48–62.

Davidson, Roger. 1981. "Subcommittee Government: New Channels for Policymaking." In *The New Congress,* ed. Thomas E. Mann and Norman J. Ornstein. Washington, D.C.: American Enterprise Institute.

Davidson, Roger. 1996. "Building a Republican Regime on Capitol Hill." *Extension of Remarks,* December 1–2.

Deering, Christopher. 1982. "Subcommittee Government in the U.S. House: An Analysis of Bill Management." *Legislative Studies Quarterly* 7:533–46.

Derthick, Martha. 1979. *Policymaking for Social Security.* Washington, D.C.: Brookings Institution.

Derthick, Martha, and Paul Quirk. 1985. *The Politics of Deregulation.* Washington, D.C.: Brookings Institution.

Dion, Douglas. 1992. "The Robustness of the Structure-Induced Equilibrium." *American Journal of Political Science* 36:462–82.

Dion, Douglas. 1995. "Trampled Underfoot: Minority Rights and Procedural Change in the U.S. House of Representatives." Department of Political Science, University of Michigan, Ann Arbor. Typescript.

Dodd, Lawrence C. 1977. "Congress and the Quest for Power." In *Congress Reconsidered,* ed. Lawrence C. Dodd and Bruce I. Oppenheimer. New York: Praeger.

Dodd, Lawrence C., and Bruce I. Oppenheimer. 1985. "The House in Transition: Partisanship and Opposition." In *Congress Reconsidered,* 3rd ed., ed. Lawrence C. Dodd and Bruce I. Oppenheimer. Washington, D.C.: CQ Press.

Dodd, Lawrence C., and Bruce I. Oppenheimer. 1993. "Maintaining Order in the House: The Struggle for Institutional Equilibrium." In *Congress Reconsidered,* 5th ed., ed. Lawrence C. Dodd and Bruce I. Oppenheimer. Washington, D.C.: CQ Press.

Downs, Anthony. 1957. *An Economic Theory of Democracy.* New York: Harper & Row.

Economic Research Service. 1984a. "Dairy: Background for 1985 Farm Legislation." Washington, D.C.: U.S. Department of Agriculture.

Economic Research Service. 1984b. "Peanuts: Background for 1985 Farm Legislation." Washington, D.C.: U.S. Department of Agriculture.

Eulau, Heinz. 1984. "Legislative Committee Assignments." *Legislative Studies Quarterly* 9:587–633.

Eulau, Heinz, and Paul D. Karps. 1977. "The Puzzle of Representation: Specifying Components of Responsiveness." *Legislative Studies Quarterly* 2:233–54.

Eulau, Heinz, and Vera McCluggage. 1984. "Standing Committees in Legislatures: Three Decades of Research." *Legislative Studies Quarterly* 9:195–270.

Eulau, Heinz, John C. Wahlke, William Buchanan, and Leroy C. Ferguson. 1959. "The Role of the Representative: Some Empirical Observations on the Theory of Edmund Burke." *American Political Science Review* 53:742–56.

Evans, C. Lawrence. 1991. *Leadership in Committee.* Ann Arbor: University of Michigan Press.

Fenno, Richard F., Jr. 1962. "The House Appropriations Committee as a Political System." *American Political Science Review* 56:310–24.

Fenno, Richard F., Jr. 1966. *The Power of the Purse.* Boston: Little, Brown.

Fenno, Richard F., Jr. 1971. "The Freshman Congressman: His View of the House." In *Congressional Behavior,* ed. Nelson W. Polsby. New York: Random House.

Fenno, Richard F., Jr. 1973a. *Congressmen in Committees.* Boston: Little, Brown.

Fenno, Richard F., Jr. 1973b. "The Internal Distribution of Influence: The House." In *The Congress and America's Future,* ed. David B. Truman. Englewood Cliffs, N.J.: Prentice-Hall.

Fenno, Richard F., Jr. 1975. "If, as Ralph Nader Says, Congress is 'the Broken Branch,' Why Do We Love Our Congressmen So Much?" In *Congress in Change: Evolution and Reform,* ed. Norman J. Ornstein. New York: Praeger.

Fenno, Richard F., Jr. 1978. *Home Style.* Boston: Little, Brown.

Fenno, Richard F., Jr. 1986. "Observation, Context, and Sequence in the Study of Politics." *American Political Science Review* 80: 3–16.

Ferejohn, John. 1975. "Logrolling in an Institutional Context: A Case Study of Food Stamps Legislation." In *Congress and Policy Change,* ed. Gerald C. Wright et al. New York: Agathon.

Ferejohn, John. 1983. "Congress and Redistribution." In *Making Economic Policy in Congress,* ed. Allen Schick. Washington, D.C.: American Enterprise Institute.

Ferejohn, John, and Morris P. Fiorina. 1975. "Purposive Models of Legislative Behavior." *American Economic Review* 65:407–14.

Fiorina, Morris P. 1974. *Representatives, Roll Calls, and Constituencies.* Boston: D. C. Heath.

Fiorina, Morris P. 1975. "Formal Models in Political Science." *American Journal of Political Science* 19:133–59.

Fiorina, Morris P. 1981. *Retrospective Voting in American National Elections.* New Haven, Conn.: Yale University Press.

Fiorina, Morris P. 1989. *Congress: Keystone of the Washington Establishment,* 2nd ed. New Haven, Conn.: Yale University Press.

Forshee, Richard A. 1994. "The President, Committees, and the Legislative Agenda." Ph.D. diss., University of Michigan, Ann Arbor.

Fox, Harrison W., Jr., and Susan Webb Hammond. 1977. *Congressional Staffs: The Invisible Force in American Lawmaking.* New York: Free Press.

Gertzog, Irwin N. 1976. "The Routinization of Committee Assignments in the U.S. House of Representatives." *American Journal of Political Science* 20:693–713.

Gilligan, Thomas, and Keith Krehbiel. 1987. "Collective Decision-Making and Standing Committees: An Informational Rationale for Restrictive Amendment Procedures." *Journal of Law, Economics, and Organization* 3:287–335.

Gilligan, Thomas, and Keith Krehbiel. 1989. "Asymmetric Information and Legislative Rules with a Heterogeneous Committee." *American Journal of Political Science* 33: 459–90.

Gilligan, Thomas, and Keith Krehbiel. 1990. "Organization of Informative Committees by a Rational Legislature." *American Journal of Political Science* 34:531–64.

Gilligan, Thomas, and Keith Krehbiel. 1994. "The Gains from Exchange Hypothesis of Legislative Organizations." *Legislative Studies Quarterly* 19:181–214.

Grenzke, Janet M. 1989. "Shopping in the Congressional Supermarket: The Currency Is Complex." *American Journal of Political Science* 33:1–24.

Groseclose, Timothy. 1992. "Monte Carlo Tests of Theories of Legislative Committee Composition." Carnegie-Mellon University. Typescript.

Groseclose, Timothy, and Keith Krehbiel. 1994. "Golden Parachutes, Rubber Checks, and Strategic Retirements from the 102nd House." *American Journal of Political Science* 38:75–99.

Haeberle, Steven H. 1978. "The Institutionalization of the Subcommittee in the House of Representatives." *Journal of Politics* 40:1054–65.

Hall, Richard L. 1987. "Participation and Purpose in Committee Decision Making." *American Political Science Review* 81:105–27.

Hall, Richard L. 1989. "Committee Decision Making in the Post-Reform Congress." In *Congress Reconsidered*, 4th ed., ed. Lawrence C. Dodd and Bruce I. Oppenheimer. Washington, D.C.: CQ Press.

Hall, Richard L. 1992. "Measuring Legislative Influence." *Legislative Studies Quarterly* 17:205–31.

Hall, Richard L. 1993. "Participation, Abdication, and Representation in Committees." In *Congress Reconsidered*, 5th ed., ed. Lawrence C. Dodd and Bruce I. Oppenheimer. Washington, D.C.: CQ Press.

Hall, Richard L. 1994a. "Mobilizing Bias: Private Groups and Public Lobbies in Law Making and Rule Making." Department of Political Science, University of Michigan, Ann Arbor. Typescript.

Hall, Richard L. 1994b. "Review of *Information and Legislative Organization*." *American Political Science Review* 88:495–97.

Hall, Richard L. 1995. "Empiricism and Progress in Positive Theories of Legislative Institutions." In *Positive Theories of Congressional Institutions*, ed. Kenneth A. Shepsle and Barry R. Weingast. Ann Arbor: University of Michigan Press.

Hall, Richard L., and C. Lawrence Evans. 1990. "The Power of Subcommittees." *Journal of Politics* 52:335–54.

Hall, Richard L., and Bernard Grofman. 1990. "The Committee Assignment Process and the Conditional Nature of Committee Bias." *American Political Science Review* 84: 1149–66.

Hall, Richard L., and Colleen Heflin. 1995. "The Importance of Color in Congress:

Member Race, Ethnicity, and Minority Representation." Department of Political Science, University of Michigan, Ann Arbor. Typescript.

Hall, Richard L., and Robert Van Houweling. 1995. "Avarice and Ambition: Representatives' Decisions to Run or Retire from the U.S. House." *American Political Science Review* 89:121–36.

Hall, Richard L., and Frank W. Wayman. 1990. "Buying Time: Moneyed Interests and the Mobilization of Bias in Congressional Committees." *American Political Science Review* 84:797–820.

Hamm, Keith E. 1983. "Patterns of Influence Among Committees, Agencies, and Interest Groups." *Legislative Studies Quarterly* 8:379–426.

Hammond, Susan Webb. 1981. "The Management of Legislative Offices." In Joseph Cooper and G. Calvin Mackenzie, eds. *The House at Work*. Austin: University of Texas Press.

Hammond, Susan Webb. 1989. "Congressional Caucuses in the Policy Process." In *Congress Reconsidered,* 4th ed., ed. Lawrence C. Dodd and Bruce I. Oppenheimer. Washington, D.C.: CQ Press.

Hansen, John Mark. 1992. *Gaining Access*. Chicago: University of Chicago Press.

Hardin, Clifford M., Kenneth A. Shepsle, and Barry R. Weingast. 1983. "Government by Subcommittee," *Wall Street Journal,* June 24.

Herzog, Donald. 1989. *Happy Slaves: A Critique of Consent Theory*. Chicago: University of Chicago Press.

Hinckley, Barbara. 1971. *The Seniority System in Congress*. Bloomington: Indiana University Press.

Hinckley, Barbara. 1975. "Policy Content, Committee Membership, and Behavior." *American Journal of Political Science* 19:543–58.

House Committee on Agriculture. 1982. *Legislative Calendar of the House Committee on Agriculture, 97th Congress*. Washington, D.C.: Government Printing Office.

House Committee on Agriculture. 1983. *Report on the Activities of the Committee on Agriculture during the 97th Congress*. Washington, D.C.: Government Printing Office.

House Committee on Agriculture. 1994. *Legislative Calendar of the House Committee on Agriculture, 103rd Congress — First Session*. Washington, D.C.: Government Printing Office.

House Committee on Education and Labor. 1983a. *Legislative Calendar of the House Committee on Education and Labor, 97th Congress*. Washington, D.C.: Government Printing Office.

House Committee on Education and Labor. 1983b. *Report on the Activities of the Committee on Education and Labor during the 97th Congress*. Washington, D.C.: Government Printing Office.

House Committee on Education and Labor. 1983c. *Rules of the Committee on Education and Labor*. Washington, D.C.: Government Printing Office.

House Committee on Education and Labor. 1994. *Legislative Calendar of the House Committee on Education and Labor, 103rd Congress — First Session*. Washington, D.C.: Government Printing Office.

House Committee on Energy and Commerce. 1983a. *Rules of the House Committee on Energy and Commerce*. Washington, D.C.: Government Printing Office.

House Committee on Energy and Commerce. 1983b. *Universal Telephone Preservation Act of 1983: Report of the Committee on Energy and Commerce.* Washington, D.C.: Government Printing Office.

House Committee on Energy and Commerce. 1985a. *Legislative Calendar of the Committee on Energy and Commerce, 98th Congress.* Washington, D.C.: Government Printing Office.

House Committee on Energy and Commerce. 1985b. *Report on the Activities of the Committee on Energy and Commerce during the 98th Congress.* Washington, D.C.: Government Printing Office.

House Committee on Energy and Commerce. 1994. *Legislative Calendar of the Committee on Energy and Commerce, 103rd Congress — First Session.* Washington, D.C.: Government Printing Office.

Huitt, Ralph K. 1954. "The Congressional Committee: A Case Study." *American Political Science Review* 48:340–65.

Huitt, Ralph K. 1973. "The Internal Distribution of Influence: The Senate." In *The Congress and America's Future,* ed. David B. Truman. Englewood Cliffs, N.J.: Prentice-Hall.

Interuniversity Consortium for Political and Social Research. 1984. *Roster of United States Congressional Officeholders and Biographical Characteristics of Members of the United States Congress, 1979–1984: Merged Data.* Ann Arbor, Mich.: Interuniversity Consortium for Political and Social Research.

Jackson, Brooks. 1988. *Honest Graft.* New York: Knopf.

Jackson, John E. 1973. "Intensities, Preferences, and Electoral Politics." *Social Science Quarterly* 2:231–46.

Jackson, John E. 1974. *Constituencies and Leaders in Congress.* Cambridge: Harvard University Press.

Jackson, John E., and David C. King. 1989. "Private Interests, Public Goods, and Representation." *American Political Science Review* 83:1143–64.

Jackson, John E., and John W. Kingdon. 1992. "Ideology, Interest Group Ratings, and Roll Call Votes." *American Journal of Political Science* 36:805–23.

Jewell, Malcolm E. 1983. "Legislator-Constituency Relations and the Representative Process." *Legislative Studies Quarterly* 8:303–38.

Johannes, John R. 1988. *To Serve the People: Congress and Constituency Service.* Lincoln: University of Nebraska Press.

Jones, Bryan. 1994. *Reconceiving Decision-Making in Democratic Politics.* Chicago: University of Chicago Press.

Jones, Charles O. 1961. "Representation in Congress: The Case of the House Committee on Agriculture." *American Political Science Review* 55:358–67.

Kalt, Joseph P., and Mark A. Zupan. 1984. "Capture and Ideology in the Economic Theory of Politics." *American Economic Review* 74:279–300.

Kaplan, Abraham. 1964. *The Conduct of Inquiry.* New York: Chandler Publishing.

Kathlene, Lyn. 1994. "Power and Influence in State Legislative Policymaking: The Interaction of Gender and Position in Committee Hearing Debates." *American Political Science Review* 88:560–76.

Kau, James B., and Paul H. Rubin. 1982. *Congressmen, Constituents, and Contributors:*

Determinants of Roll Call Voting in the House of Representatives. Boston: Martinus Nijhoff.

Kiewiet, D. Roderick, and Mathew D. McCubbins. 1991. *The Logic of Delegation.* Chicago: University of Chicago Press.

King, David C. 1994. "The Nature of Congressional Committee Jurisdictions." *American Political Science Review* 88:48–62.

King, Gary. 1989. *Unifying Political Methodology: The Likelihood Theory of Statistical Inference.* New York: Cambridge University Press.

Kingdon, John W. 1977. "Models of Legislative Voting." *Journal of Politics* 39:563–95.

Kingdon, John W. 1984. *Agendas, Alternatives, and Public Policies.* Boston: Little, Brown.

Kingdon, John W. 1988. "Ideas, Politics, and Public Policies." Paper presented at the 84th annual meeting of the American Political Science Association.

Kingdon, John W. 1989. *Congressmen's Voting Decisions.* New York: Harper & Row.

Kirkland, Lane. 1982a. "A Report on Congress." *AFL-CIO News,* January.

Kirkland, Lane. 1982b. "A Report on Congress." *AFL-CIO News,* October.

Kozak, David C., and John D. McCartney. 1981. *Congress and Public Policy: A Source Book of Documents and Readings.* Chicago: Dorsey Press.

Krehbiel, Keith. 1987. "Why Are Committees Powerful?" *American Political Science Review* 81:929–45.

Krehbiel, Keith. 1988. "Spatial Models of Legislative Choice." *Legislative Studies Quarterly* 8:259–319.

Krehbiel, Keith. 1990. "Are Congressional Committees Composed of Preference Outliers?" *American Political Science Review* 84:149–63.

Krehbiel, Keith. 1991. *Information and Legislative Organization.* Ann Arbor: University of Michigan Press.

Londregan, John, and James M. Snyder. 1994. "Comparing Committee and Floor Preferences." *Legislative Studies Quarterly* 19:233–66.

McCrone, Donald J., and James H. Kuklinski. 1979. "The Delegate Theory of Representation." *American Journal of Political Science* 23:278–300.

McKissick, Gary. 1995. "Policy Entrepreneurs and Recurring Issues in Congress." University of Michigan. Typescript.

MacRae, Duncan, Jr. 1958. *Dimensions of Congressional Voting.* Los Angeles: University of California Press.

Magleby, David B., and Candice J. Nelson. 1990. *The Money Chase.* Washington, D.C.: Brookings Institution.

Malbin, Michael. 1979. *Unelected Representatives.* New York: Basic Books.

Maltzman, Forrest. 1994. "Controlling Committees." George Washington University. Typescript.

Manley, John. 1970. *The Politics of Finance.* Boston: Little, Brown.

Maraniss, David. 1983. "Power Play: Chairman's Gavel Crushes Gas Decontrol Vote." *Washington Post,* Nov. 20, A1.

March, James G., and Herbert A. Simon. 1958. *Organizations.* New York: John Wiley & Sons.

Matthews, Donald R. 1959. "The Folkways of the United States Senate: Conformity to

Group Norms and Legislative Effectiveness." *American Political Science Review* 53: 1064–89.

Matthews, Donald R. 1960. *U.S. Senators and Their World*. Chapel Hill: University of North Carolina Press.

Matthews, Donald R., and James A. Stimson. 1970. *Yeas and Nays*. New York: Wiley.

Mayhew, David. 1974. *Congress: The Electoral Connection*. New Haven, Conn.: Yale University Press.

Milbraith, Lester M. 1963. *The Washington Lobbyists*. Chicago: Rand McNally.

Mill, John Stuart. 1975 [1861]. "Considerations on Representative Government." In *Three Essays*. Oxford: Oxford University Press.

Miller, Warren E., and Donald Stokes. 1963. "Constituency Influence in Congress." *American Political Science Review* 57:45–56.

Nagel, Jack H. 1975. *The Descriptive Analysis of Power*. New Haven, Conn.: Yale University Press.

National Farmers Union. 1982a. "1981 Voting Record — House." *National Farmers Union Washington Newsletter* 5:4–8.

National Farmers Union. 1982b. "1982 Voting Record — House." *National Farmers Union Washington Newsletter* 15:4–8.

Nyhan, Paul. 1995. "Cuts in Committee Spending Approved by House Panel." *CQ Weekly Report,* Mar. 11, p. 735.

O'Donnell, Thomas. 1981. "Controlling Legislative Time." In *The House at Work,* ed. Joseph Cooper and G. Calvin Mackenzie. Austin: University of Texas Press.

Oleszek, Walter J. 1984. *Congressional Procedures and the Policy Process,* 2nd ed. Washington, D.C.: CQ Press.

Olson, Mancur, Jr. 1965. *The Logic of Collective Action*. Cambridge: Harvard University Press.

Oppenheimer, Bruce I. 1981. "Congress and the New Obstructionism: Developing an Energy Program." In *Congress Reconsidered,* 2nd ed., ed. Lawrence C. Dodd and Bruce I. Oppenheimer. Washington: Congressional Quarterly.

Ornstein, Norman J. 1972. "Information, Resources, and Legislative Decision-Making: Some Comparative Perspectives." Ph.D. diss. University of Michigan.

Ornstein, Norman J. 1981. "The House and Senate in a New Congress." In *The New Congress,* ed. Thomas E. Mann and Norman J. Ornstein. Washington, D.C.: American Enterprise Institute.

Ornstein, Norman J. 1995. "Is Speaker Gingrich Plotting to Overthrow the Committee System?" *Roll Call,* Nov. 9, pp. 5, 30.

Ornstein, Norman J., Thomas E. Mann, and Michael J. Malbin. 1984. *Vital Statistics on Congress, 1983–84*. Washington, D.C.: American Enterprise Institute.

Ornstein, Norman J., Thomas E. Mann, and Michael J. Malbin. 1987. *Vital Statistics on Congress, 1987–88*. Washington, D.C.: American Enterprise Institute.

Ornstein, Norman J., Thomas E. Mann, and Michael J. Malbin. 1996. *Vital Statistics on Congress, 1995–96*. Washington, D.C.: American Enterprise Institute.

Ornstein, Norman J., Thomas E. Mann, Michael J. Malbin, Allen Schick, and John F. Bibby. 1990. *Vital Statistics on Congress: 1984–1989 Edition*. Washington, D.C.: American Enterprise Institute.

Panning, William H. 1983. "Formal Models of Legislative Processes." *Legislative Studies Quarterly* 8:427–55.

Parker, Glenn R. 1986. *Homeward Bound.* Pittsburgh, Pa.: University of Pittsburgh Press.

Parker, Glenn R. 1989. *Characteristics of Congress.* Englewood Cliffs, N.J.: Prentice-Hall.

Parker, Glenn R., and Suzanne Parker. 1979. "Factions in Committees: The U.S. House of Representatives." *American Political Science Review* 73:85–102.

Parker, Glenn R., and Suzanne Parker. 1985. *Factions in House Committees.* Knoxville: University of Tennessee Press.

Payne, James. 1980. "Show Horses and Work Horses in the U.S. House of Representatives." *Polity* 12:428–56.

Peltzman, Samuel. 1984. "Constituent Interest and Congressional Voting." *Journal of Law and Economics* 27:181–210.

Perkins, Lynette. 1980. "Influences of Members' Goals on Their Committee Behavior: The U.S. House Judiciary Committee." *Legislative Studies Quarterly* 5:373–92.

Perkins, Lynette. 1981. "Member Recruitment to a Mixed Goal Committee: The House Judiciary Committee." *Journal of Politics* 43:348–64.

Peterson, Mark A. 1990. *Legislating Together.* Cambridge: Harvard University Press.

Pitkin, Hannah F. 1967. *The Concept of Representation.* Berkeley: University of California Press.

Price, David E. 1972. *Who Makes the Laws? Creativity and Power in Senate Committees.* Cambridge, Mass.: Schenkman.

Price, David E. 1978. "Policymaking in Congressional Committees: The Impact of Environmental Factors." *American Political Science Review* 72:548–74.

Price, David E. 1985. "Congressional Committees in the Policy Process." In *Congress Reconsidered,* 3rd ed., ed. Lawrence C. Dodd and Bruce I. Oppenheimer. Washington, D.C.: Congressional Quarterly.

Quirk, Paul J. 1990. "Deregulation and the Politics of Ideas in Congress." In *Beyond Self-Interest,* ed. Jane J. Mansbridge. Chicago: University of Chicago Press.

Reeves, Andre. 1993. *Congressional Committee Chairmen: Three Who Made an Evolution.* Lexington: University of Kentucky Press.

Reid, T. R. 1980. *Congressional Odyssey.* San Francisco: W. H. Freeman.

Riker, William H., and Peter C. Ordeshook. 1973. *An Introduction to Positive Political Theory.* Englewood Cliffs, N.J.: Prentice-Hall.

Ripley, Randall B. 1969. *Power in the Senate.* New York: St. Martin's Press.

Rohde, David W. 1974. "Committee Reform in the House of Representatives and the Subcommittee Bill of Rights." *Annals of the American Academy of Political and Social Science* 411:39–47.

Rohde, David W. 1988. "Studying Congressional Norms: Concepts and Evidence." *Congress and the Presidency* 15:139–45.

Rohde, David W. 1991. *Parties and Leaders in the Postreform House.* Chicago: University of Chicago Press.

Rohde, David W. 1995. "Parties and Committees in the House: Member Motivations, Issues, and Institutional Arrangements." In *Positive Theories of Congressional Institu-*

tions, ed. Kenneth A. Shepsle and Barry R. Weingast. Ann Arbor: University of Michigan Press.

Rosenstone, Steven, and John Mark Hansen. 1993. *Mobilization, Participation, and Democracy in America.* Chicago: University of Chicago Press.

Rundquist, Barry S., and Gerald S. Strom. 1987. "Bill Construction in Legislative Committees: A Study of the U.S. House." *Legislative Studies Quarterly* 12:97–114.

Salisbury, Robert H., and Kenneth A. Shepsle. 1981a. "Congressional Staff Turnover and the Ties-That-Bind." *American Political Science Review* 75:381–96.

Salisbury, Robert H., and Kenneth A. Shepsle. 1981b. "Congressman as Enterprise." *Legislative Studies Quarterly* 6:559–76.

Schamel, Charles E., et al. 1989. *Guide to the Records of the United States House of Representatives at the National Archives: 1789–1989 Bicentennial Edition.* Washington, D.C.: National Archives.

Schattschneider, E. E. 1960. *The Semisovereign People.* Hinsdale, Ill.: Dryden.

Schick, Allen. 1983. "The Distributive Congress." In *Making Economic Policy in Congress,* ed. Allen Schick. Washington, D.C.: American Enterprise Institute.

Schlesinger, Joseph A. 1966. *Ambition and Politics.* Chicago: Rand McNally.

Searing, Donald D. 1978. "Measuring Politicians' Values: Administration and Assessment of a Ranking Technique in the British House of Commons." *American Political Science Review* 72:65–79.

Shepsle, Kenneth A. 1978. *The Giant Jigsaw Puzzle: Democratic Committee Assignments in the Modern House.* Chicago: University of Chicago Press.

Shepsle, Kenneth A. 1979. "Institutional Arrangements and Equilibrium in Multidimensional Voting Models." *American Journal of Political Science* 23:27–59.

Shepsle, Kenneth A. 1986. "Institutional Equilibrium and Equilibrium Institutions." In *Political Science: The Science of Politics,* ed. Herbert F. Weisberg. New York: Agathon Press.

Shepsle, Kenneth A. 1989. "The Changing Textbook Congress." In *Can the Government Govern,* ed. John Chubb and Paul Peterson. Washington, D.C.: Brookings Institution.

Shepsle, Kenneth A., and Barry R. Weingast. 1987a. "The Institutional Foundations of Committee Power." *American Political Science Review* 81:85–104.

Shepsle, Kenneth A., and Barry R. Weingast. 1987b. "Why Are Committees Powerful?" *American Political Science Review* 81:929–45.

Shepsle, Kenneth A., and Barry R. Weingast. 1994. "Positive Theories of Congressional Institutions." *Legislative Studies Quarterly* 19:149–80.

Shepsle, Kenneth A., and Barry R. Weingast, eds. 1995. *Positive Theories of Congressional Institutions.* Ann Arbor: University of Michigan Press.

Simon, Herbert A. 1957. *Models of Man.* New York: John Wiley & Sons.

Sinclair, Barbara. 1983a. *Majority Party Leadership in the U.S. House.* Baltimore, Md.: Johns Hopkins University Press.

Sinclair, Barbara. 1983b. "Purposive Behavior in the U.S. Congress: A Review Essay." *Legislative Studies Quarterly* 8:117–31.

Sinclair, Barbara. 1986. "Senate Styles and Senate Decision Making, 1955–1980." *Journal of Politics* 46:877–908.

Sinclair, Barbara. 1989. *The Transformation of the U.S. Senate.* Baltimore, Md.: Johns Hopkins University Press.

Smith, Richard A. 1984. "Advocacy, Interpretation, and Influence in the U.S. Congress." *American Political Science Review* 78:44–63

Smith, Steven S. 1988. "An Essay on Sequence, Position, Goals, and Committee Power." *Legislative Studies Quarterly* 13:151–76.

Smith, Steven S. 1989. *Call to Order*. Washington, D.C.: Brookings Institution.

Smith, Steven S., and Christopher Deering. 1984. *Committees in Congress*. Washington: Congressional Quarterly.

Snyder, James M. 1992. "Artificial Extremism in Interest Group Ratings." *Legislative Studies Quarterly* 17:319–45.

Strahan, Randall. 1989. "Members' Goals and Coalition-Building Strategies in the House: The Case of Tax Reform." *Journal of Politics* 51:373–84.

Swain, Carol M. 1993. *Black Faces, Black Interests*. Cambridge: Harvard University Press.

Thomas, Sue. 1994. *How Women Legislate*. New York: Oxford University Press.

Unekis, Joseph, and Leroy Reiselbach. 1983. "Congressional Committee Leadership, 1971–1978." *Legislative Studies Quarterly* 8:251–70.

Unekis, Joseph, and Leroy Reiselbach. 1984. *Congressional Committee Politics*. New York: Praeger.

U.S. Bureau of the Census. 1980. "Fuels and Financial Characteristics: Congressional Districts of the 97th Congress." Washington, D.C.: Government Printing Office.

U.S. Bureau of the Census. 1981. *Annual Census of the United States*. Washington, D.C.: Government Printing Office.

U.S. Congress. 1981. *Official Congressional Directory*. Washington, D.C.: Government Printing Office.

U.S. Congress. 1983. *Official Congressional Directory*. Washington, D.C.: Government Printing Office.

U.S. Congress, Commission on Administrative Review, House. 1977. *Final Report*. 2 vols. 95th Congress, First Session. Washington, D.C.: Government Printing Office.

U.S. Congress, House Committee on Agriculture. 1981a. *Minutes of the Business Meetings and Hearings of the House Committee on Agriculture*. Washington, D.C.: Government Printing Office.

U.S. Congress, House Committee on Agriculture. 1981b. *Rules of the Committee on Education and Labor*. Washington, D.C.: Government Printing Office.

U.S. Congress, House Committee on Agriculture. 1982. *Minutes of the Business Meetings and Hearings of the House Committee on Agriculture*. Washington, D.C.: Government Printing Office.

U.S. Congress, House Committee on Agriculture. 1994. *Minutes of the Business Meetings and Hearings of the House Committee on Agriculture*. Washington, D.C.: Government Printing Office.

U.S. Congress, Office of the House Clerk. 1982. "Salaries of Officers and Employees of the House of Representatives from January 1 to March 31, 1982." In *Report of the House Clerk*. Washington, D.C.: Government Printing Office.

U.S. Congress, Office of the House Clerk. 1984. "Salaries of Officers and Employees of the House of Representatives from January 1 to March 31, 1984." In *Report of the House Clerk*. Washington, D.C.: Government Printing Office.

U.S. Department of Agriculture. 1981. "Biennial Report: Congressional District Ranking by Selected Programs and Commodities, 97th Congress." Washington, D.C.: U.S. Department of Agriculture.

U.S. Department of Agriculture. 1984a. "Dairy: Background for 1985 Farm Legislation," Washington, D.C.: Government Printing Office.

U.S. Department of Agriculture. 1984b. "Peanuts: Background for 1985 Farm Legislation," Washington, D.C.: Government Printing Office.

U.S. Senate, Select Committee to Study the Senate Committee System. 1984. *Hearing of the Temporary Select Committee to Study the Senate Committee System,* Pts. 1 and 2, 98th Congress. Washington, D.C.: Government Printing Office.

Verba, Sidney, and Norman Nie. 1972. *Participation in America.* New York: Harper & Row.

Waldman, Steven. 1995. *The Bill.* New York: Viking Press.

Walker, Jack L. 1977. "Setting the Agenda in the U.S. Senate." *British Journal of Political Science* 7:423–45.

Weingast, Barry R. 1979. "A Rational Choice Perspective on Congressional Norms." *American Journal of Political Science* 23:245–62.

Weingast, Barry R. 1989. "Floor Behavior in the U.S. Congress: Committee Power Under the Open Rule." *American Political Science Review* 83:795–815.

Weingast, Barry R., and William Marshall. 1988. "The Industrial Organization of Congress." *Journal of Political Economy* 96:132–63.

Weisberg, Herbert, Thomas Boyd, Marshall Goodman, and Debra Gross. 1982. "Reelection and Constituency Service as State Legislator Goals: It's Just Part of the Job." Presented at the 78th annual meeting of the American Political Science Association, Denver, Colo.

Weissberg, Robert. 1978. "Collective vs. Dyadic Representation in Congress." *American Political Science Review* 72:535–47.

Whiteman, David. 1985. "The Fate of Policy Analysis in Congressional Decision Making: Three Types of Use in Committees." *Western Political Quarterly* 38:294–311.

Whiteman, David. 1987. "What Do They Know and When Do They Know It? Health Staff on the Hill." *PS* 20:221–25.

Wilson, Woodrow. 1956 [1885]. *Congressional Government.* New York: Meridian Books.

Wright, John R. 1985. "PACs, Contributions, and Roll Calls: An Organizational Perspective." *American Political Science Review* 79:400–414.

Wright, John R. 1990. "Contributions, Lobbying, and Committee Voting in the U.S. House of Representatives." *American Political Science Review* 84:417–38.

Index

A Note on the Type
The text of this book was set in a digitized
version of Sabon, a type face originally designed
by well-known typographer Jan Tschichold. It was
named for earlier type founder Jacques Sabon.
It was composed by Keystone Typesetting
Services of Orwigsburg, Pennsylvania.